how to draw
100 things
for kids

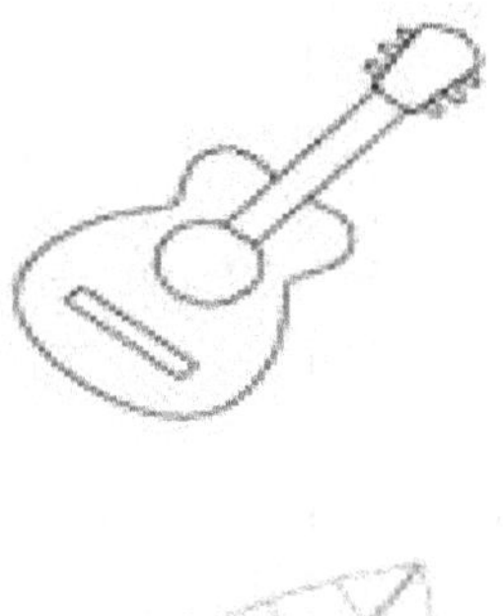 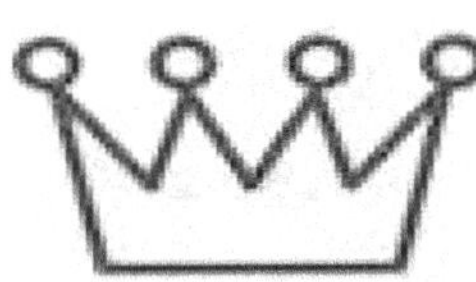 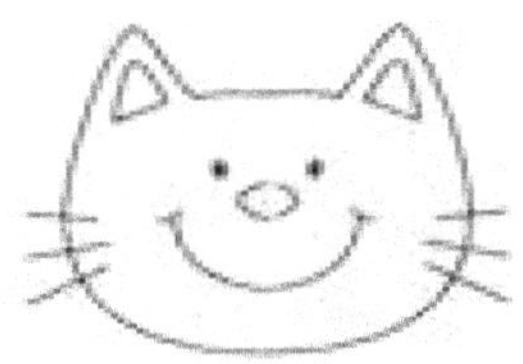 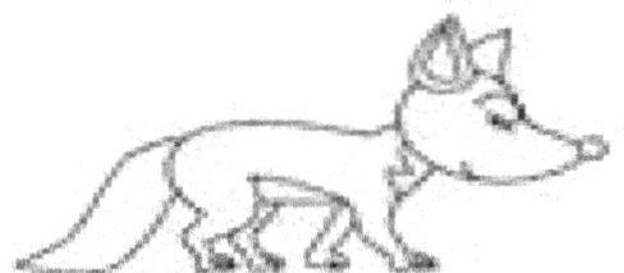

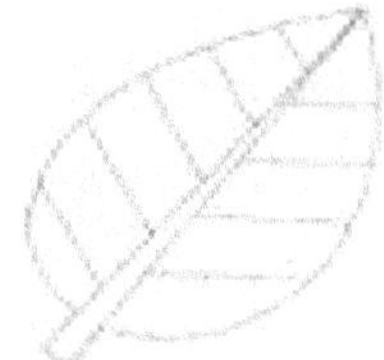 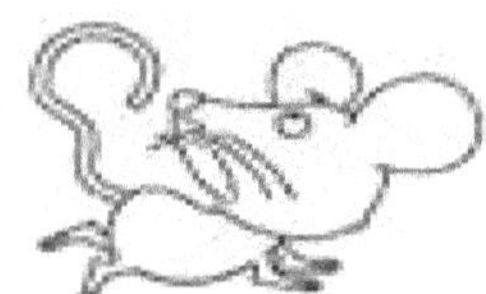  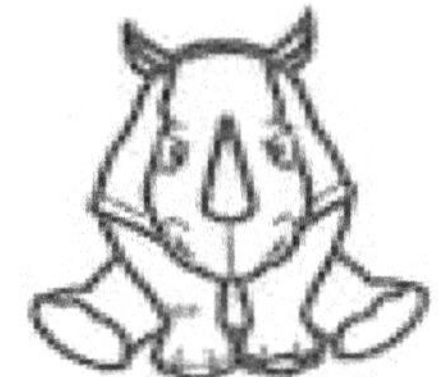

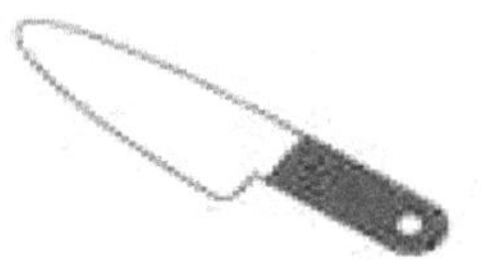 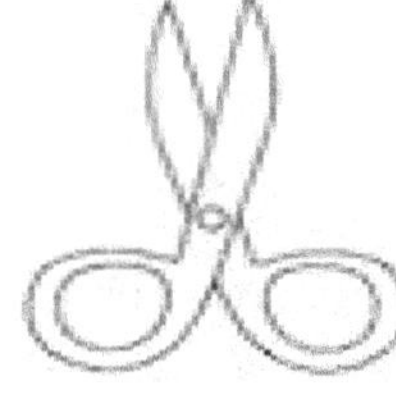 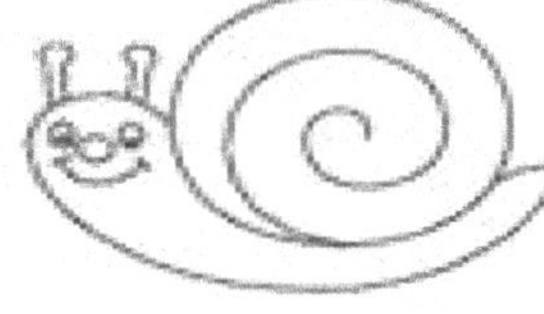 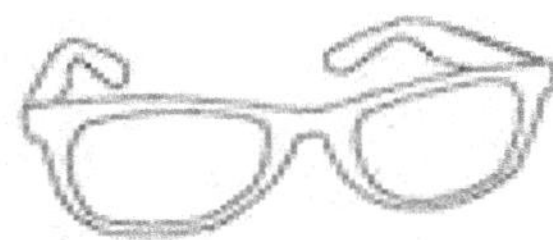

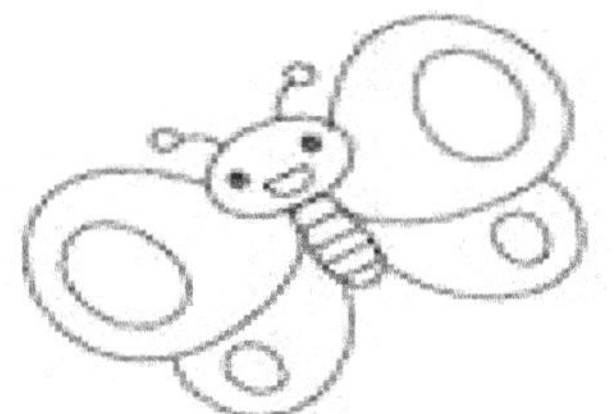 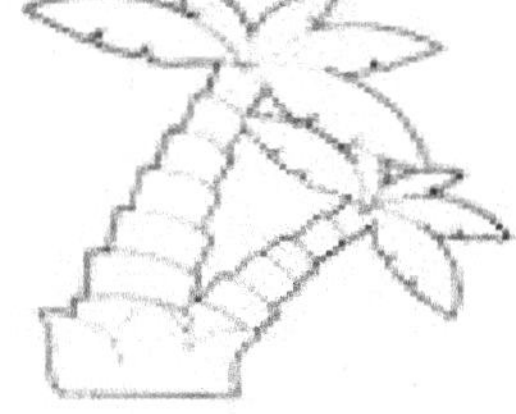 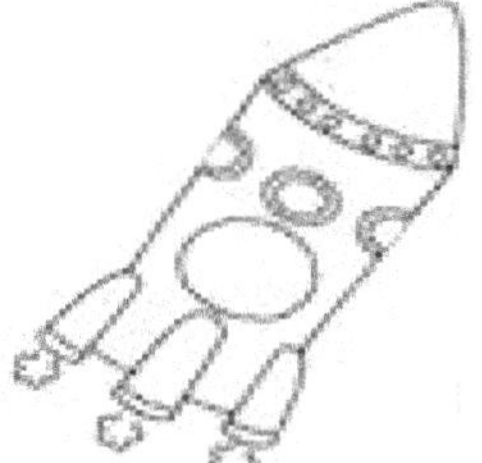 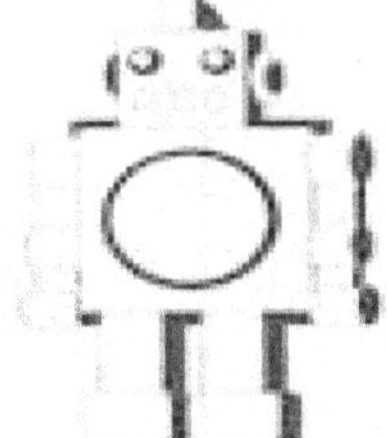

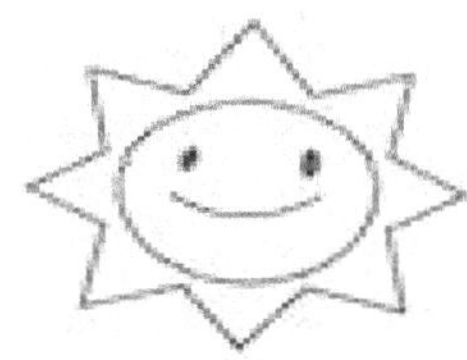 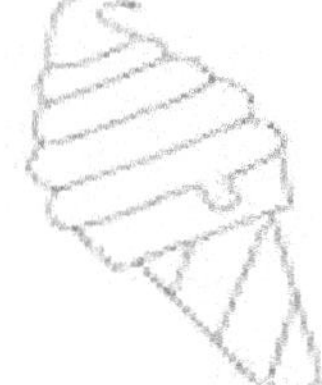 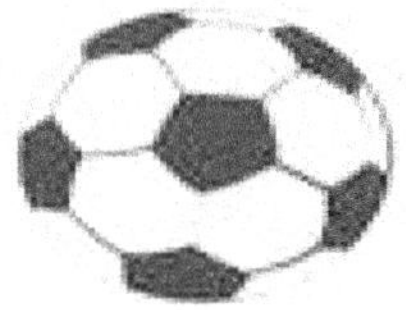 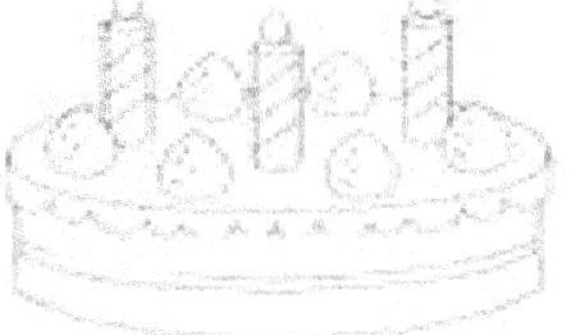

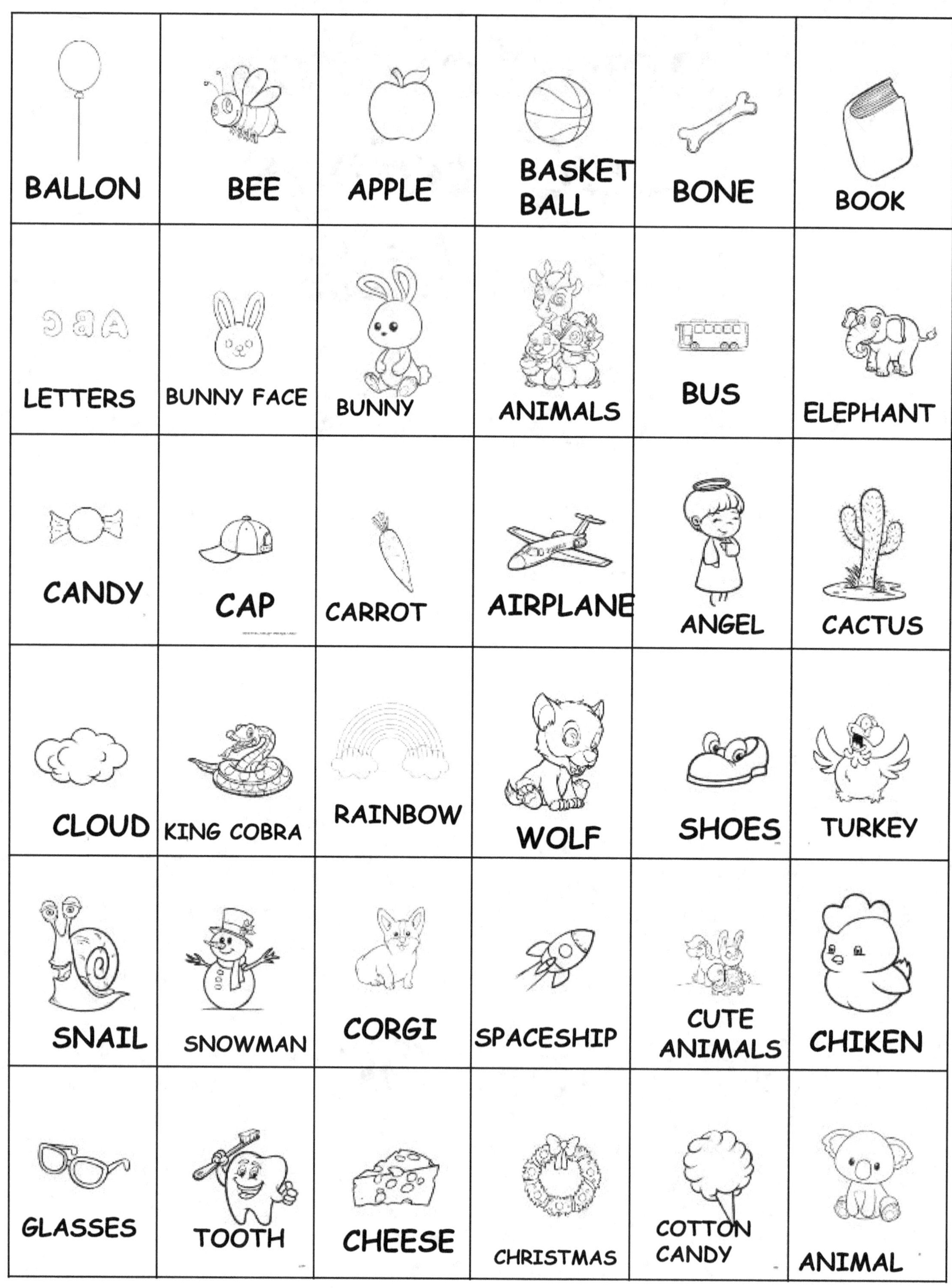

BALLON	BEE	APPLE	BASKET BALL	BONE	BOOK
LETTERS	BUNNY FACE	BUNNY	ANIMALS	BUS	ELEPHANT
CANDY	CAP	CARROT	AIRPLANE	ANGEL	CACTUS
CLOUD	KING COBRA	RAINBOW	WOLF	SHOES	TURKEY
SNAIL	SNOWMAN	CORGI	SPACESHIP	CUTE ANIMALS	CHIKEN
GLASSES	TOOTH	CHEESE	CHRISTMAS	COTTON CANDY	ANIMAL

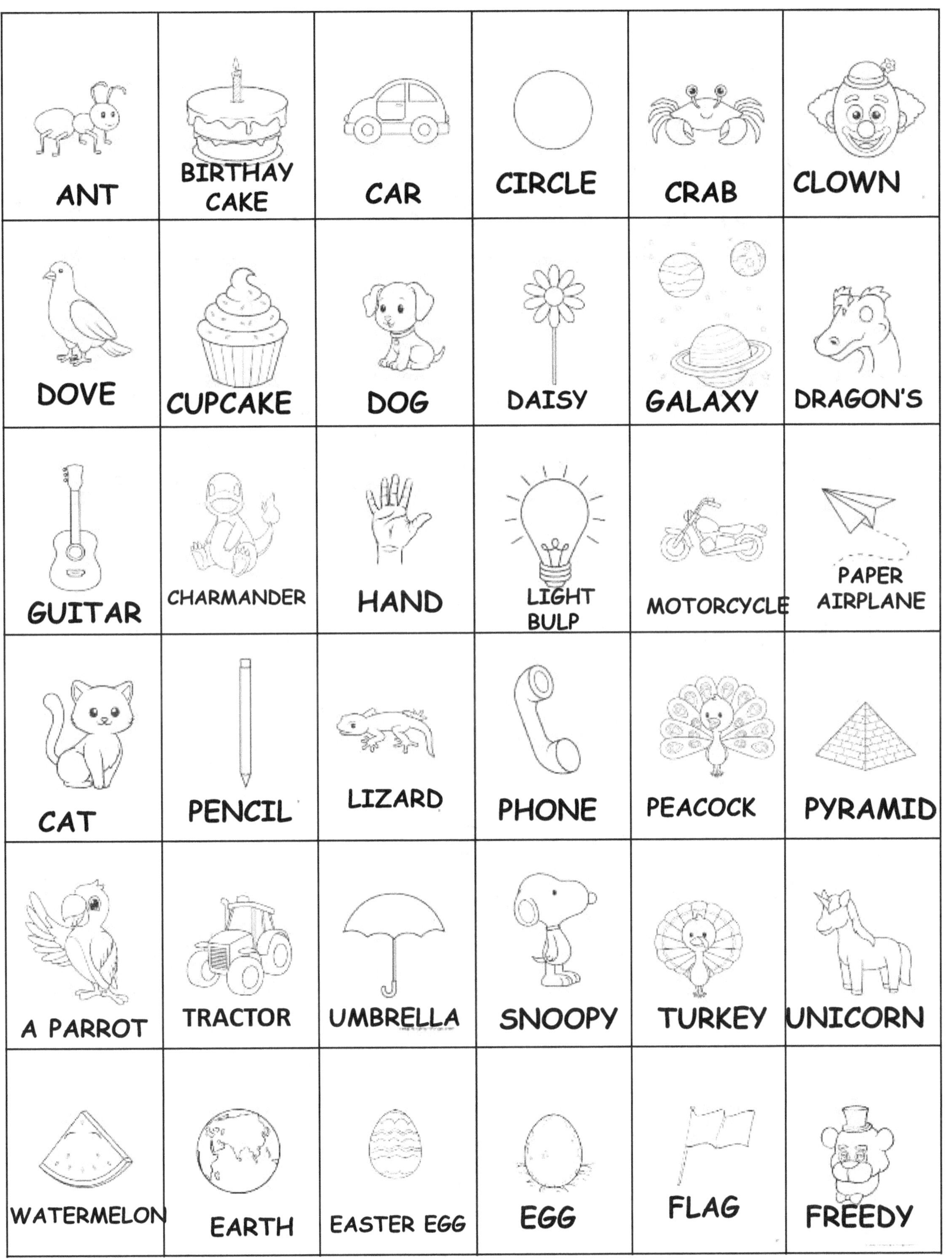

ANT
BIRTHAY CAKE
CAR
CIRCLE
CRAB
CLOWN
DOVE
CUPCAKE
DOG
DAISY
GALAXY
DRAGON'S
GUITAR
CHARMANDER
HAND
LIGHT BULP
MOTORCYCLE
PAPER AIRPLANE
CAT
PENCIL
LIZARD
PHONE
PEACOCK
PYRAMID
A PARROT
TRACTOR
UMBRELLA
SNOOPY
TURKEY
UNICORN
WATERMELON
EARTH
EASTER EGG
EGG
FLAG
FREEDY

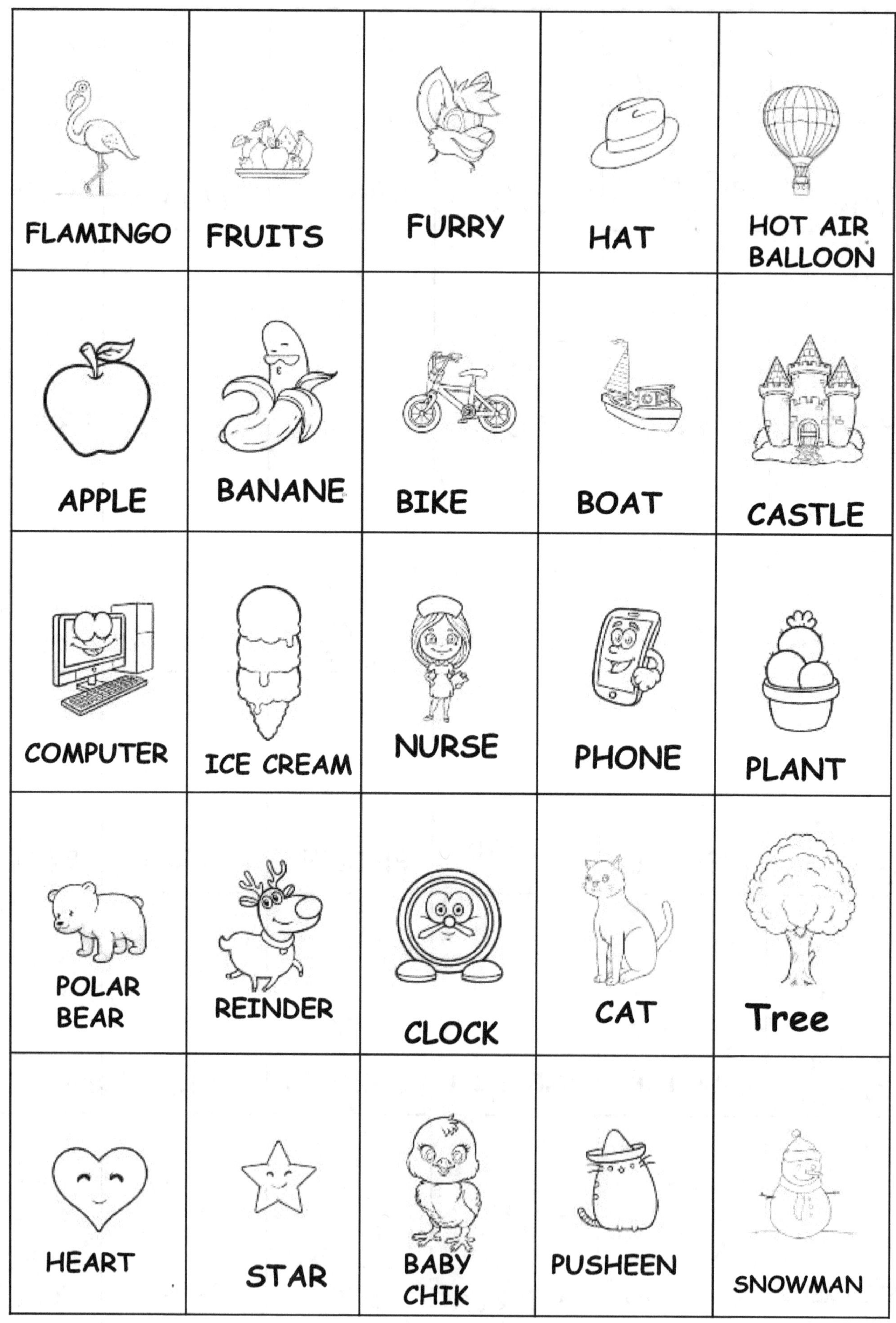

FLAMINGO
FRUITS
FURRY
HAT
HOT AIR BALLOON
APPLE
BANANE
BIKE
BOAT
CASTLE
COMPUTER
ICE CREAM
NURSE
PHONE
PLANT
POLAR BEAR
REINDER
CLOCK
CAT
Tree
HEART
STAR
BABY CHIK
PUSHEEN
SNOWMAN

BALLON

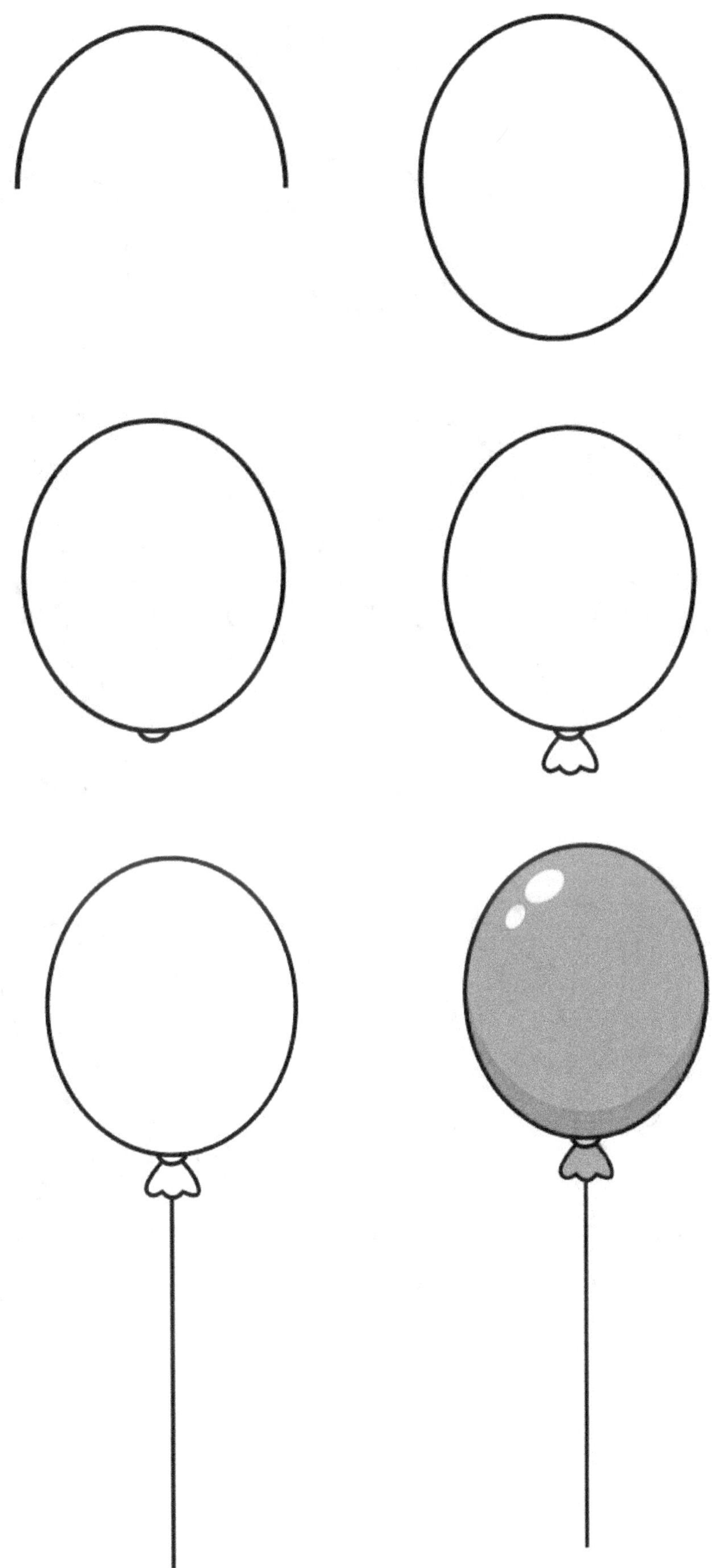

BEE

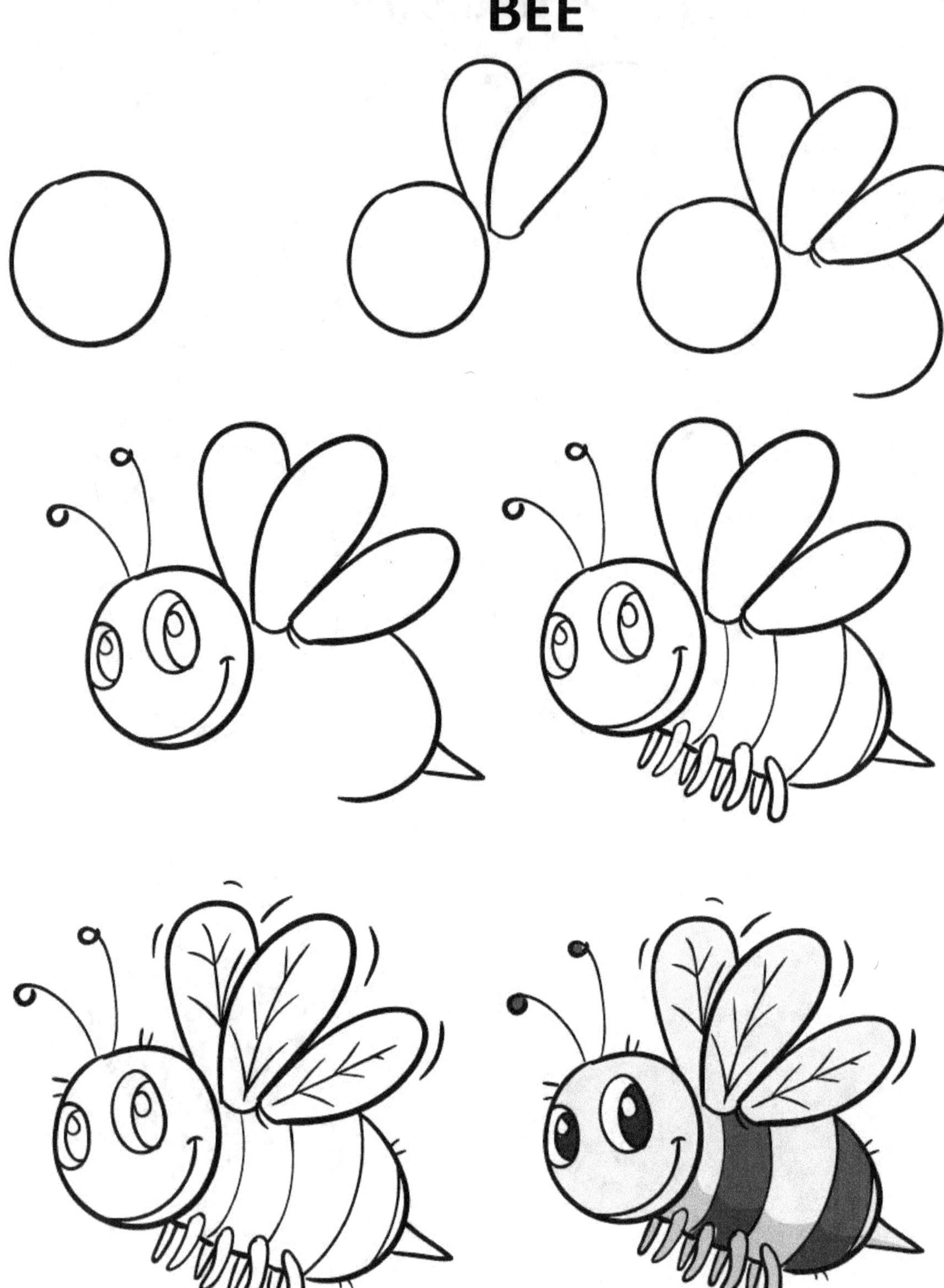

APPLE

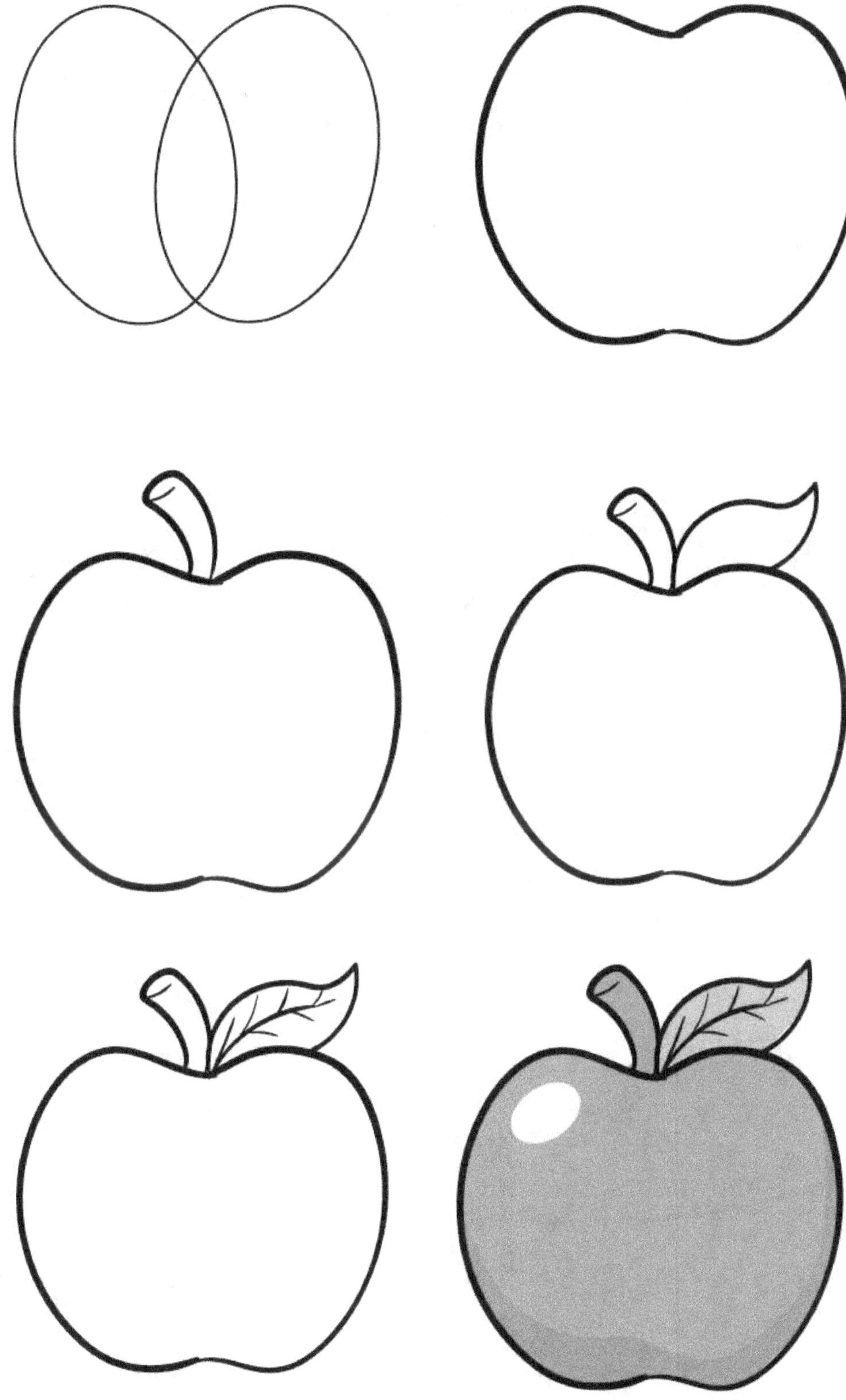

BASKET BALL

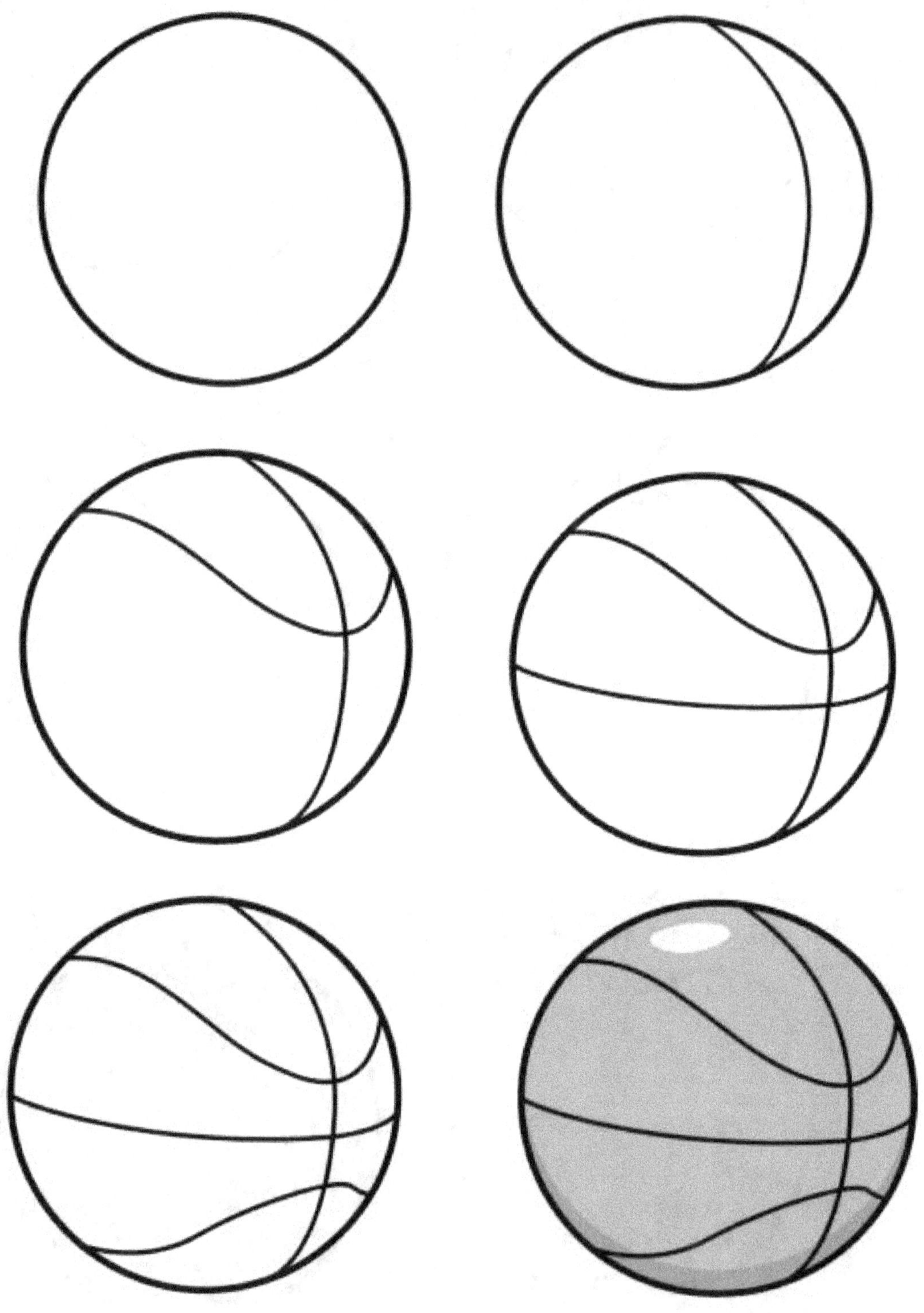

BONE

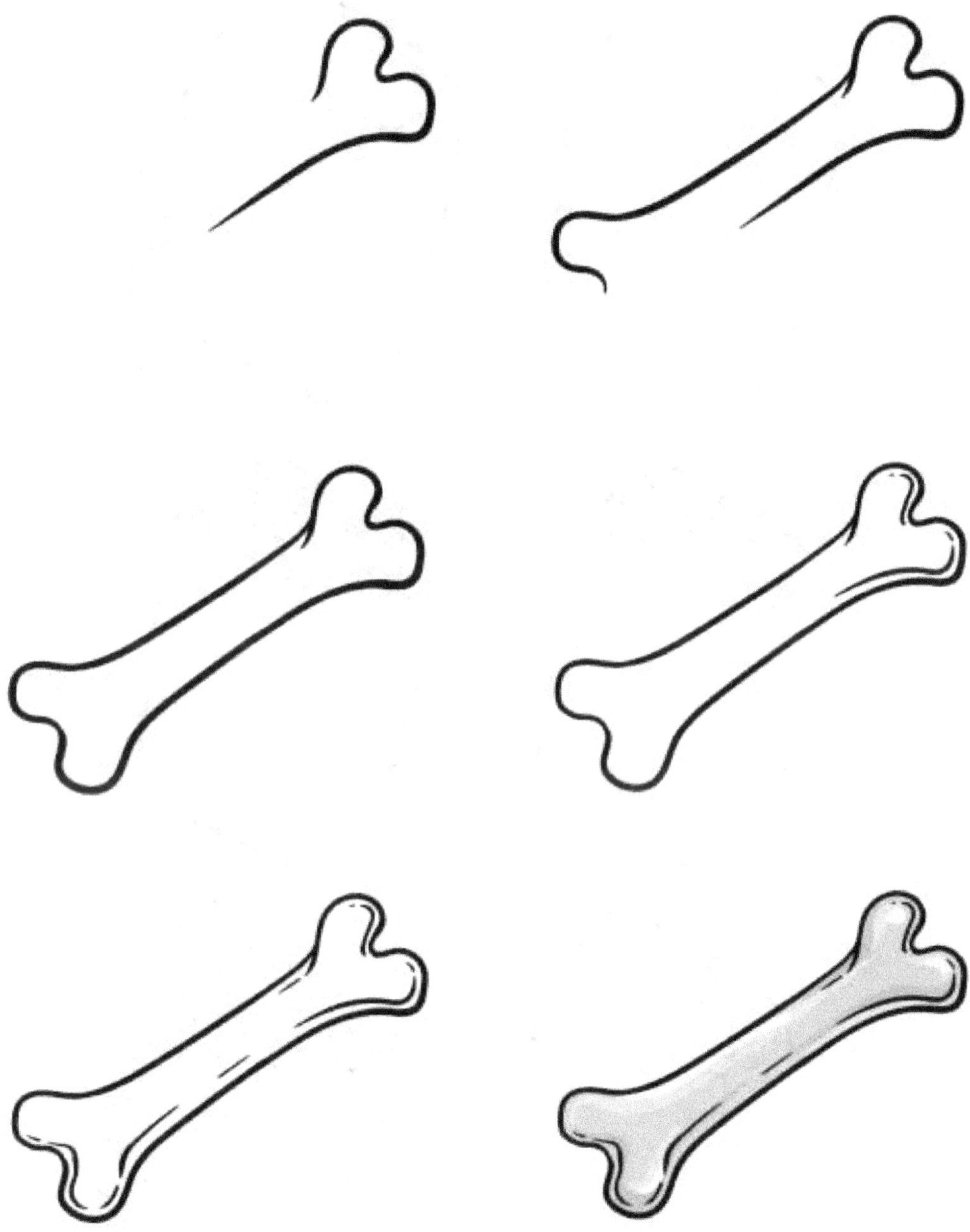

BOOK

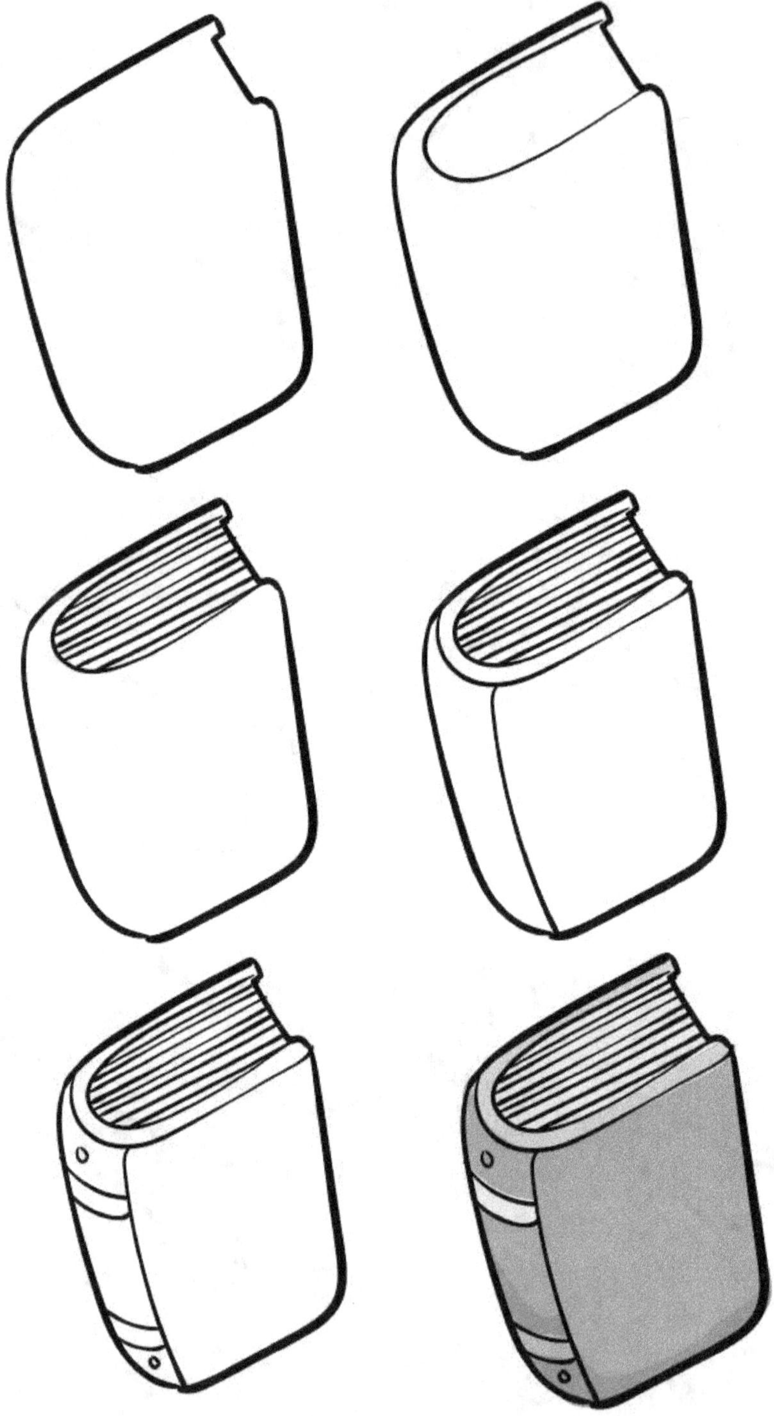

LETTERS

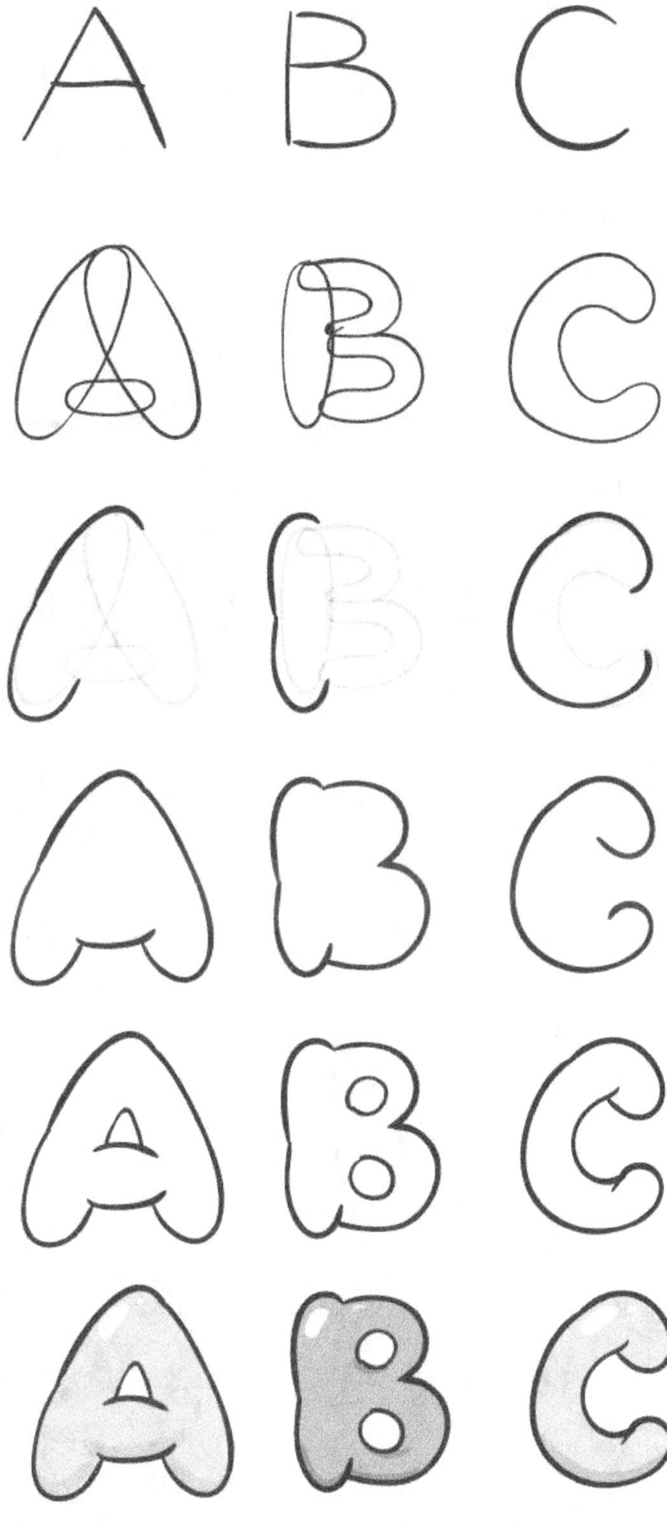

BUNNY FACE

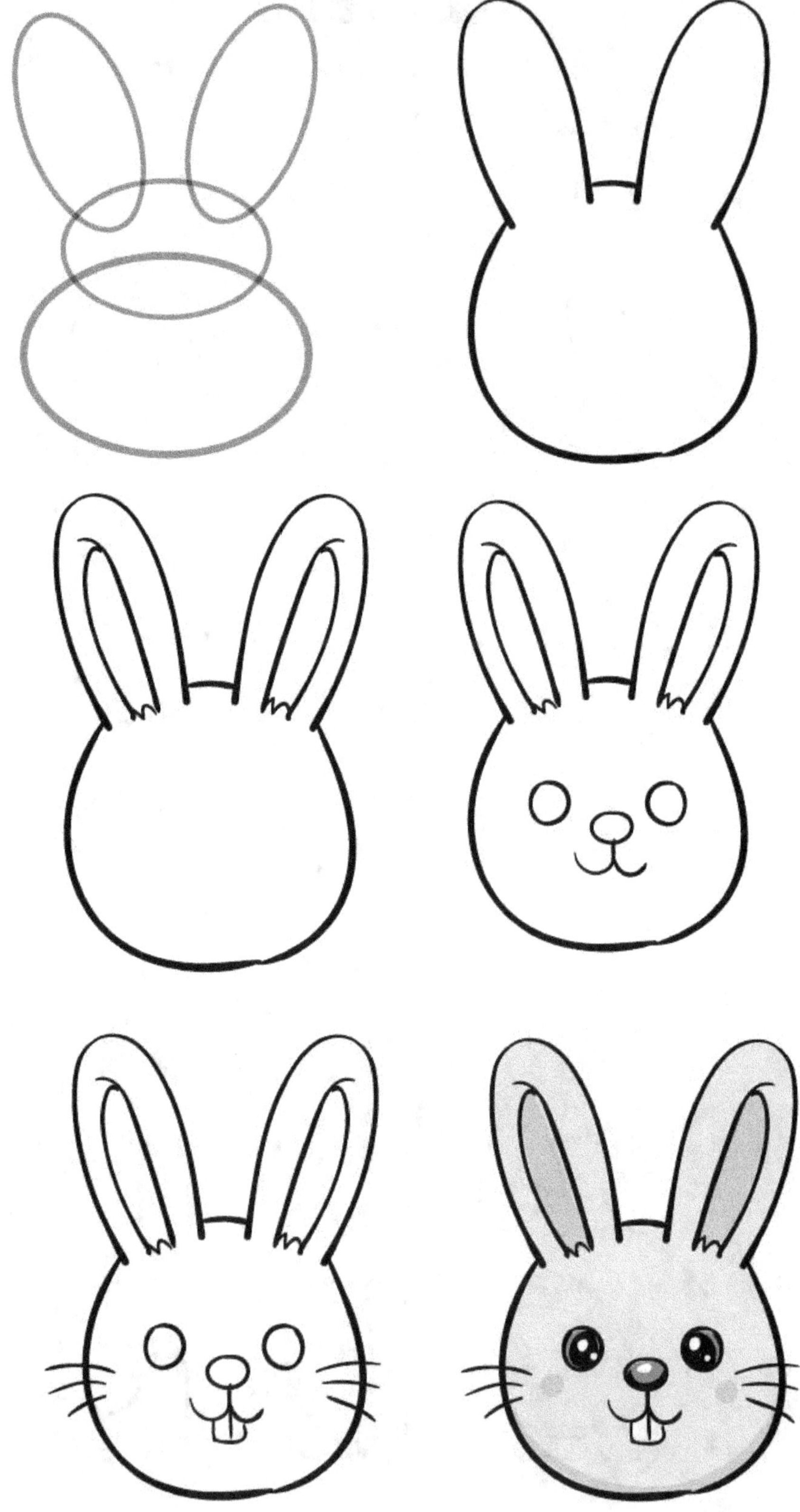

BUNNY

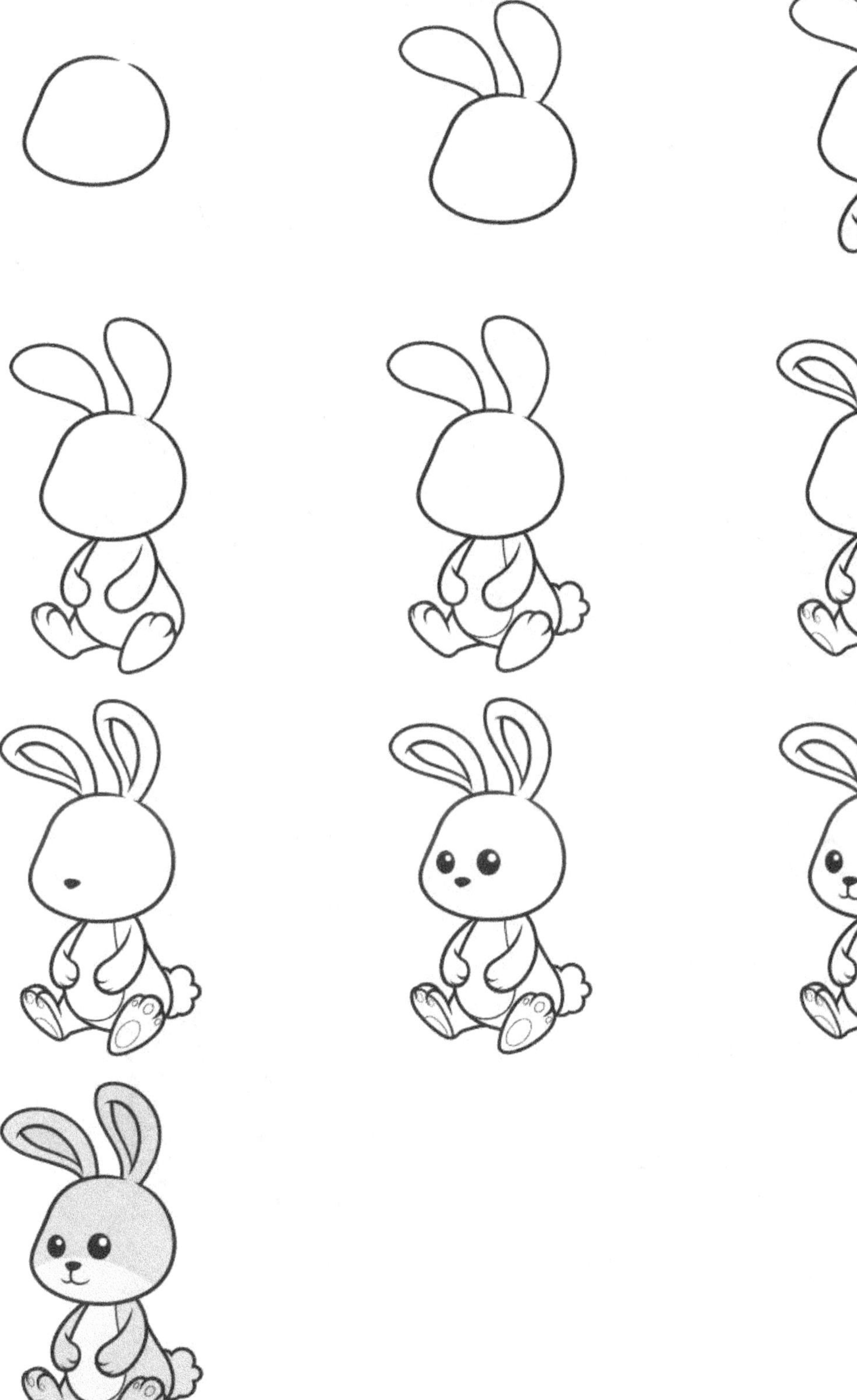

ANIMALS

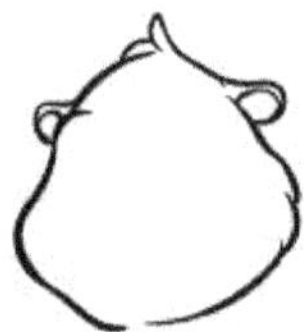 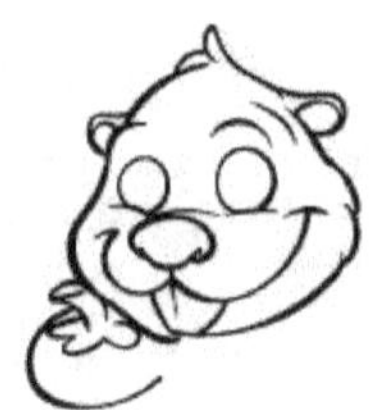

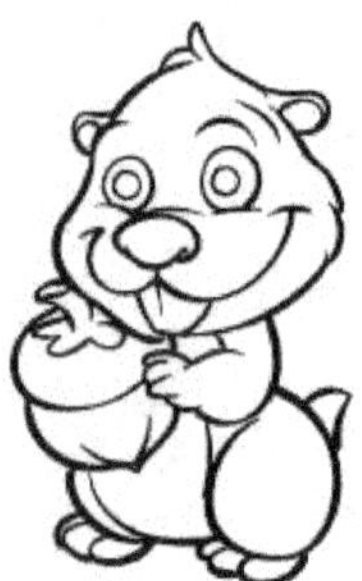 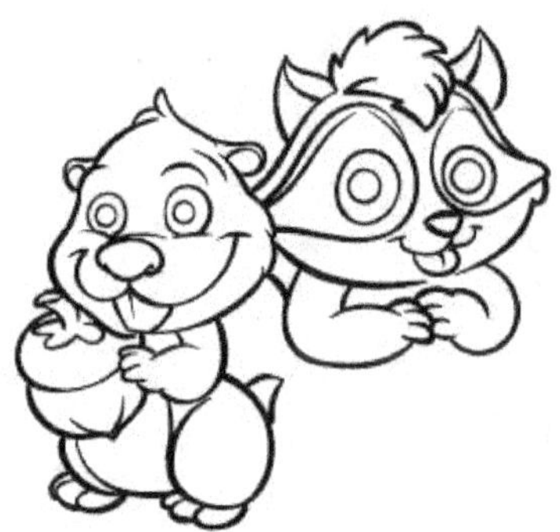

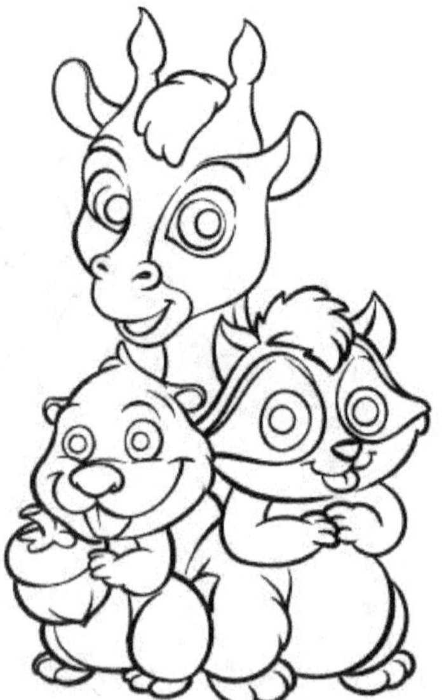 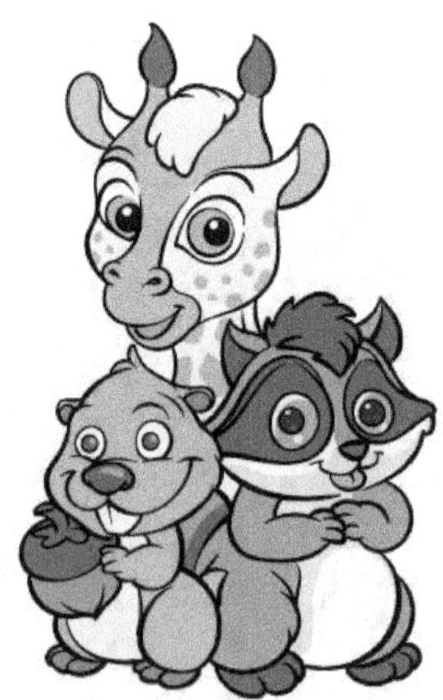

BUS

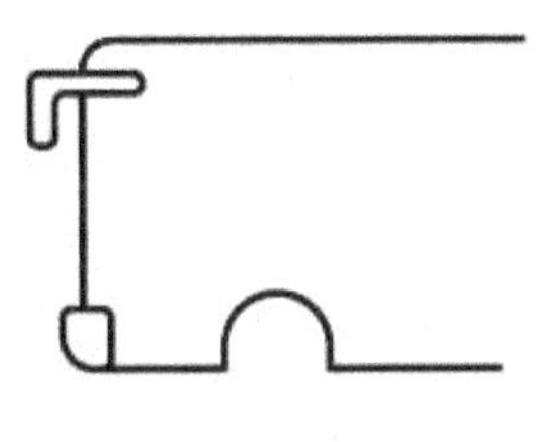 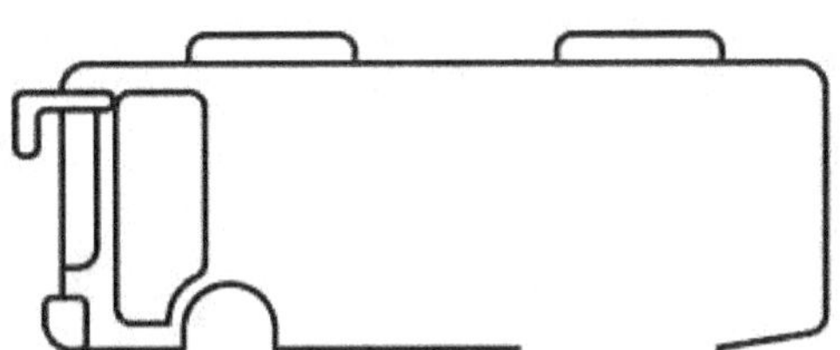

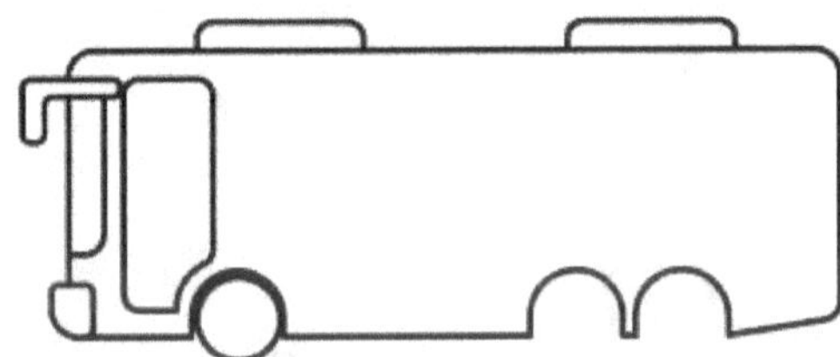 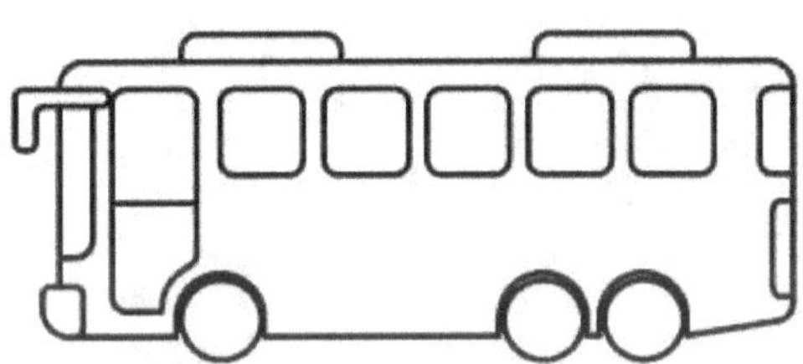

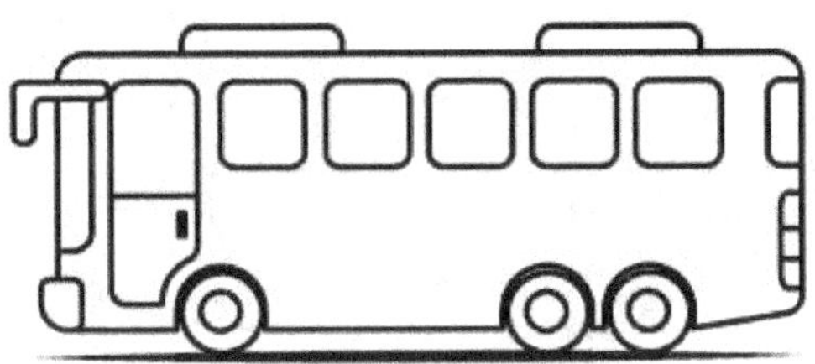 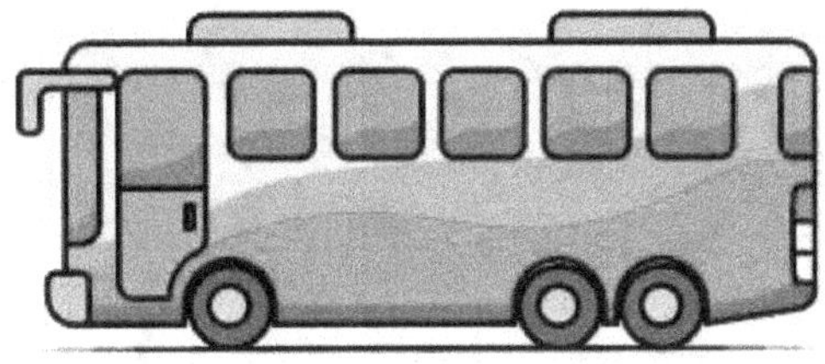

ELEPHANT

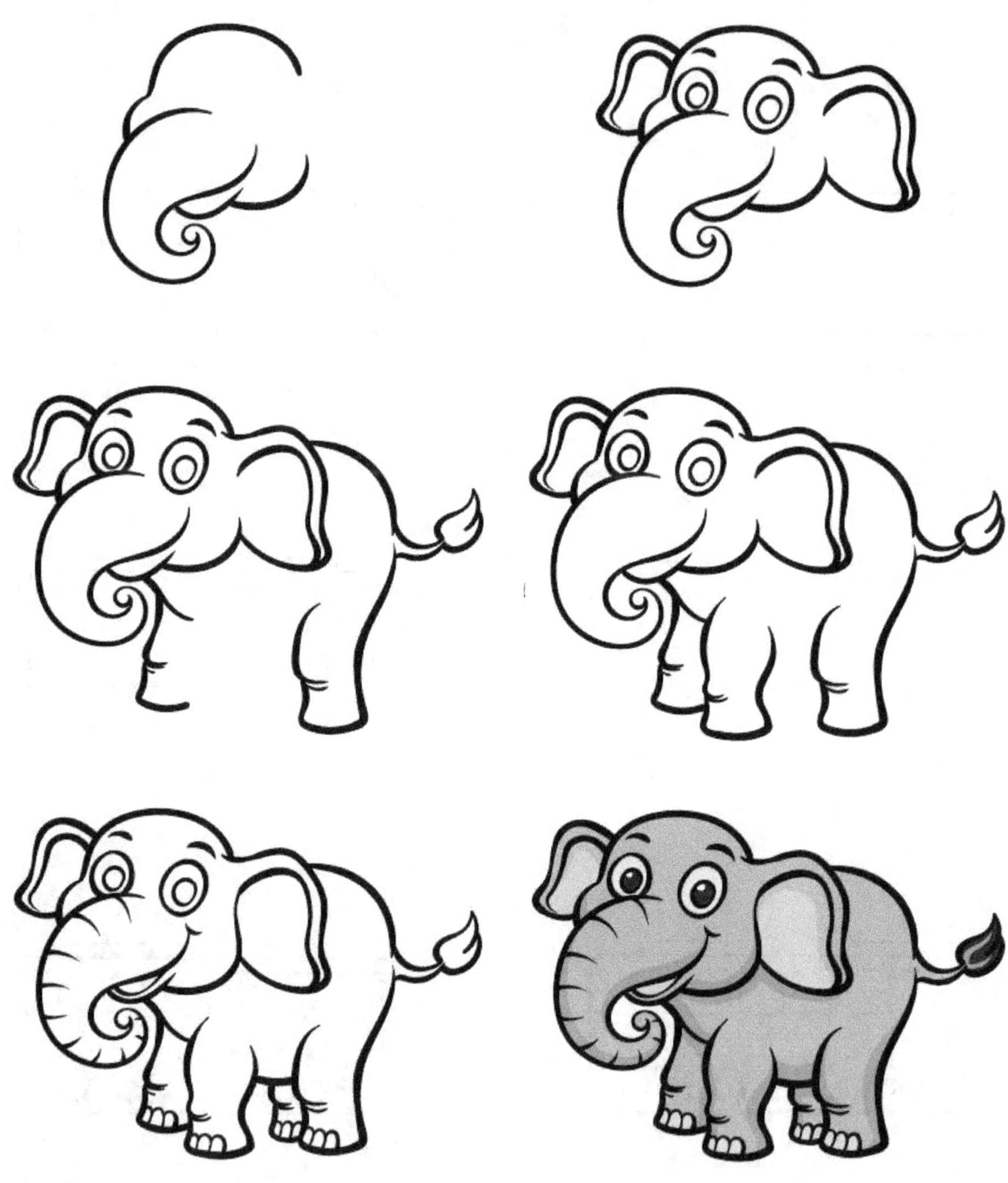

CANDY

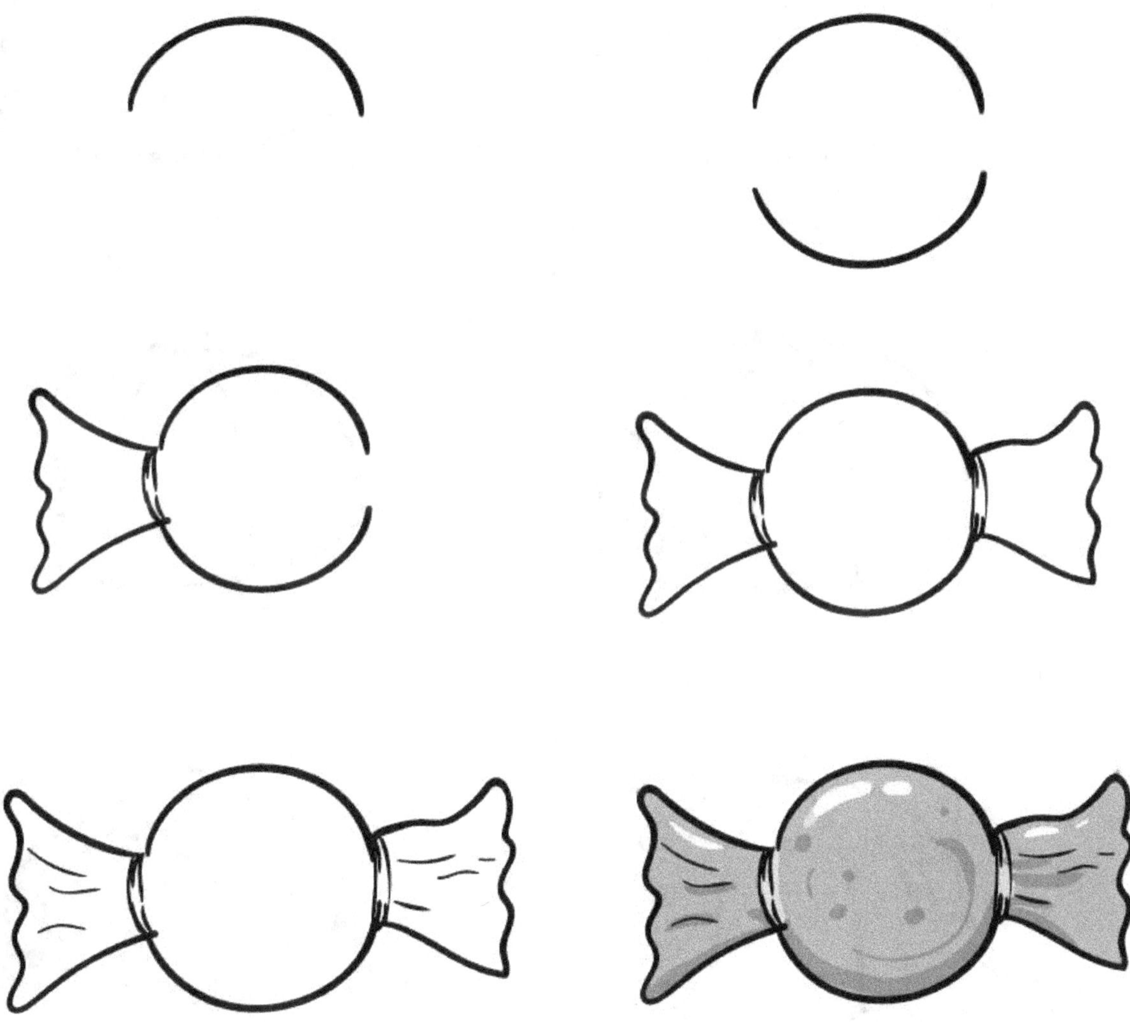

CAP

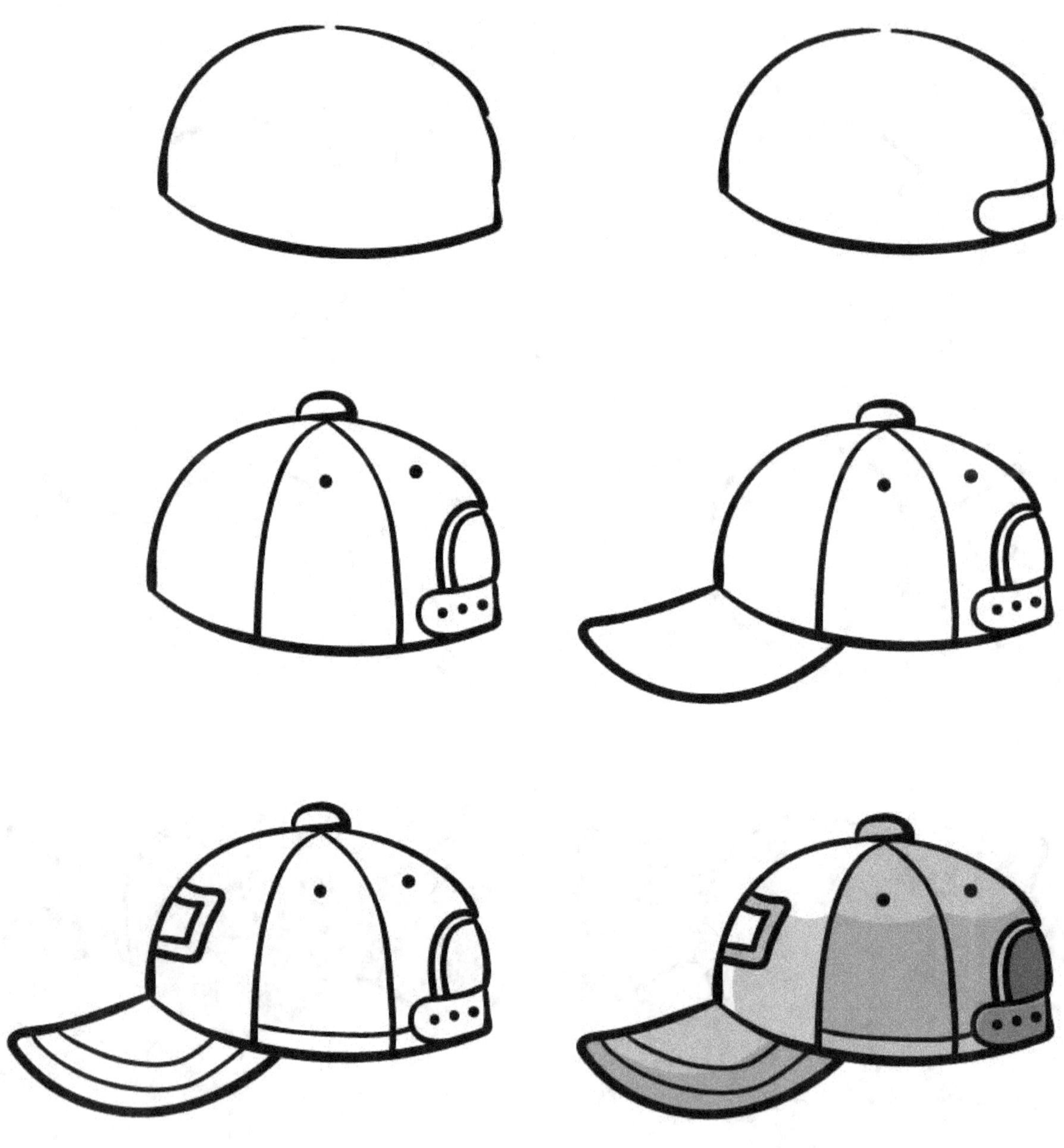

CARROT

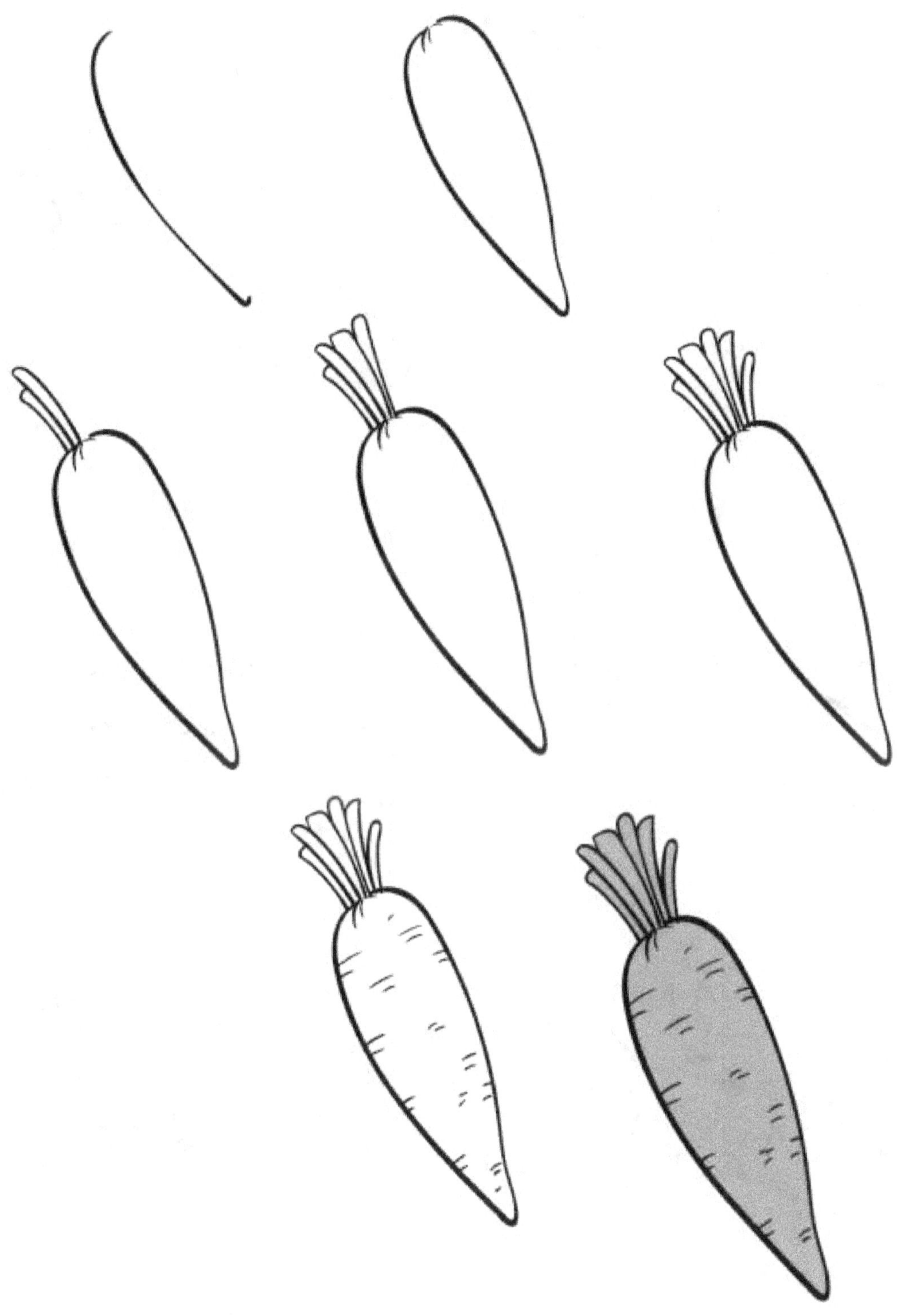

AIR PLANE

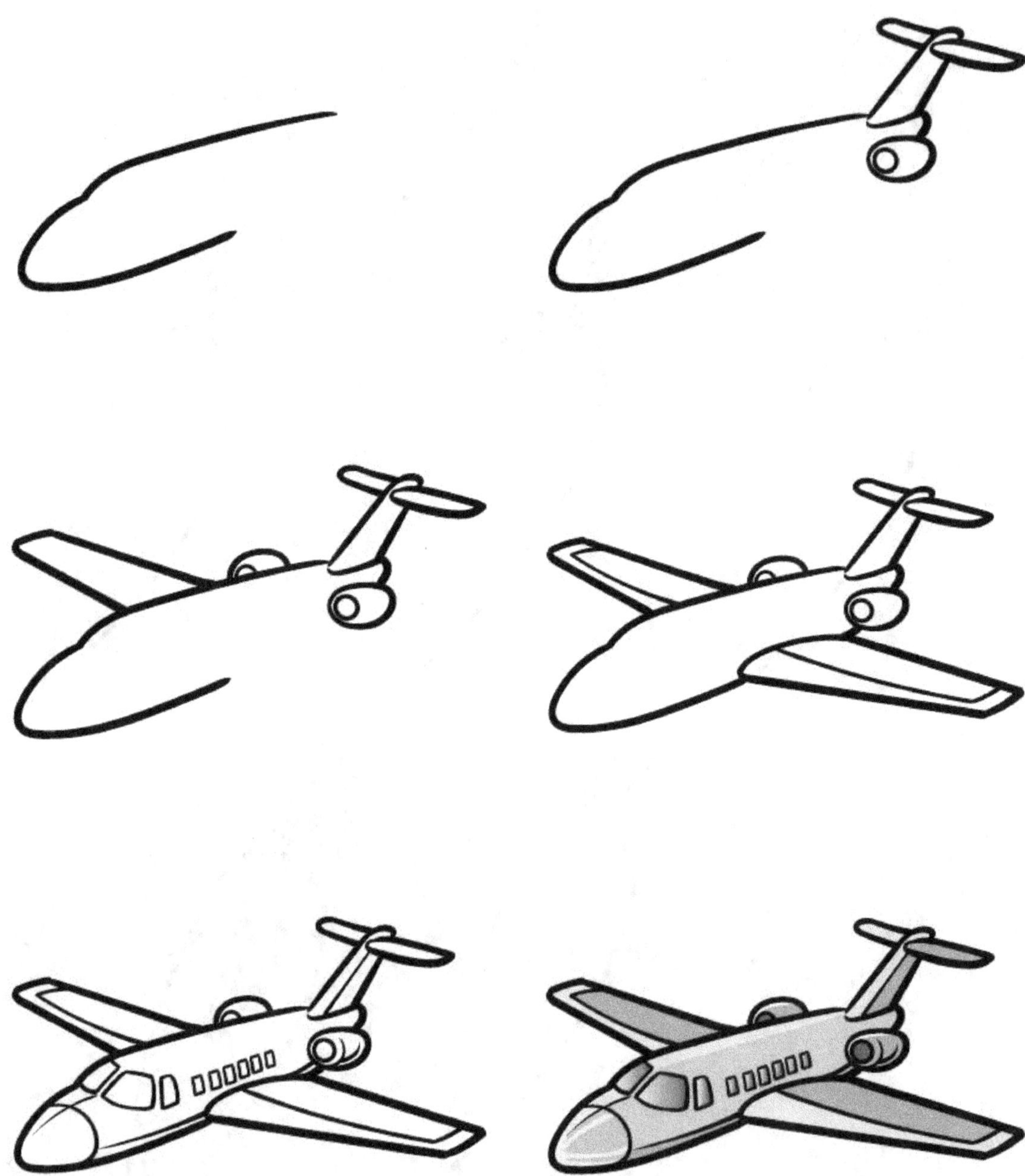

ANGEL

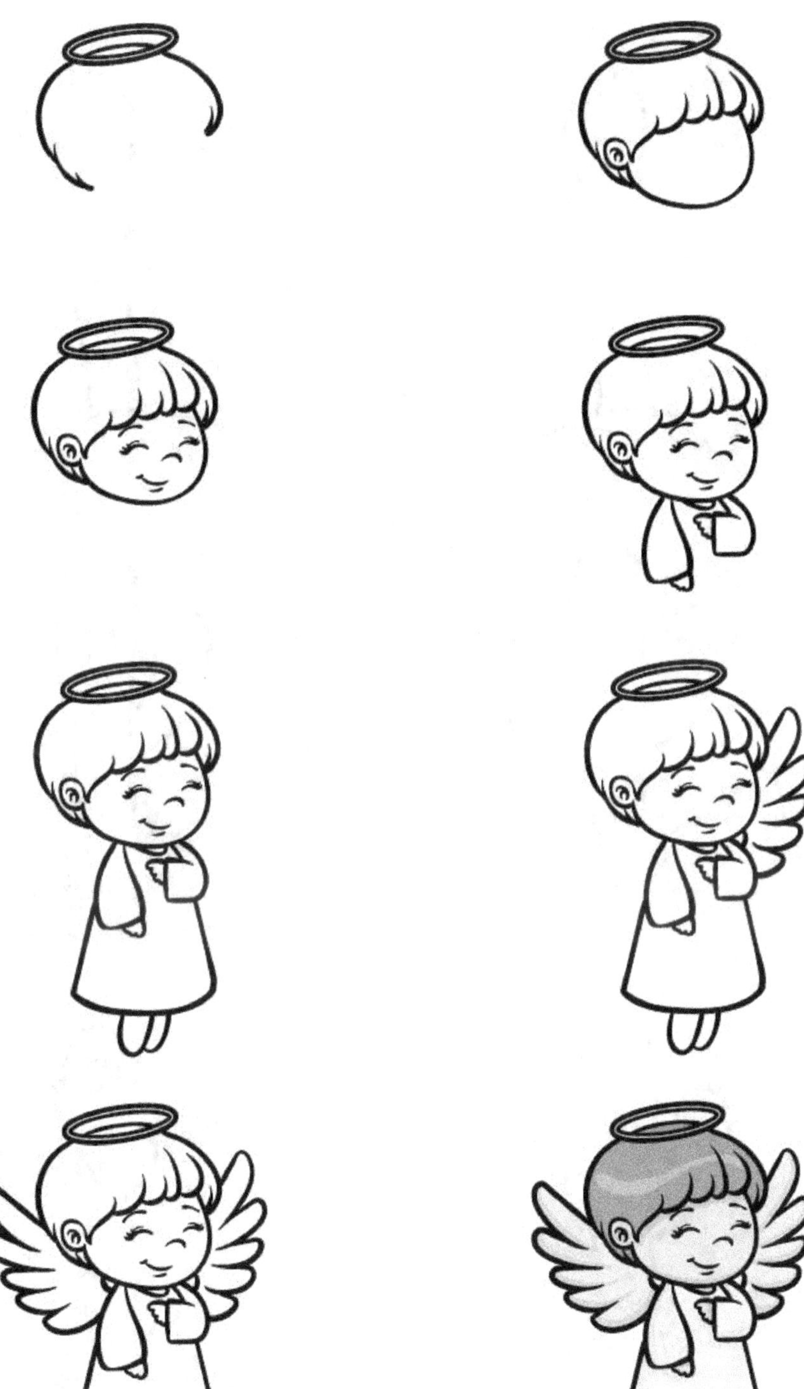

CACTUS

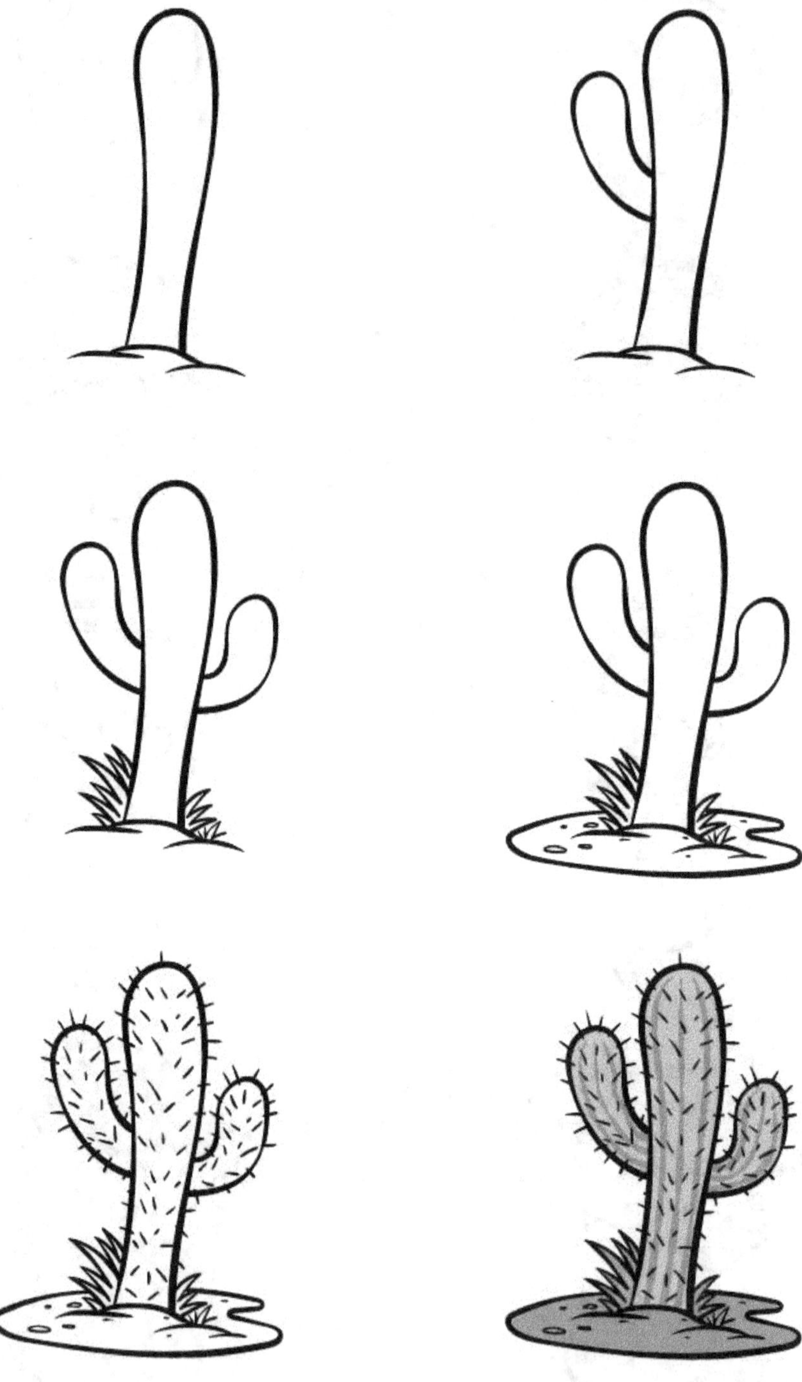

CLOUD

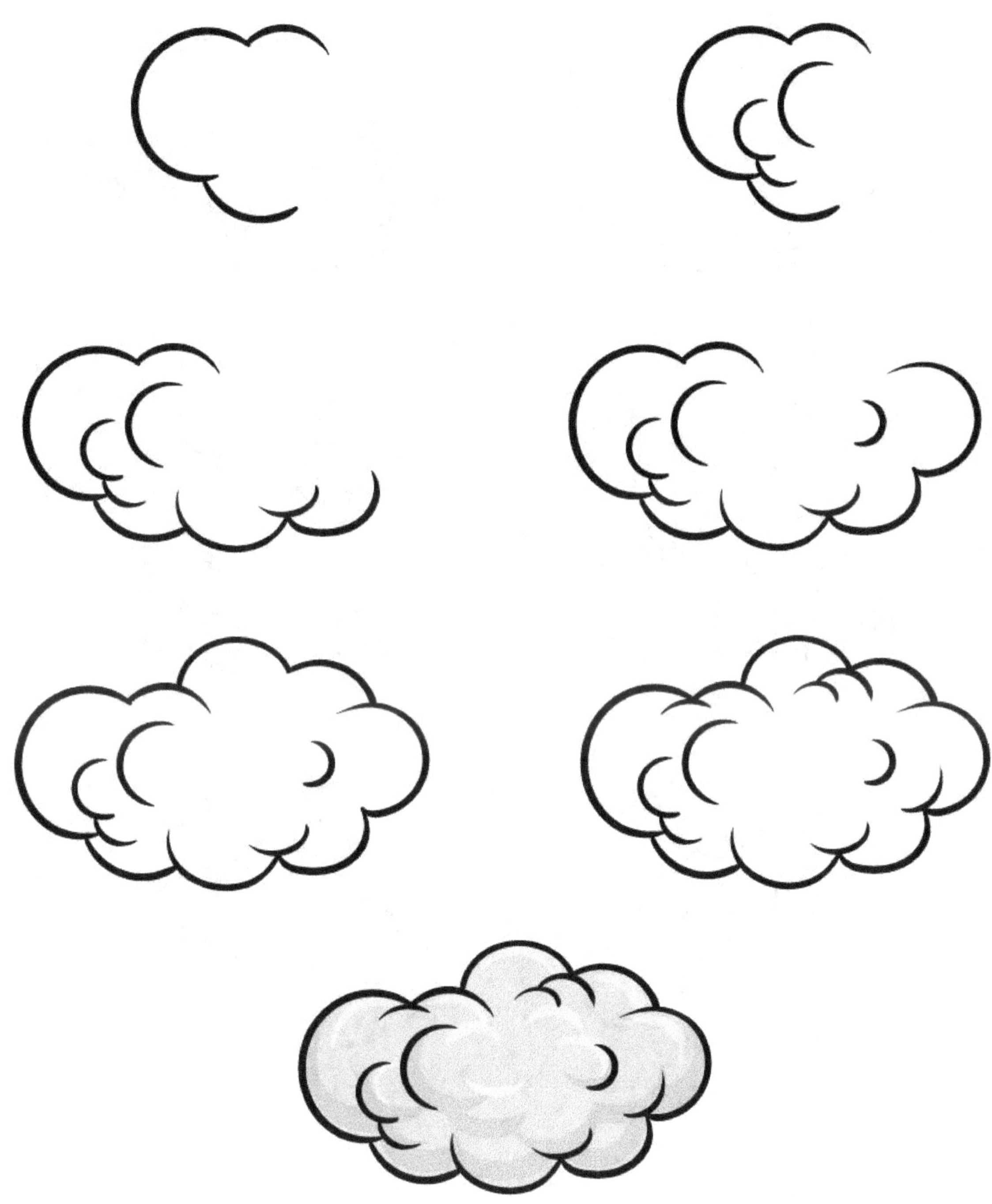

KING COBRA

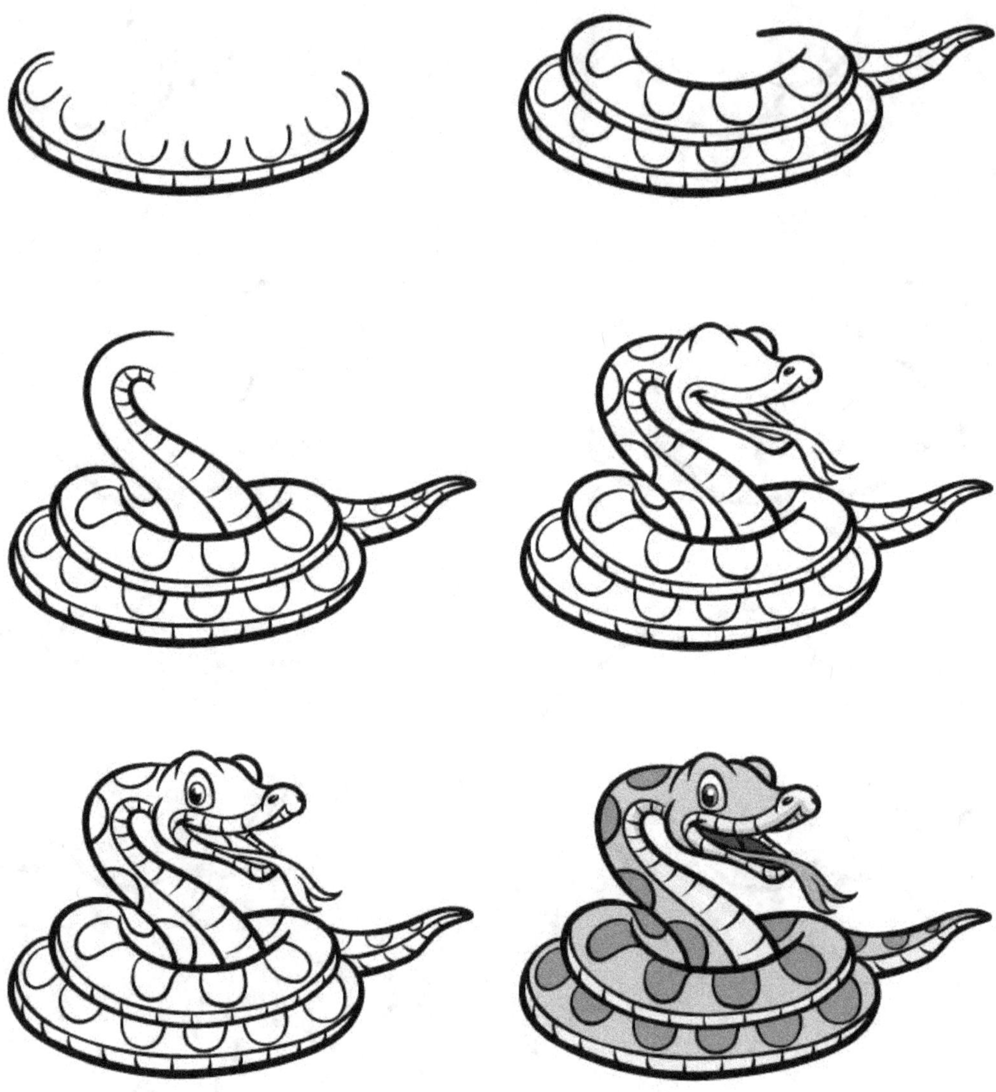

RAINBOWS

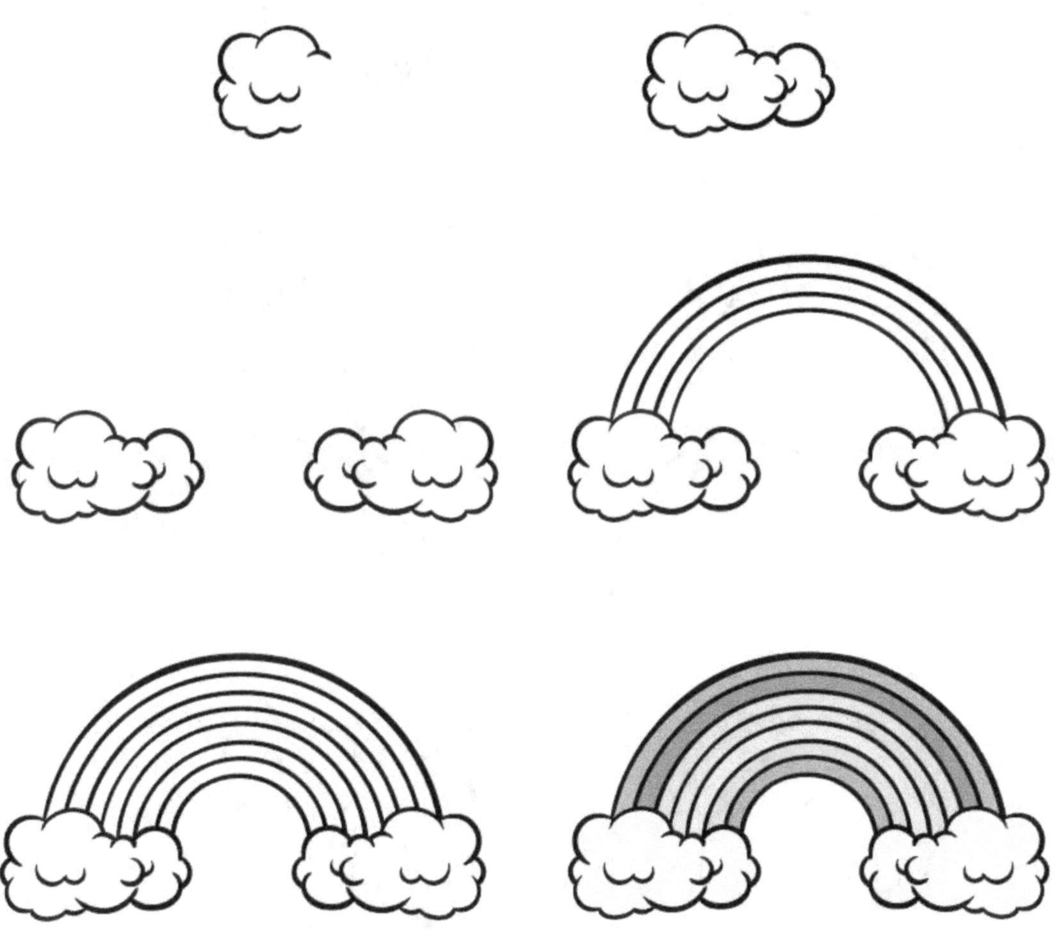

WOLF

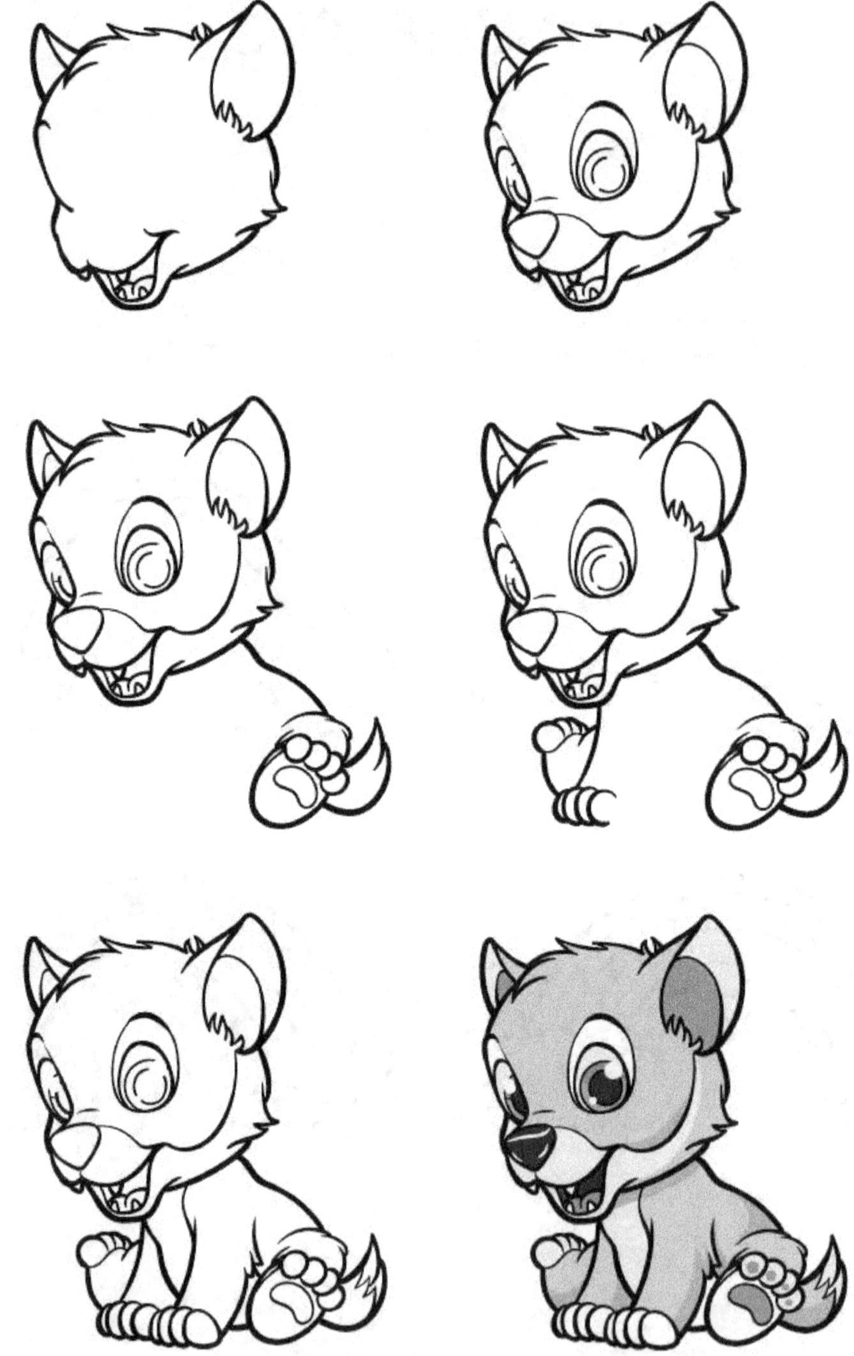

SHOES

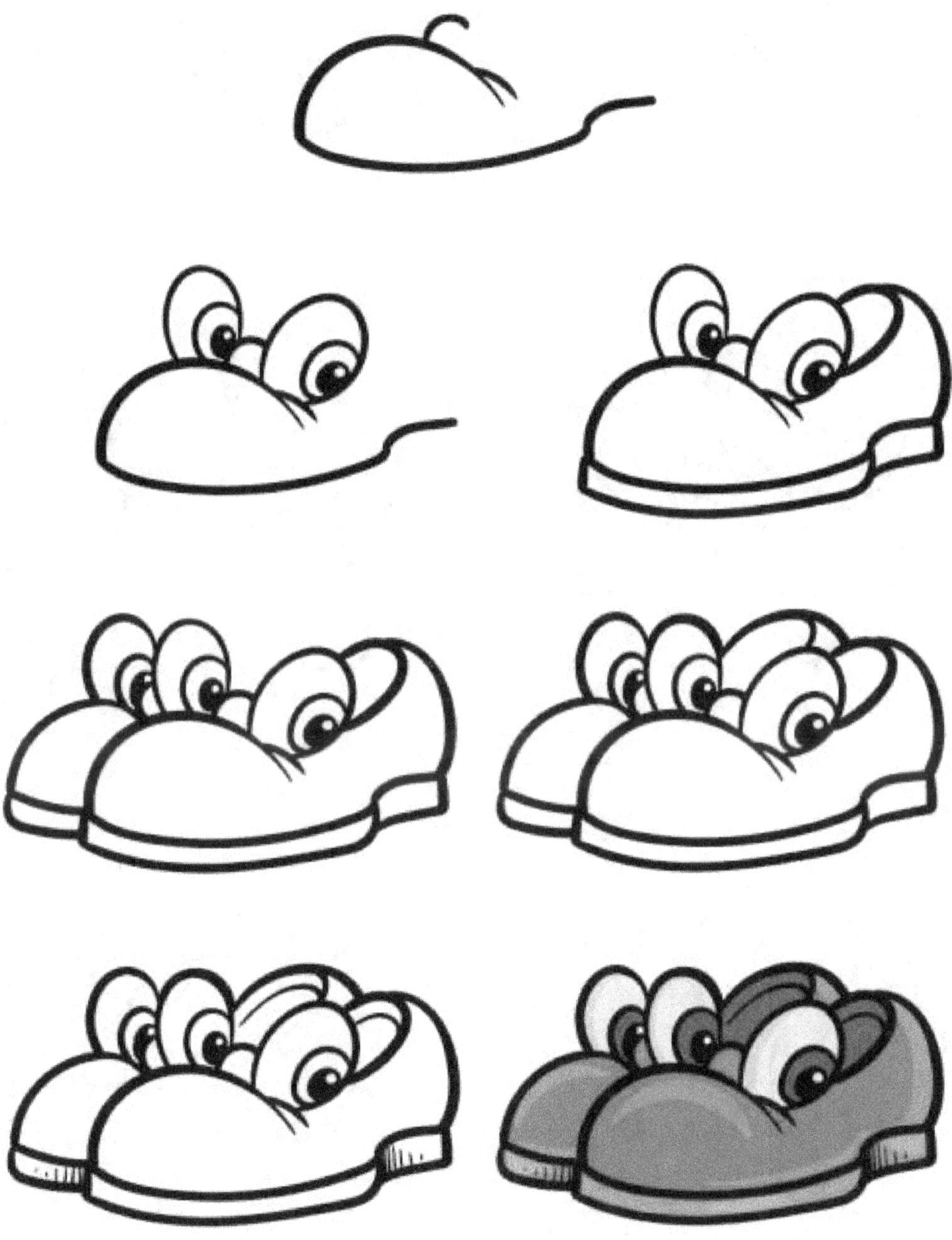

TURKEY

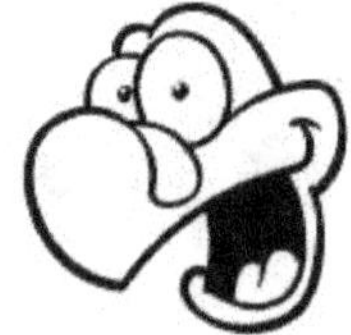
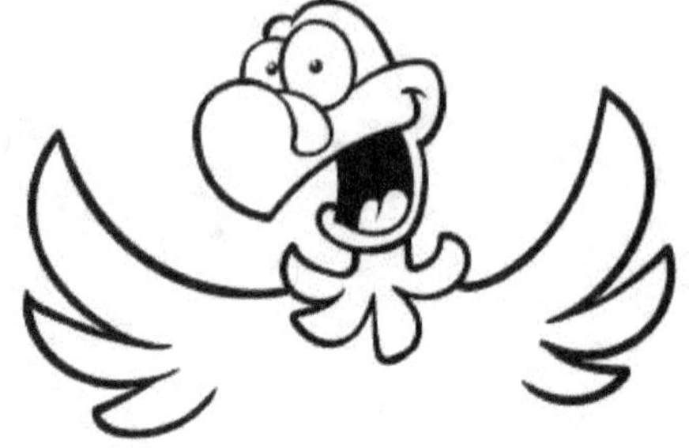
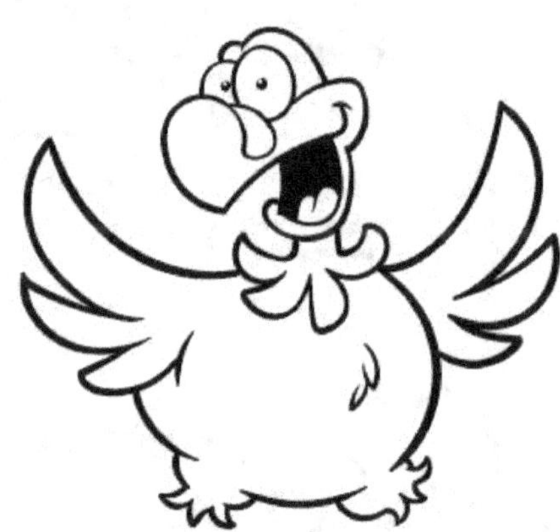
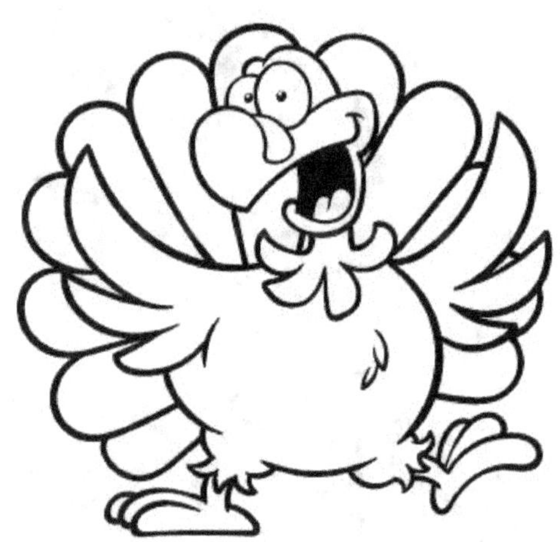
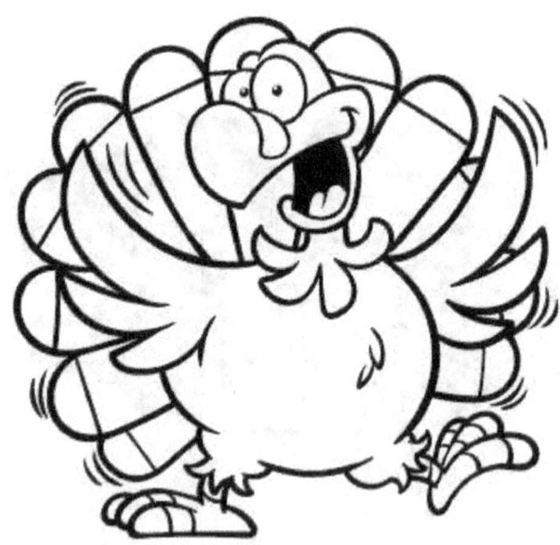
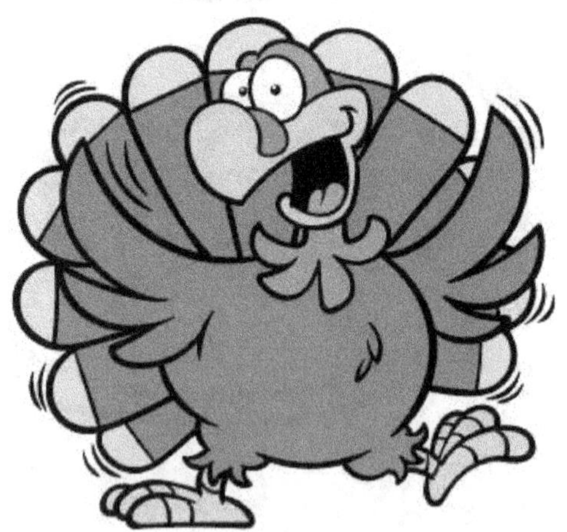

SNAIL

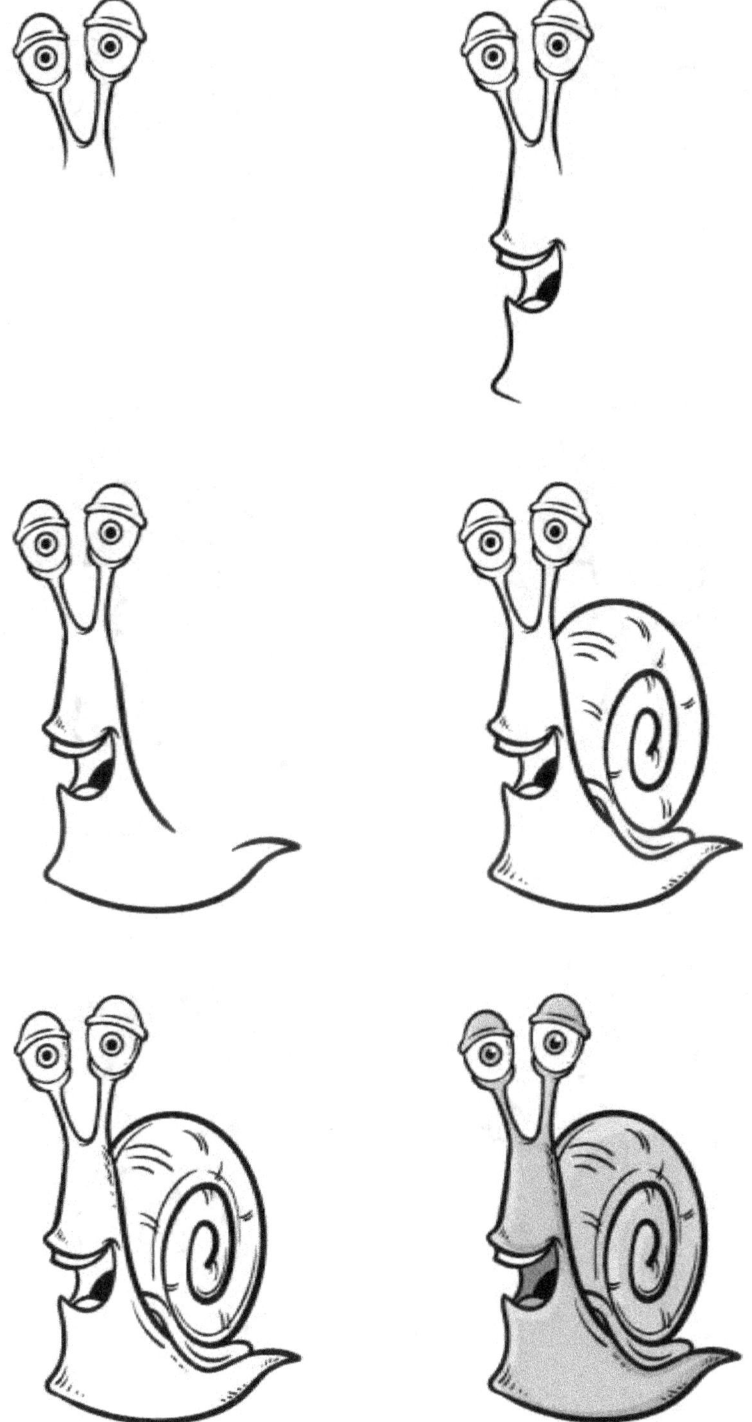

SNOWMAN

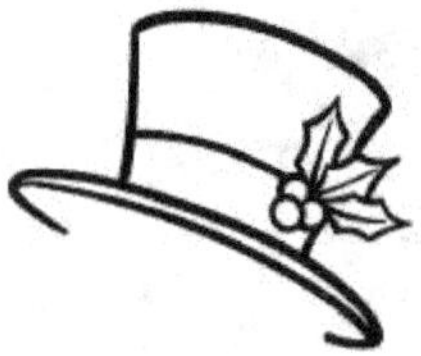 

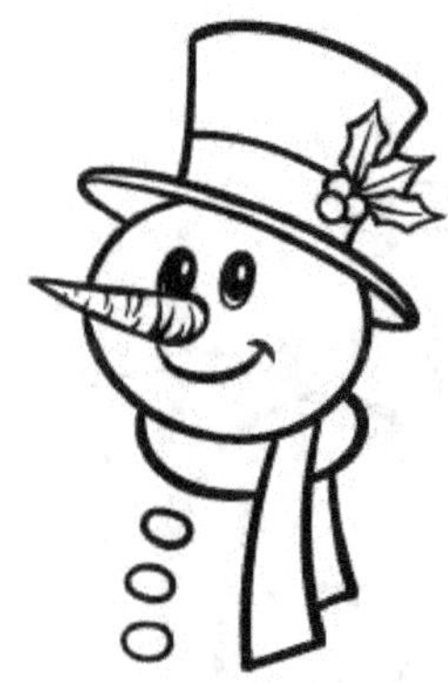 

CORGI

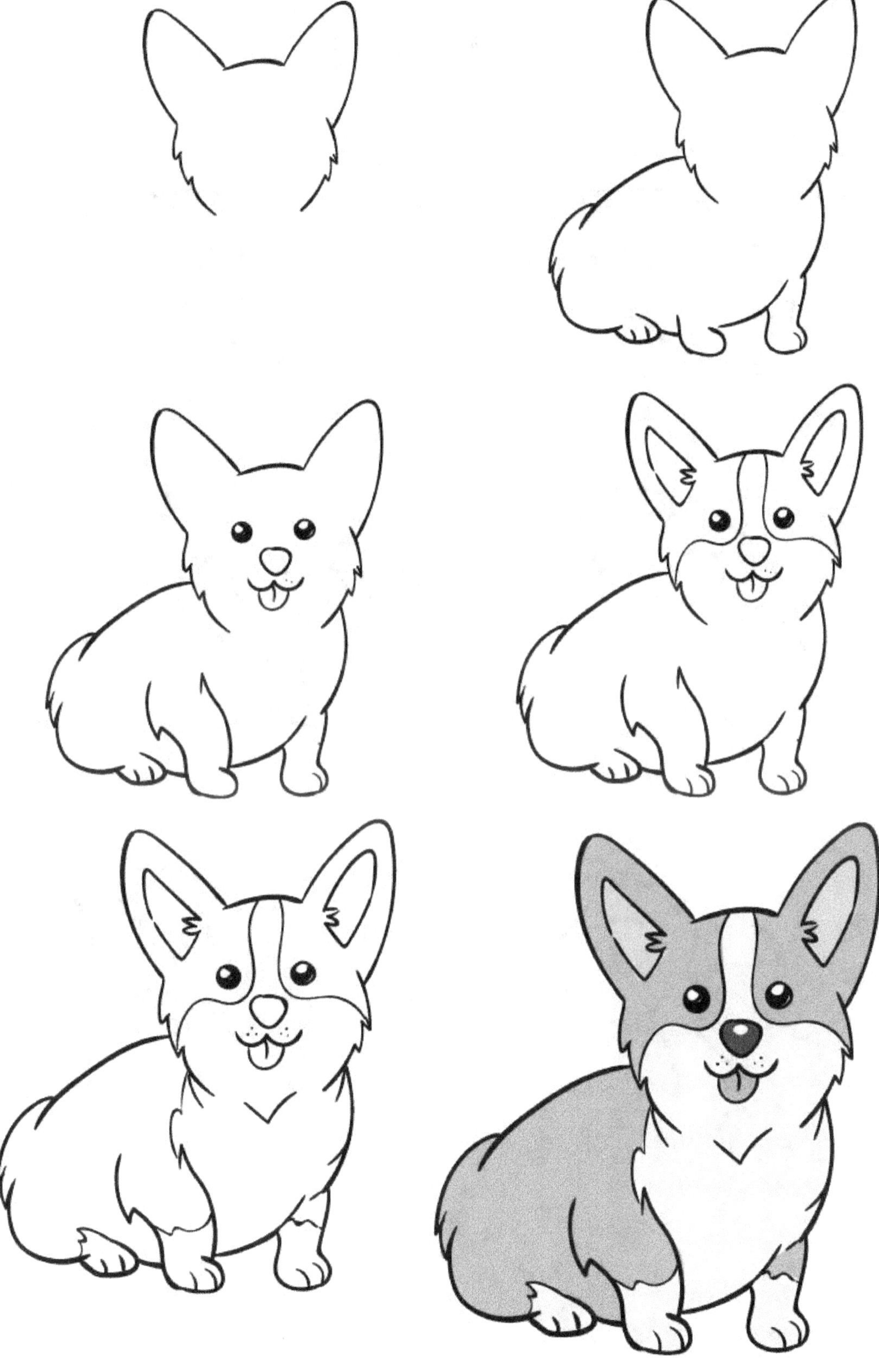

SPACE SHIP

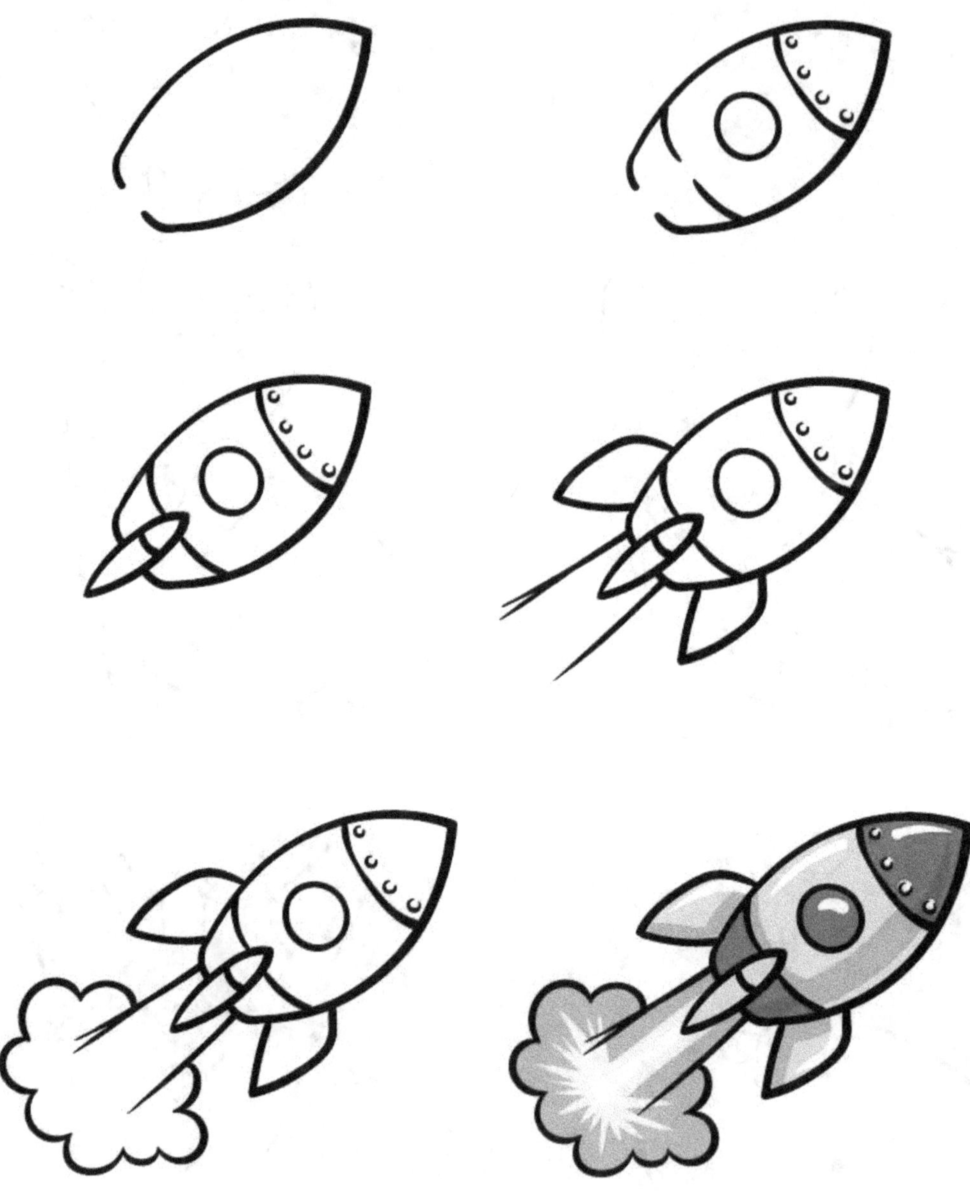

CUTE ANIMALS

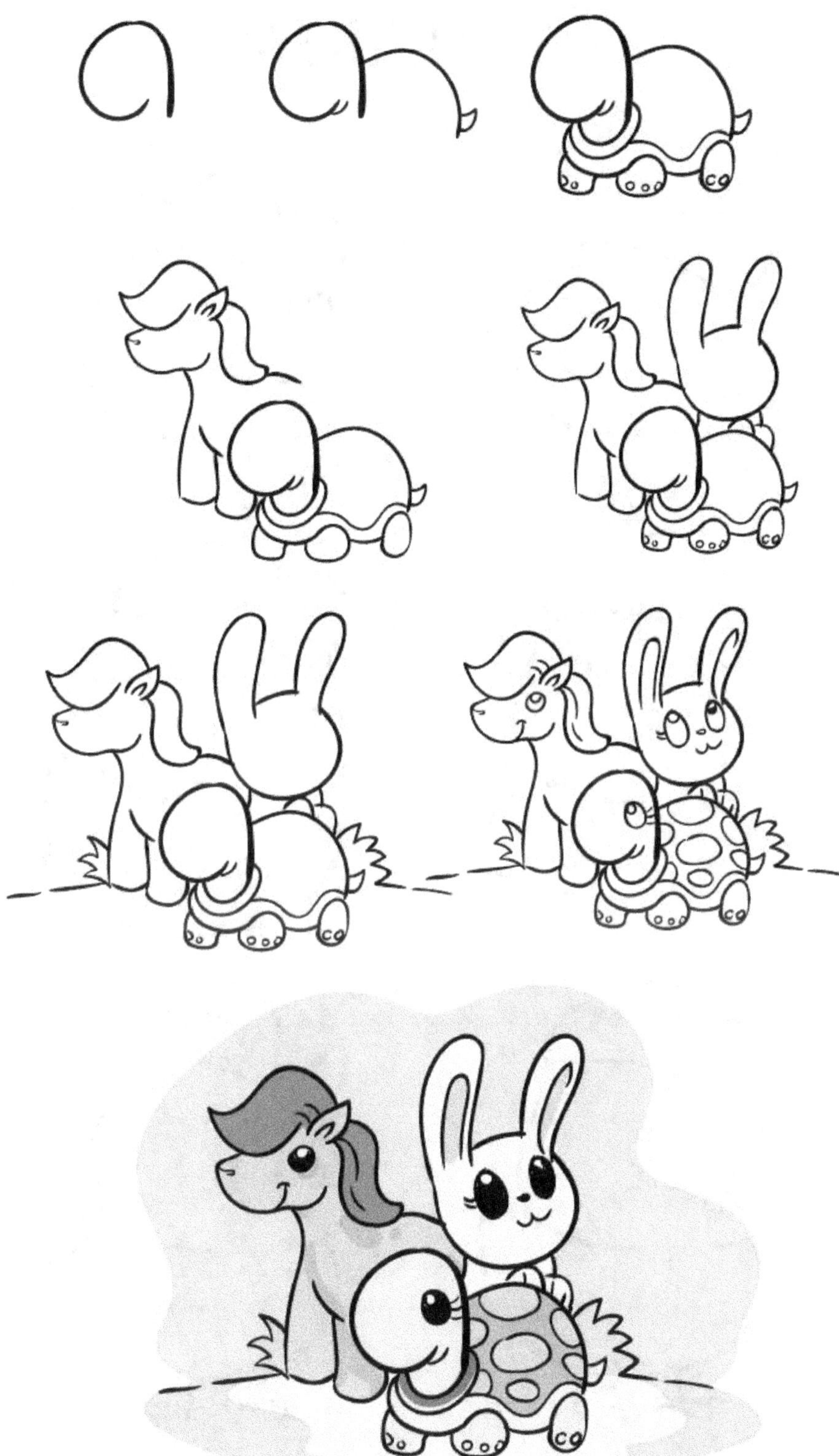

CHIKKEN

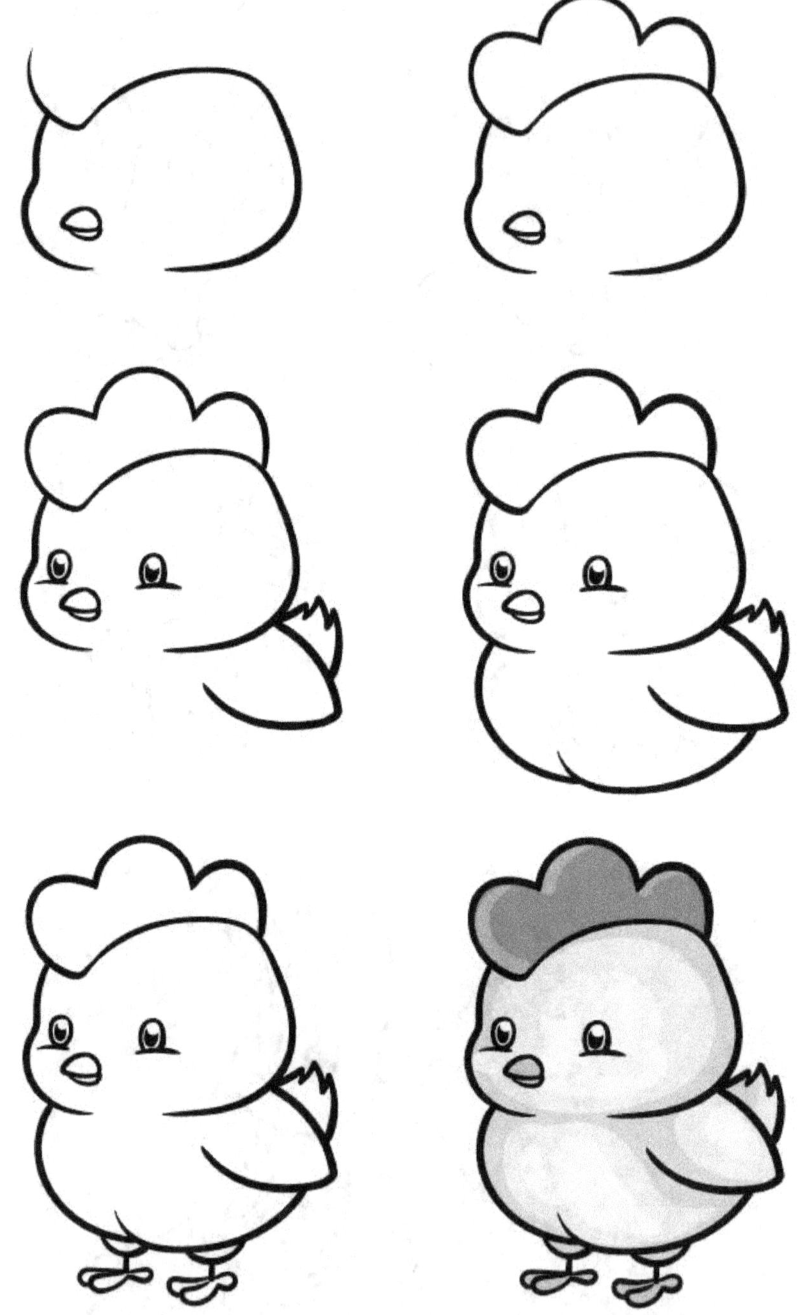

GLASSES

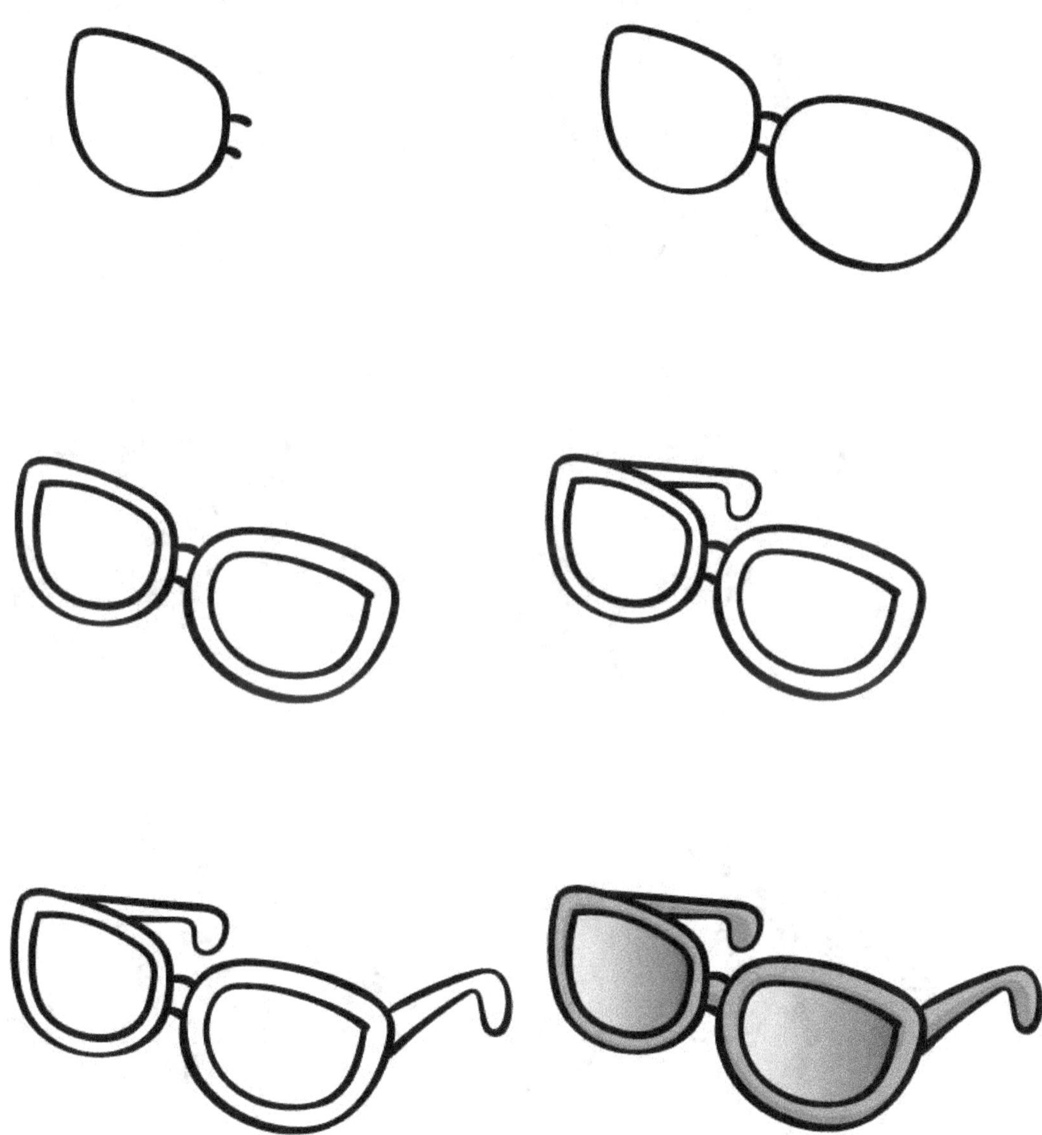

TOOTH

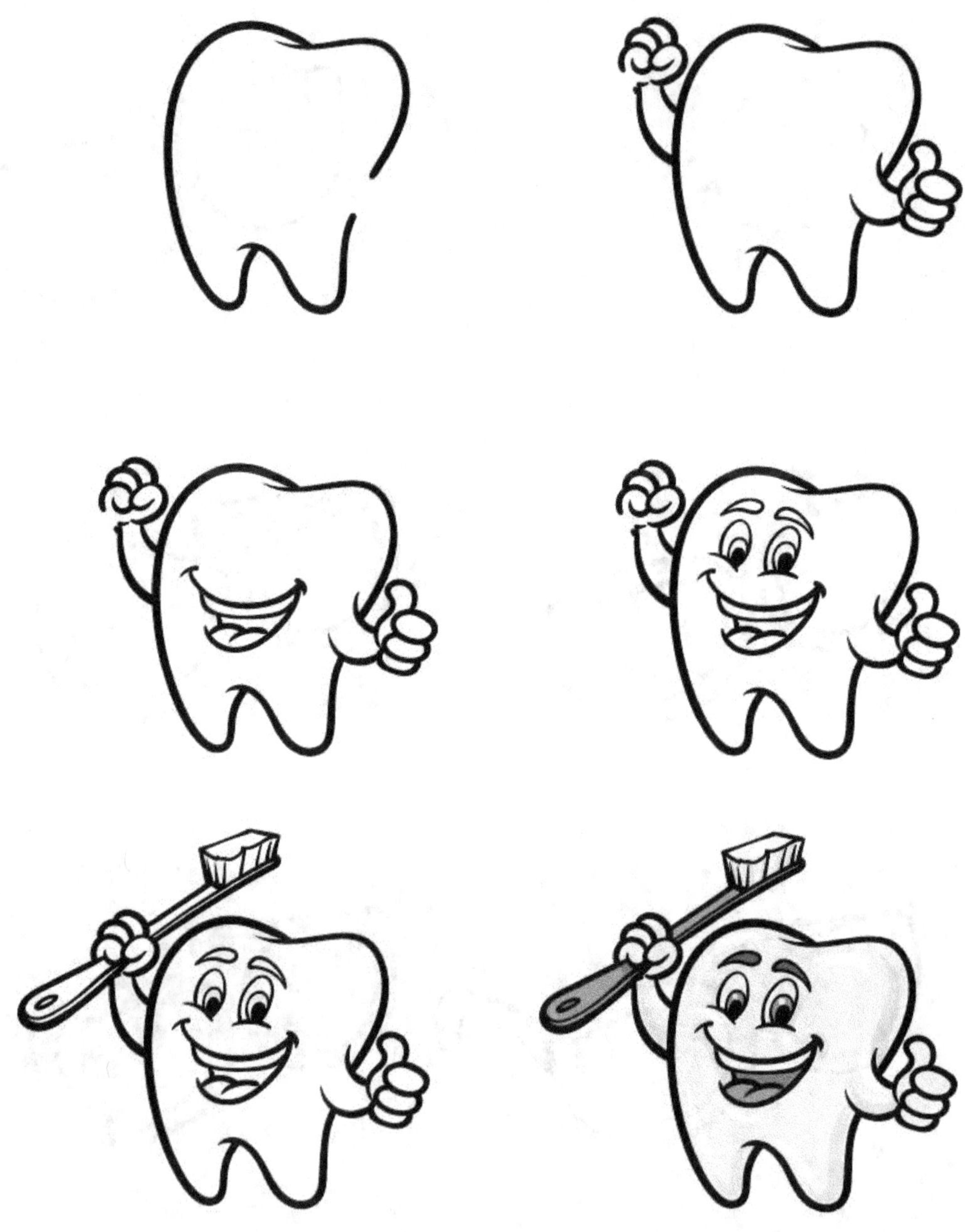

CHEESE

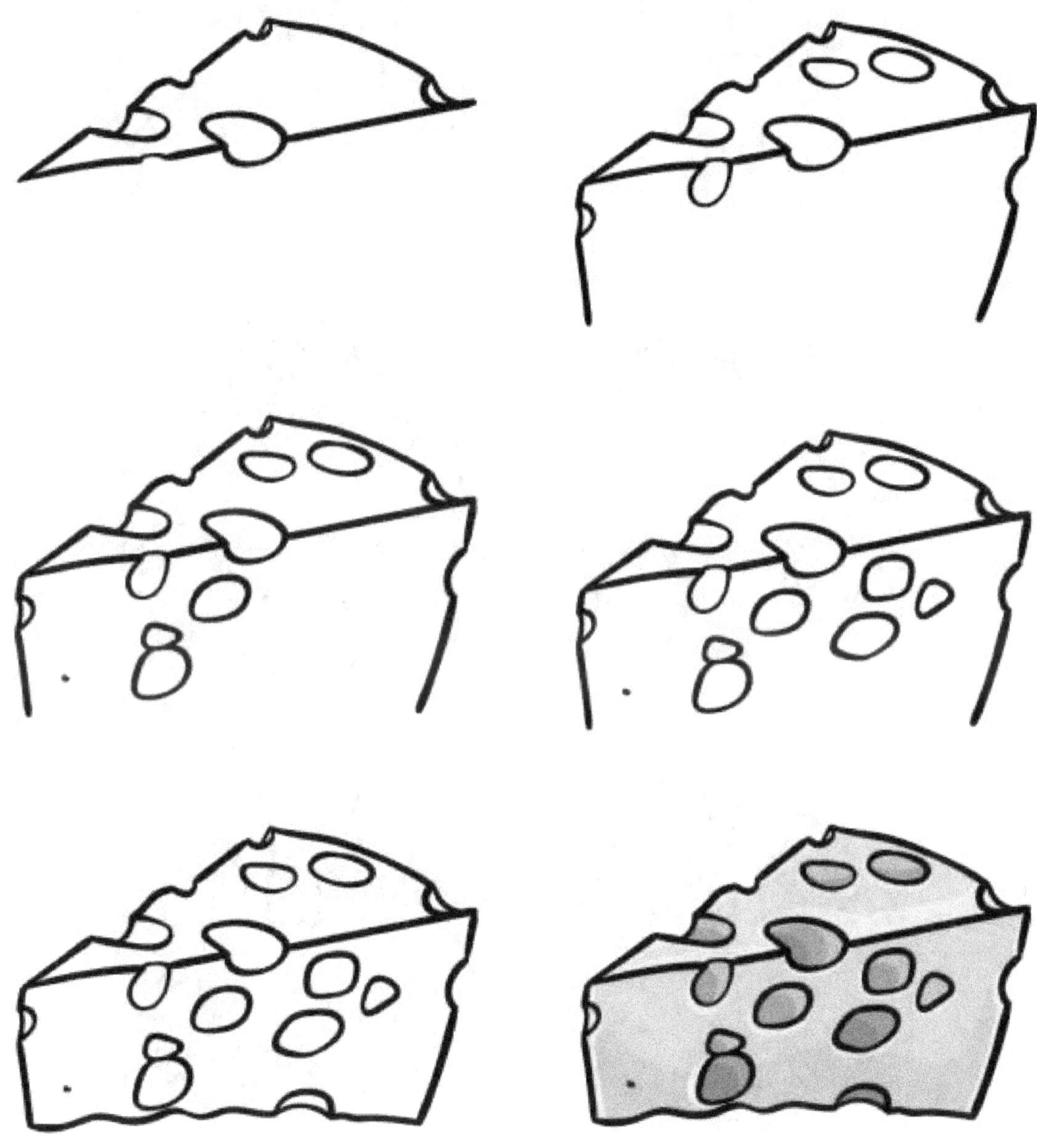

CHRISTMAS

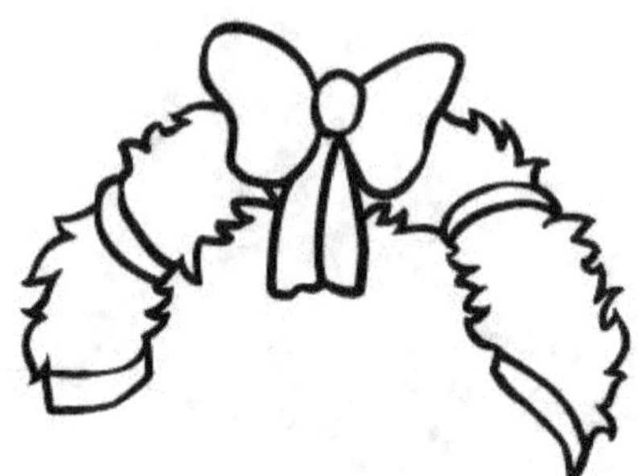

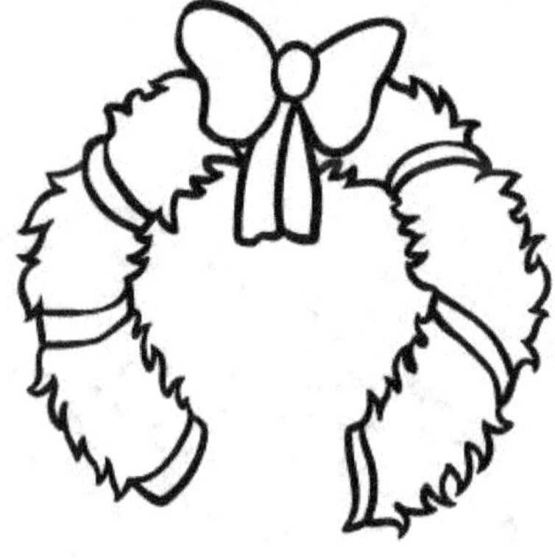

COTTON CANDY

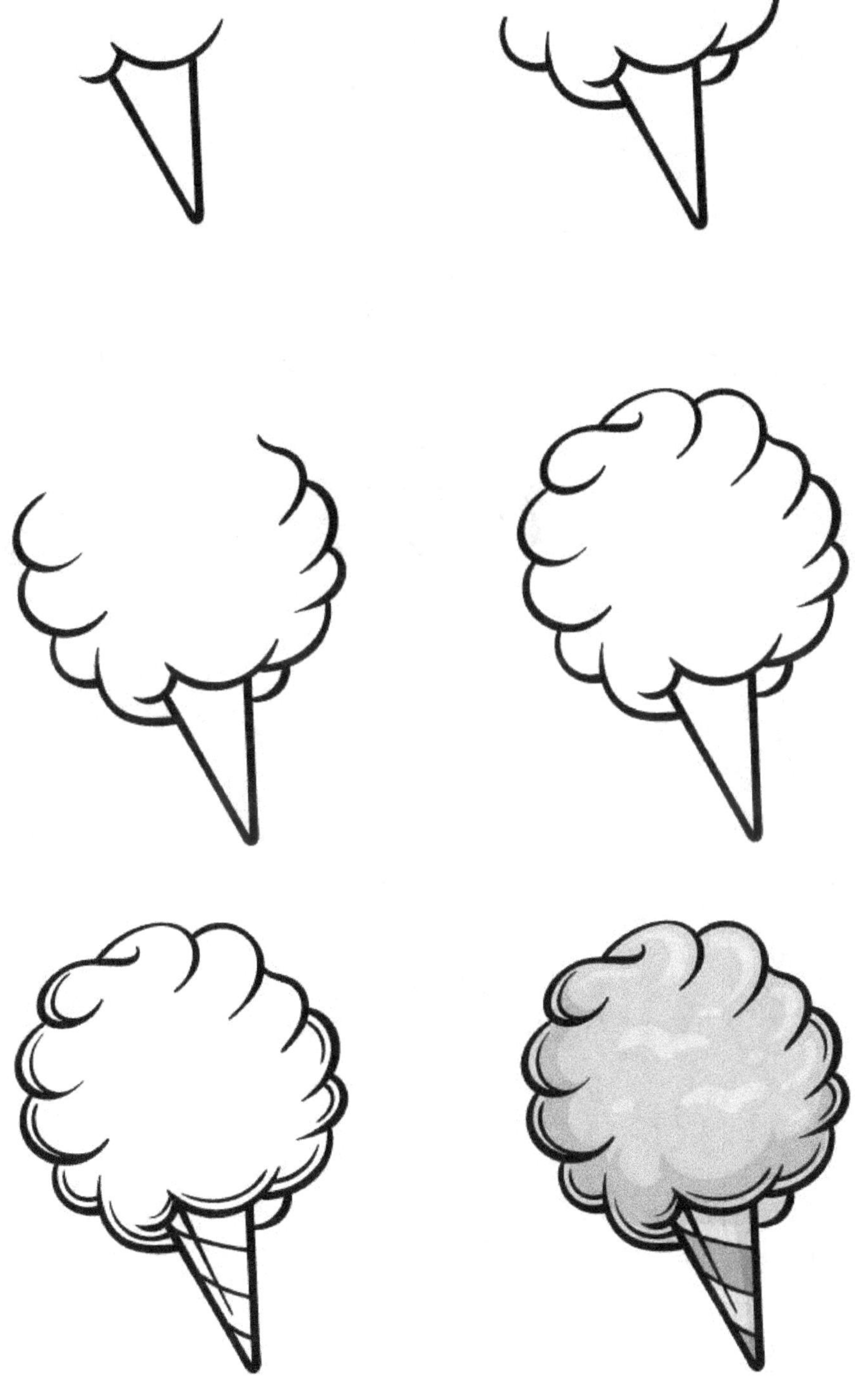

ANIMAL

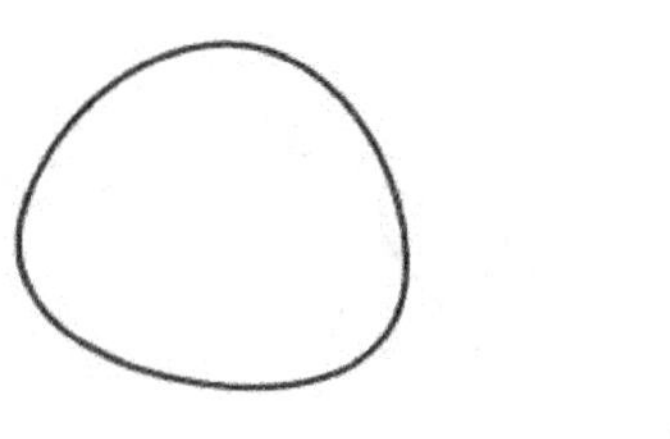 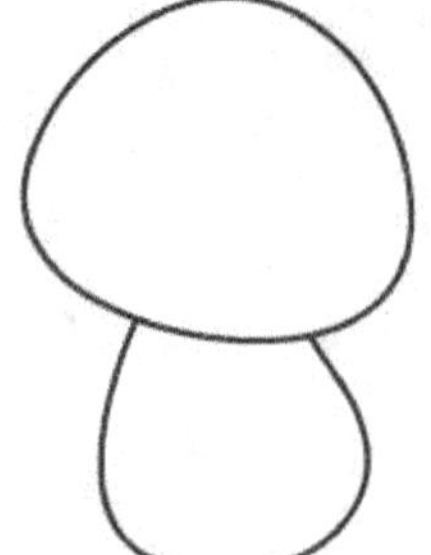 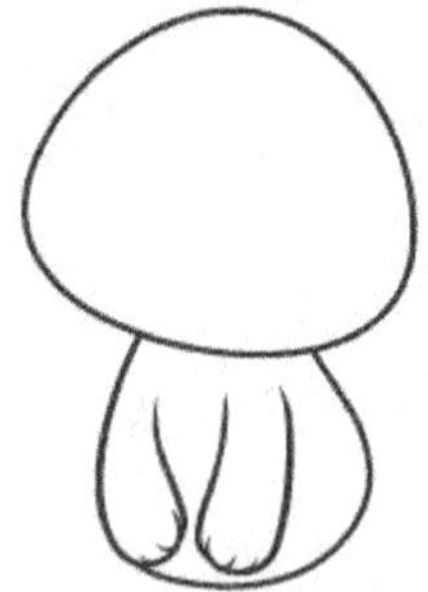

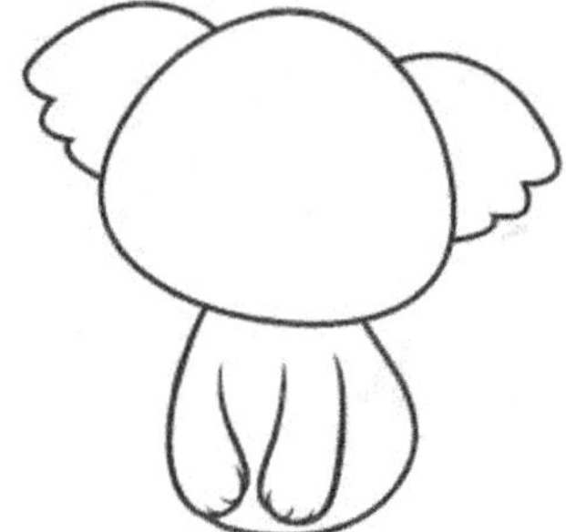 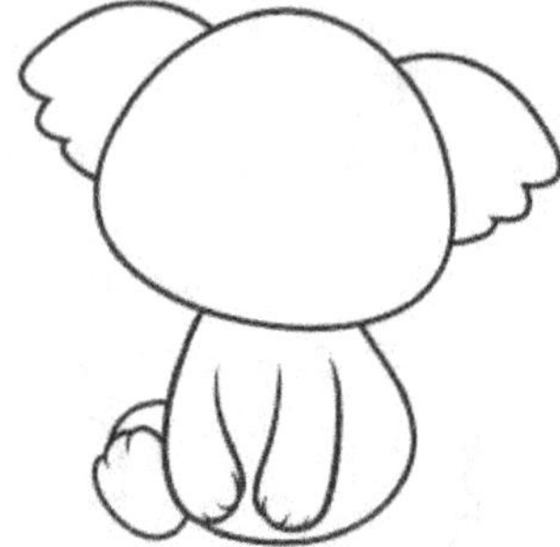 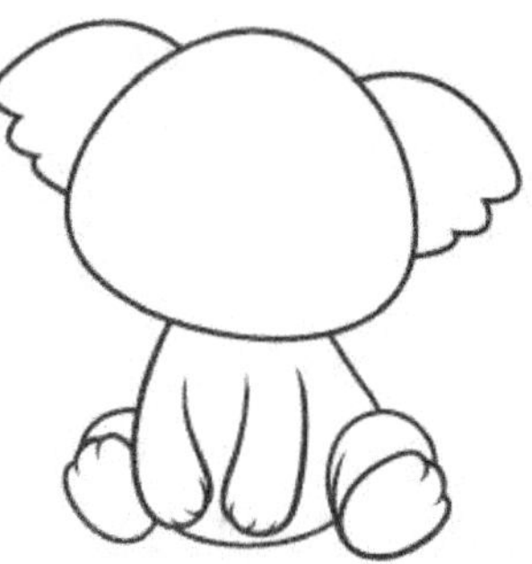

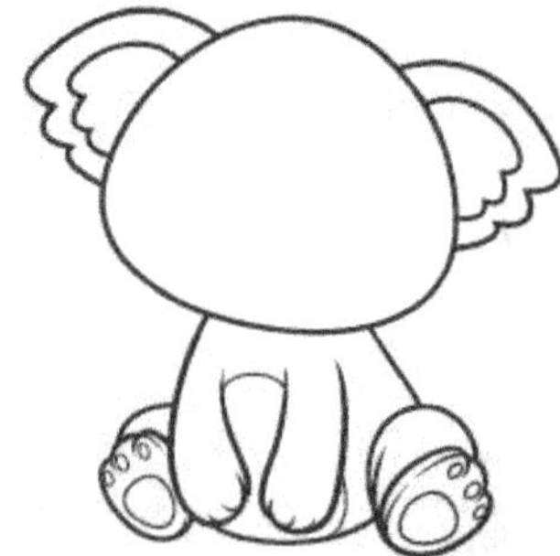 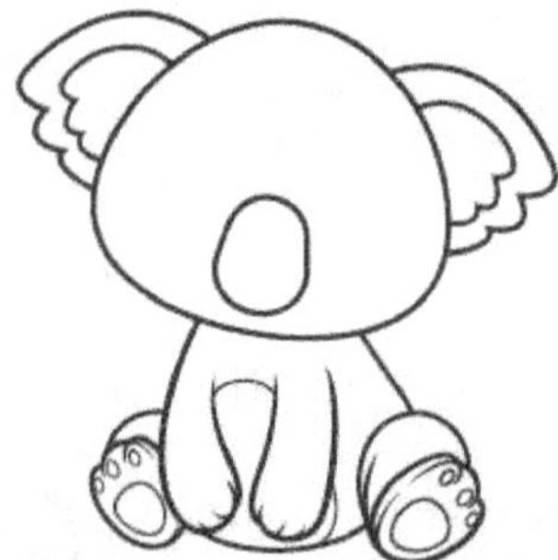 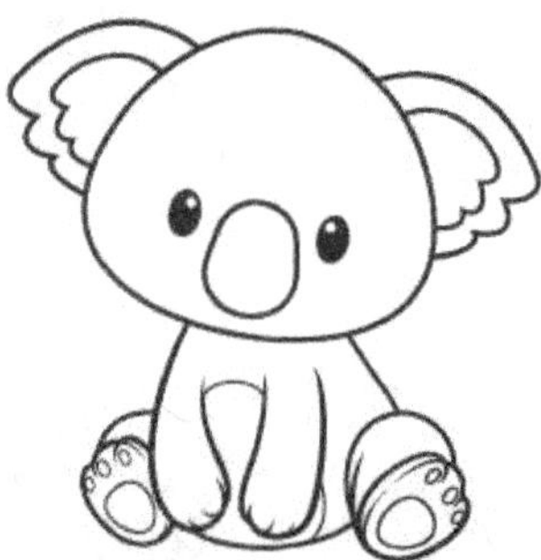

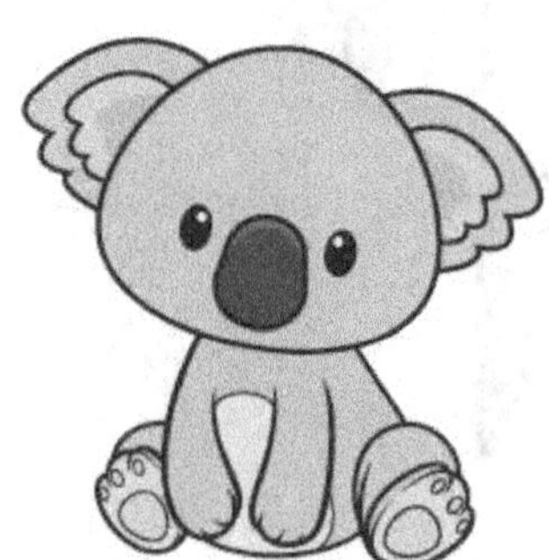

ANT

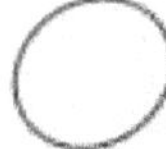 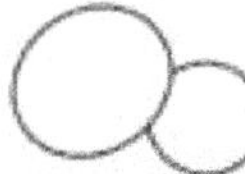 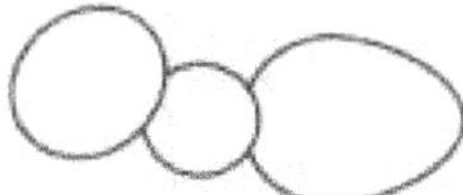

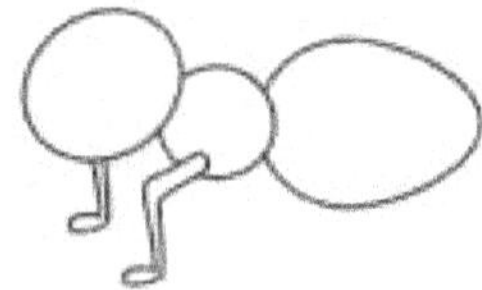 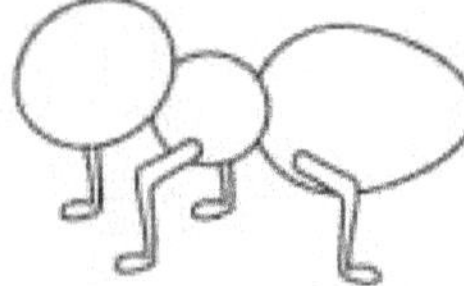 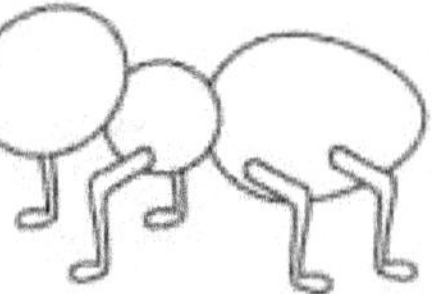

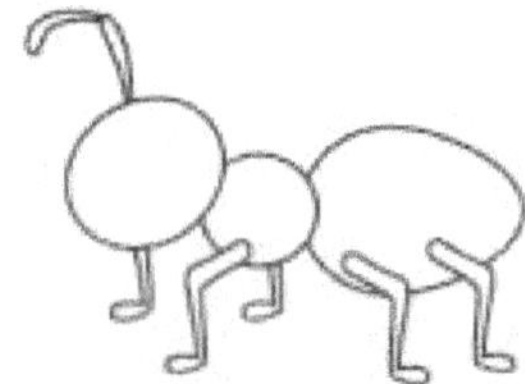 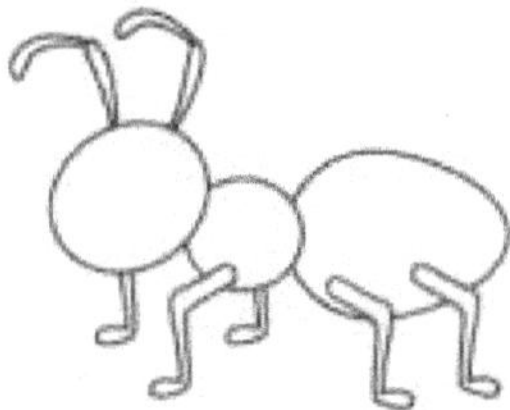 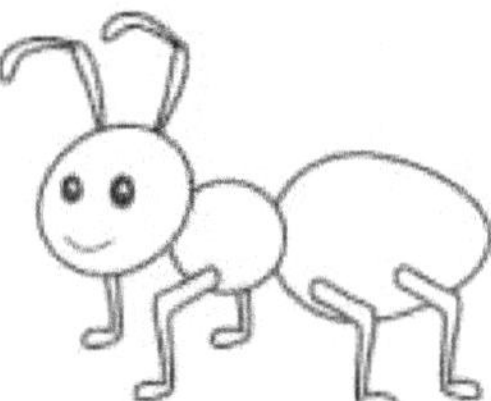

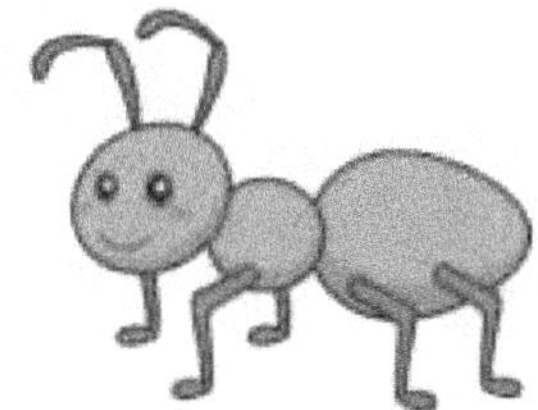

BRITHAY CAKE

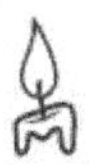 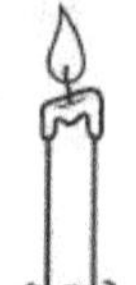 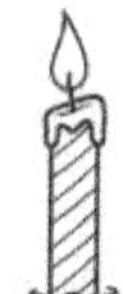

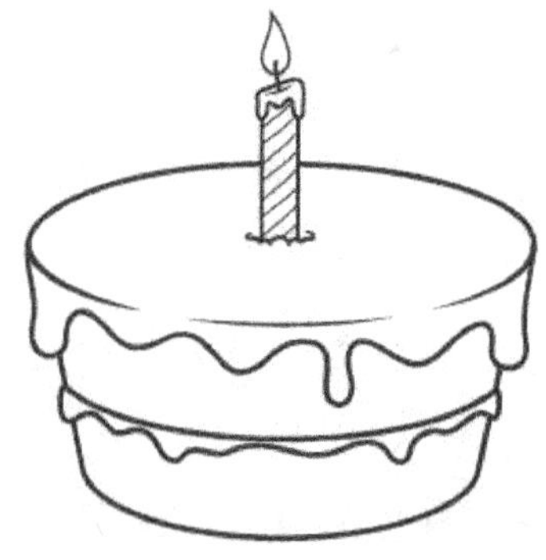  

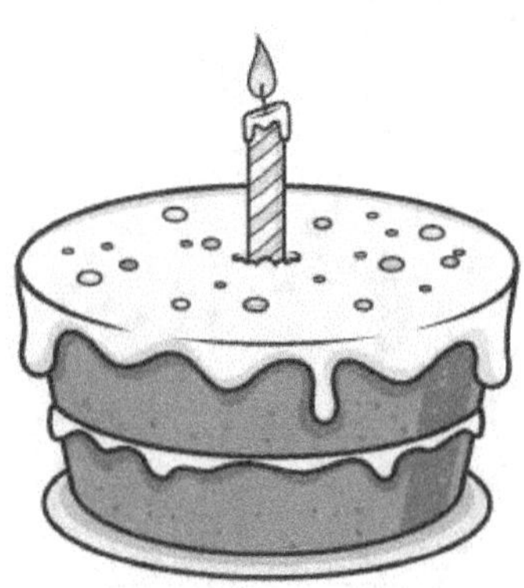

CAR

 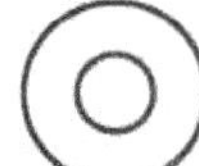 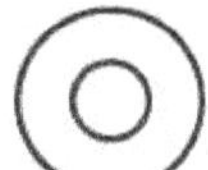 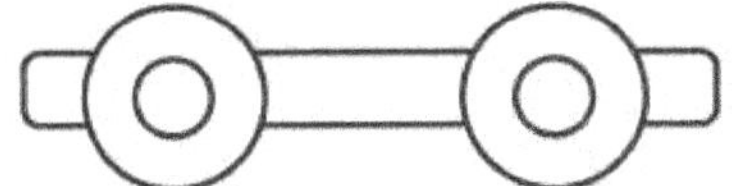

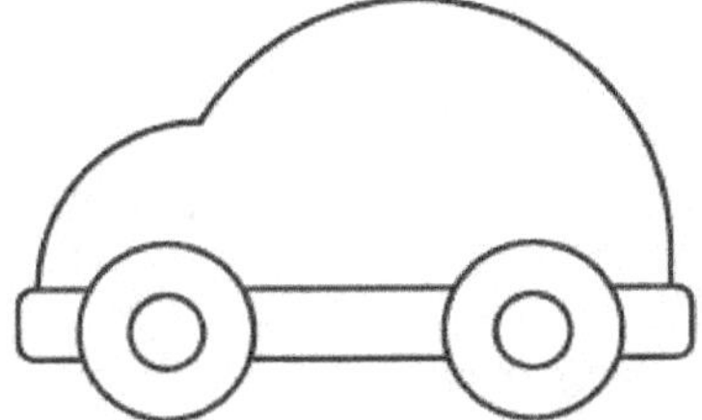 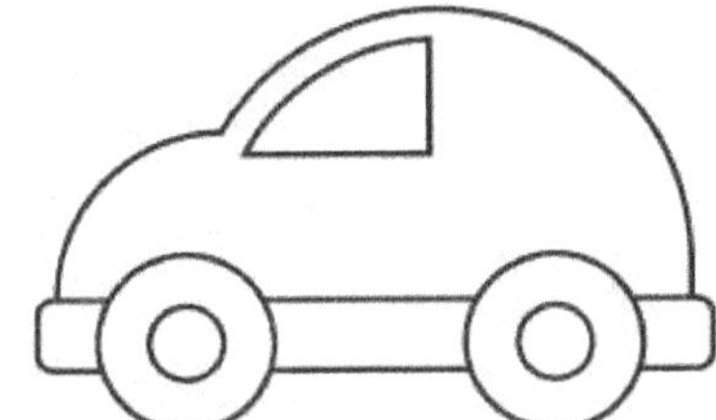 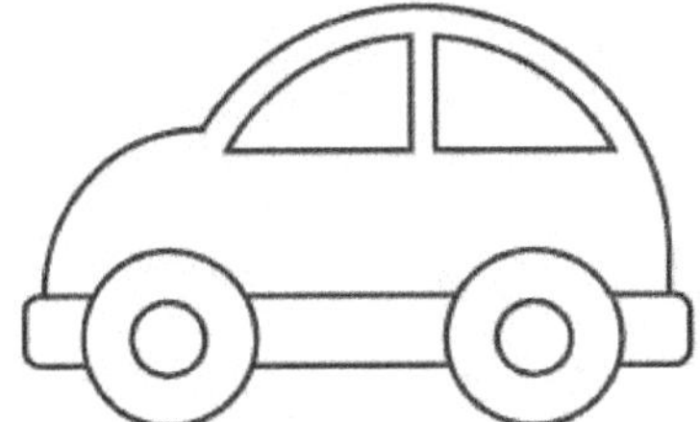

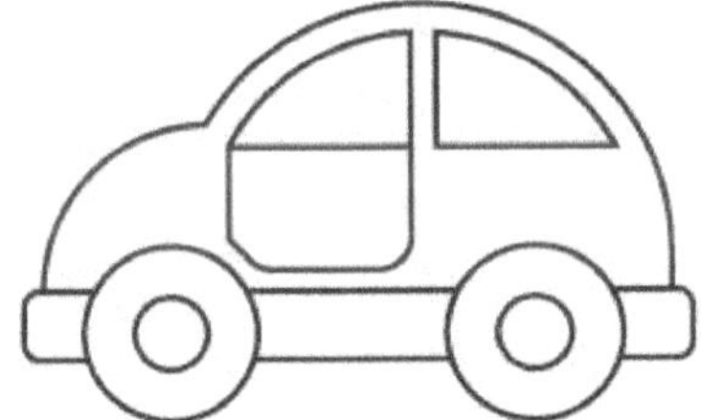 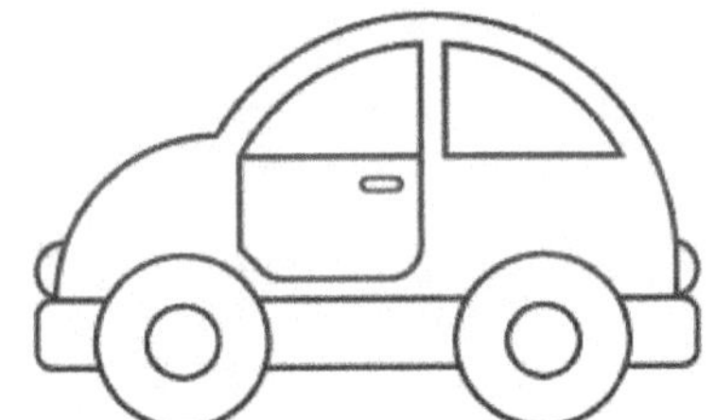 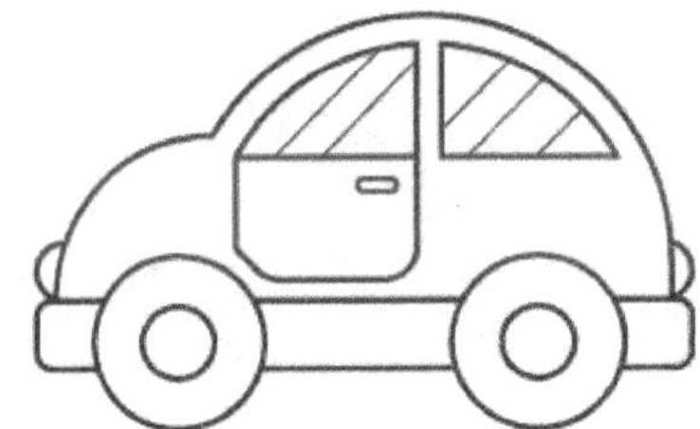

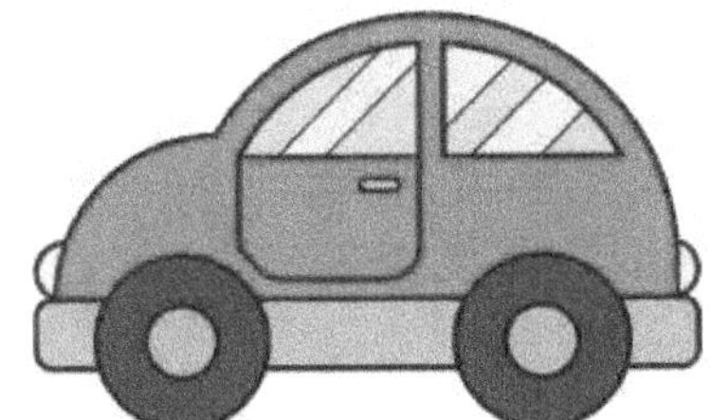

CIRCLE

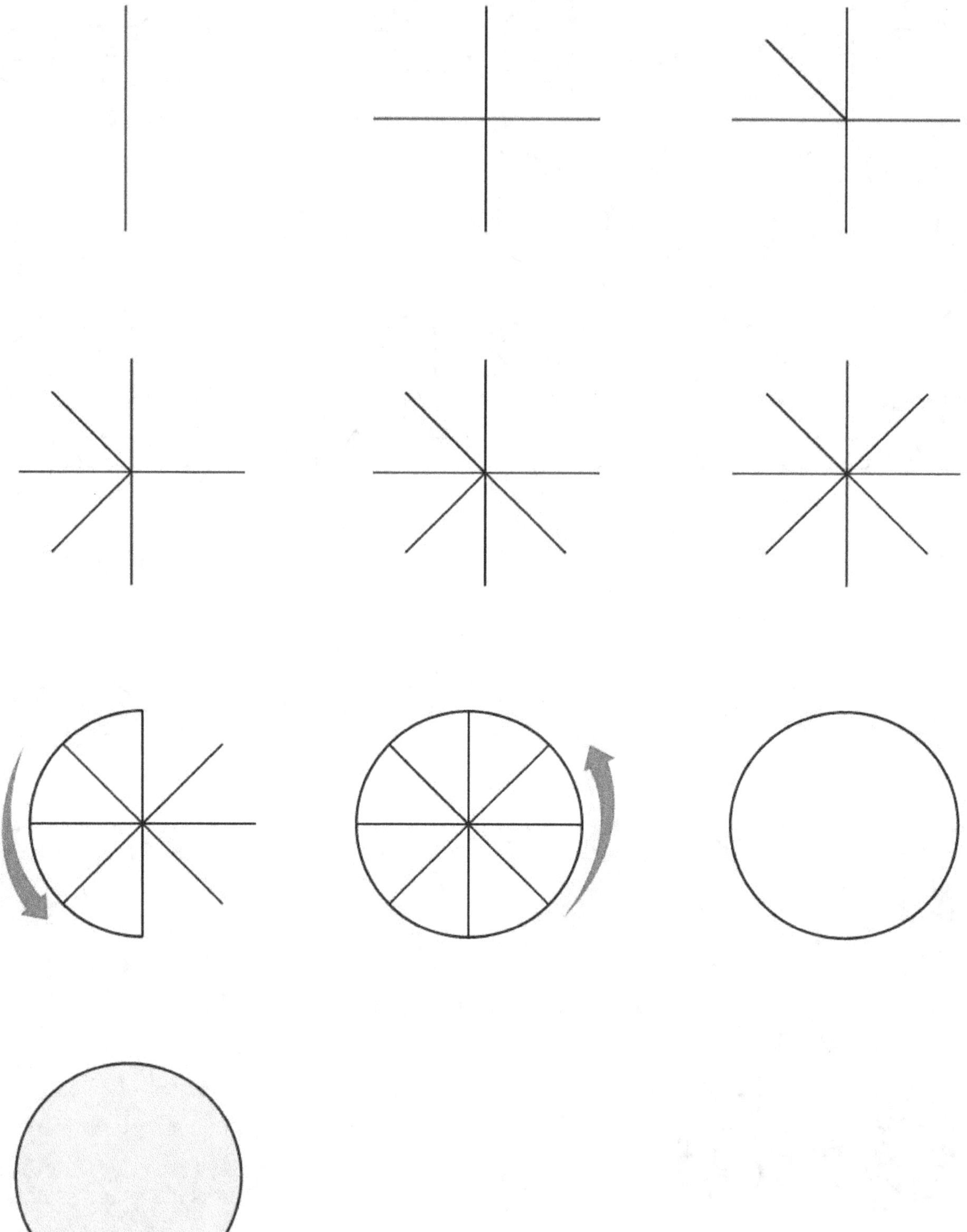

CRAP

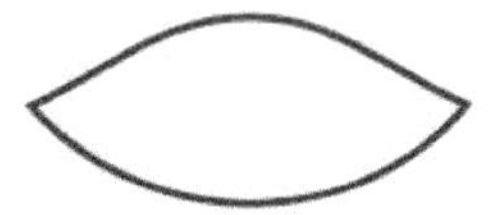
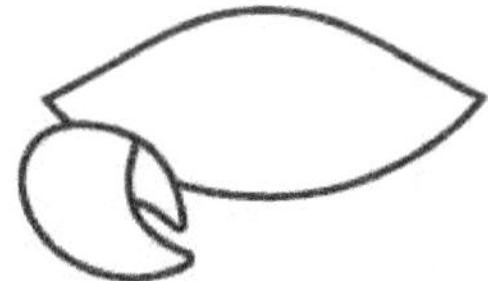
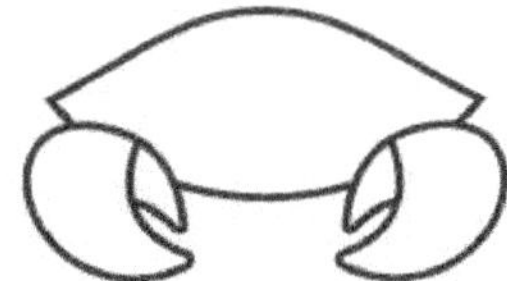
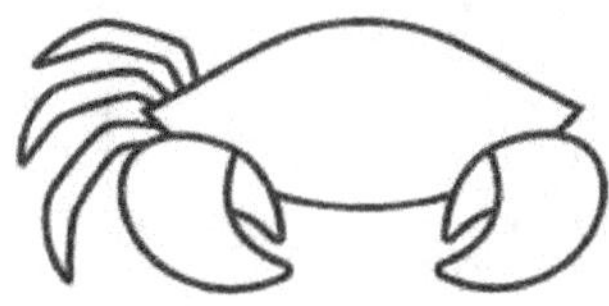
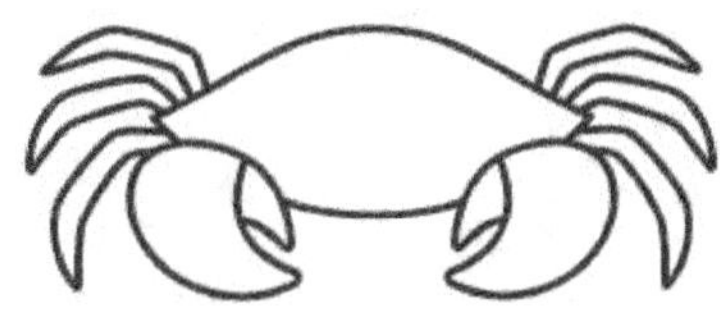
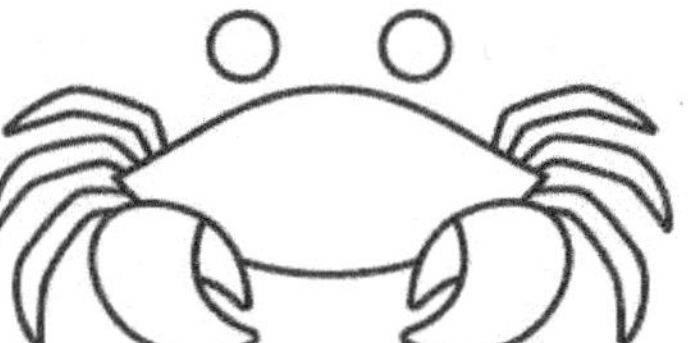
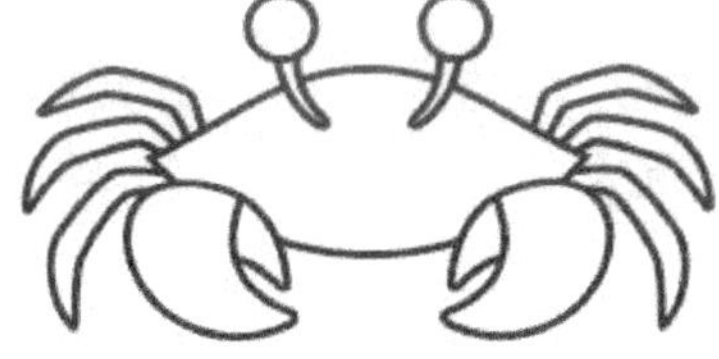
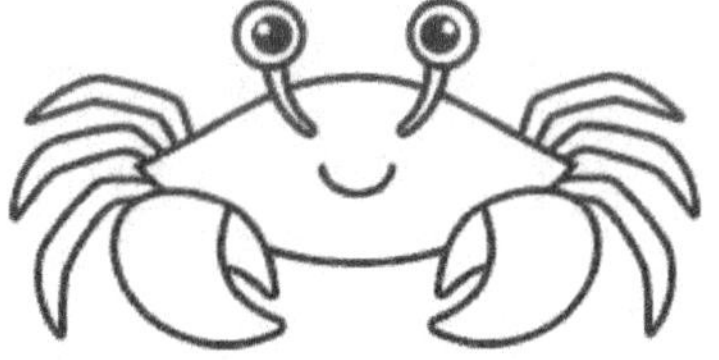
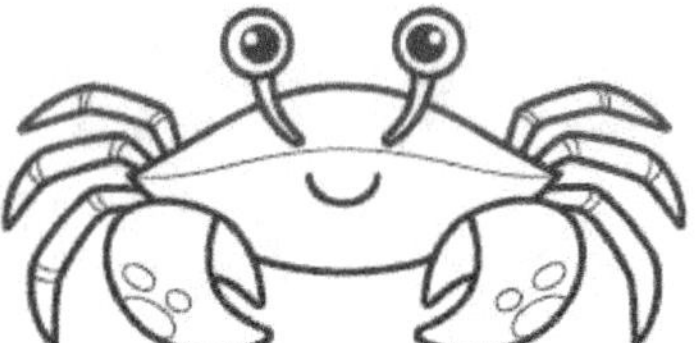
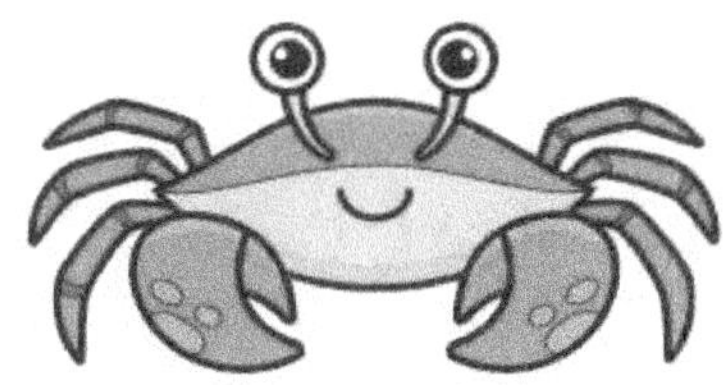

CLOWN

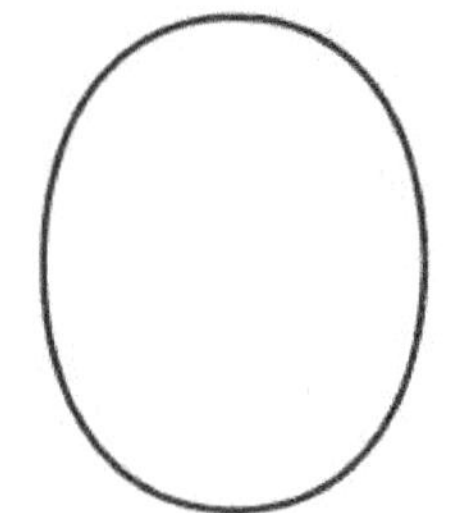
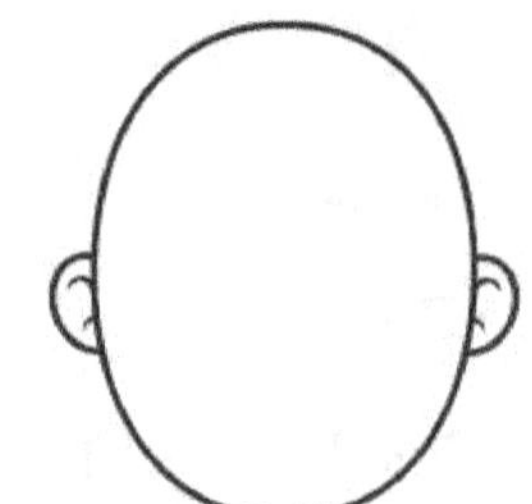
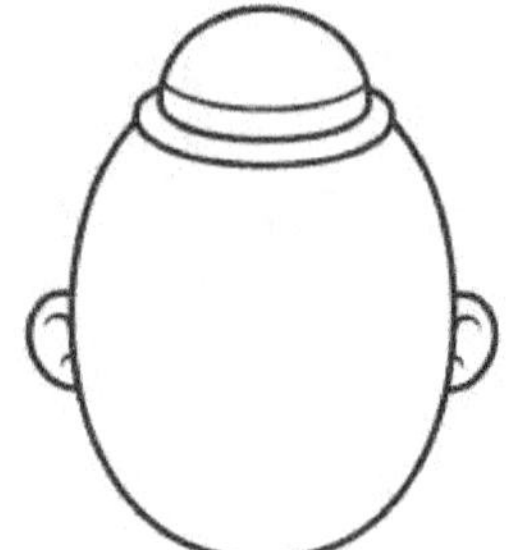
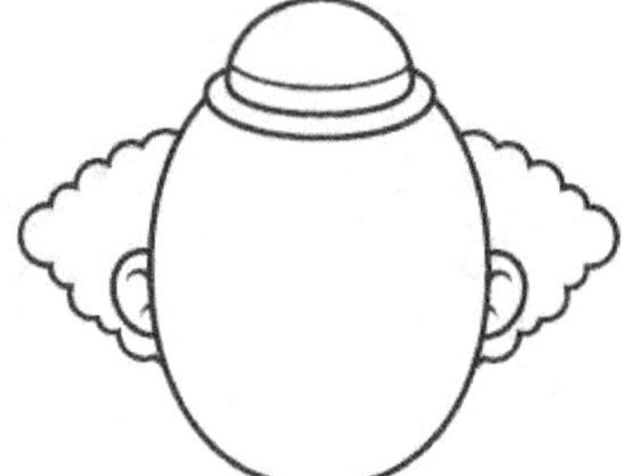
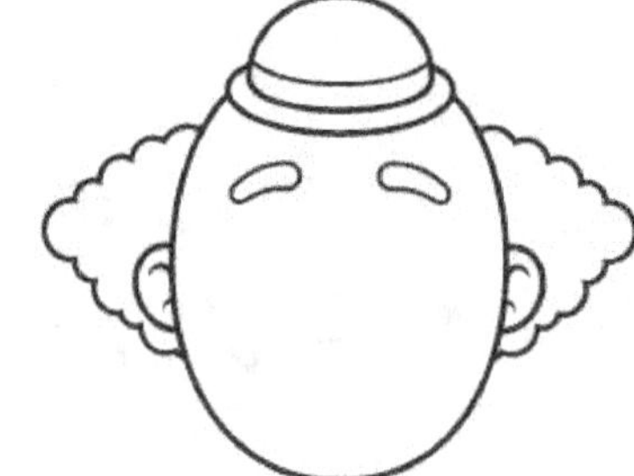
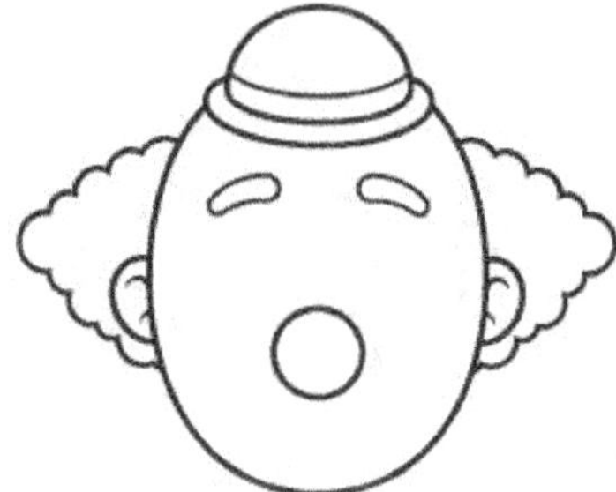
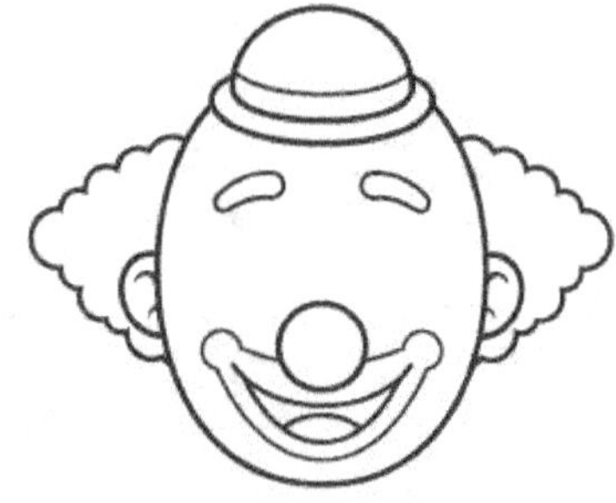
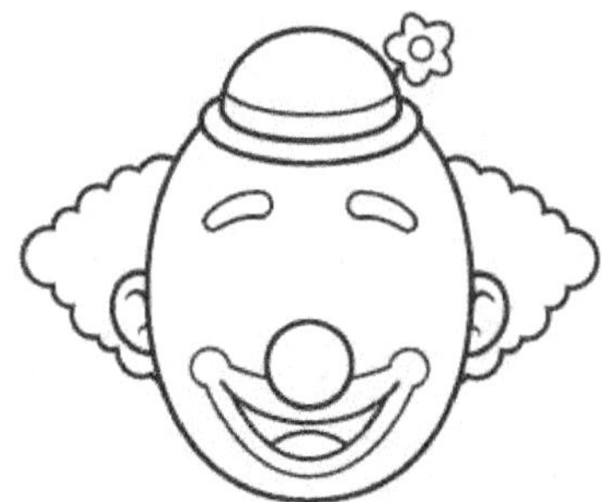
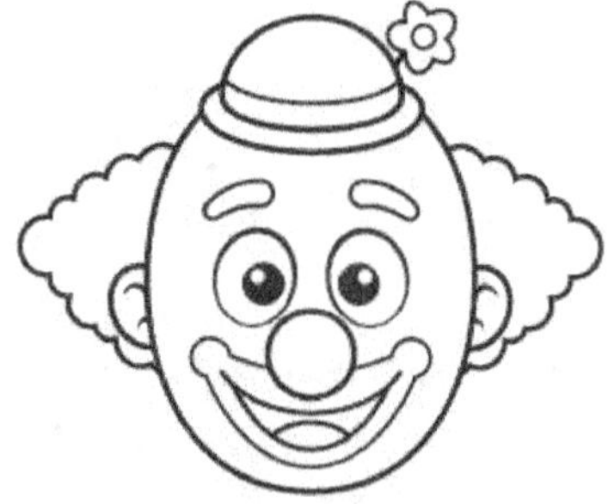

DOVE

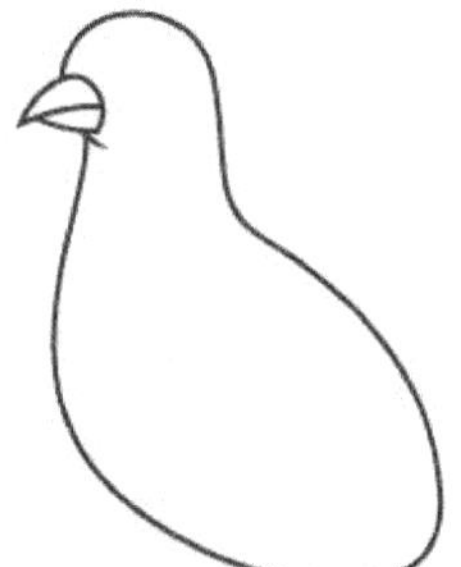
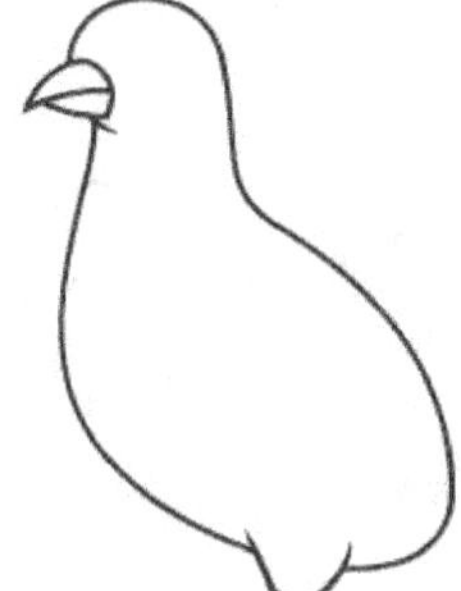
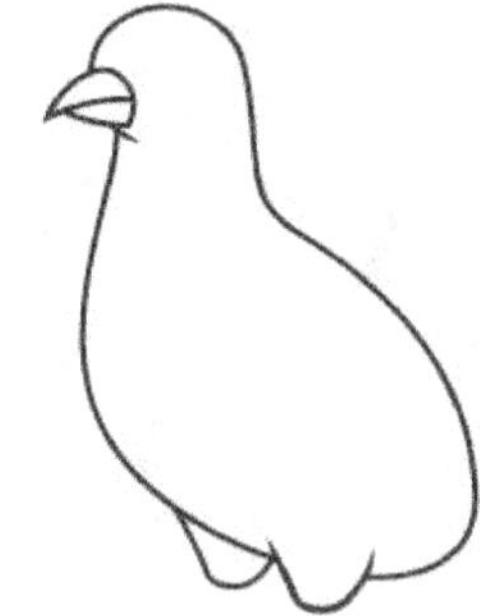
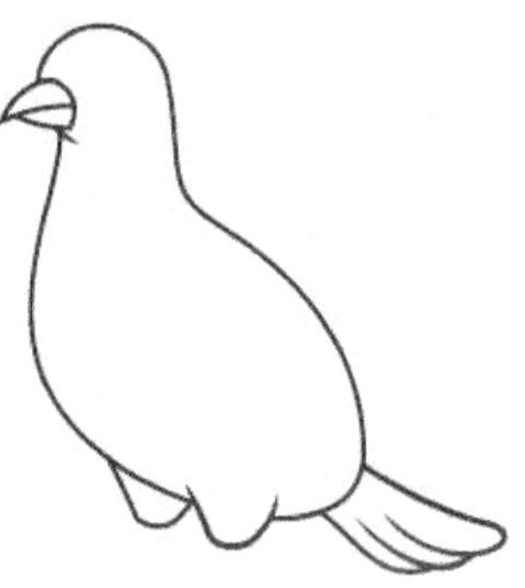
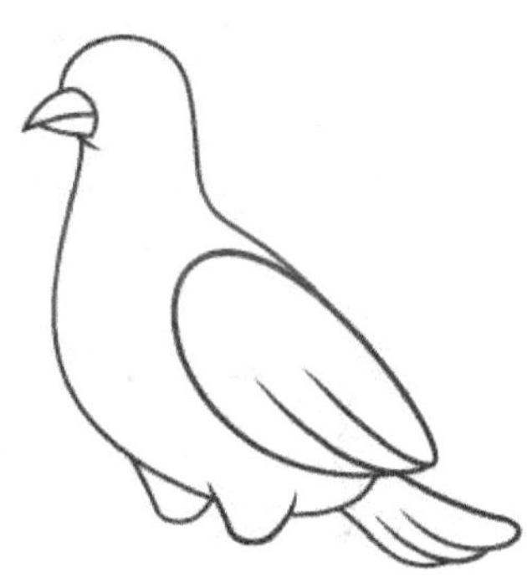
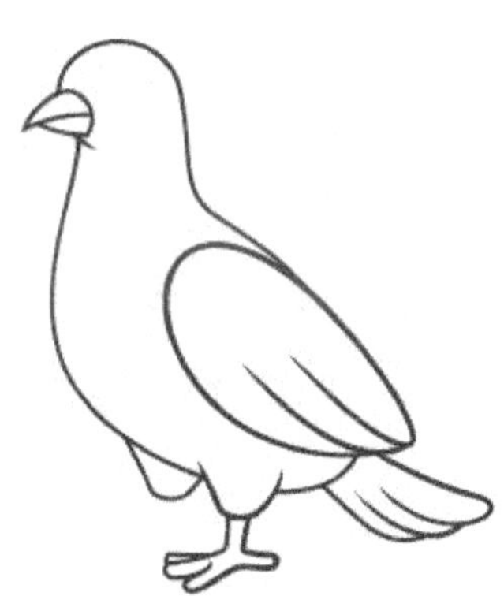
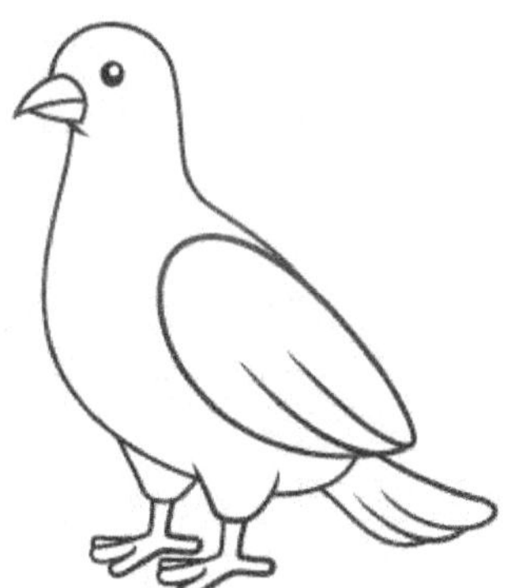
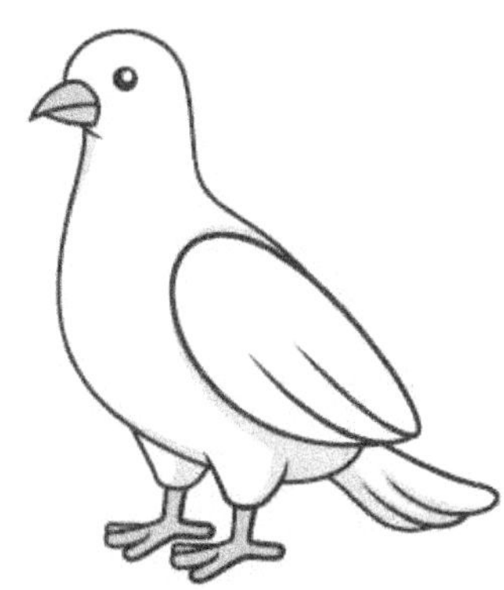

CUPCAKE

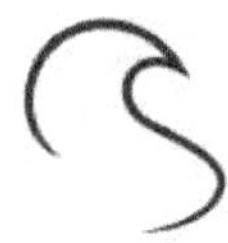

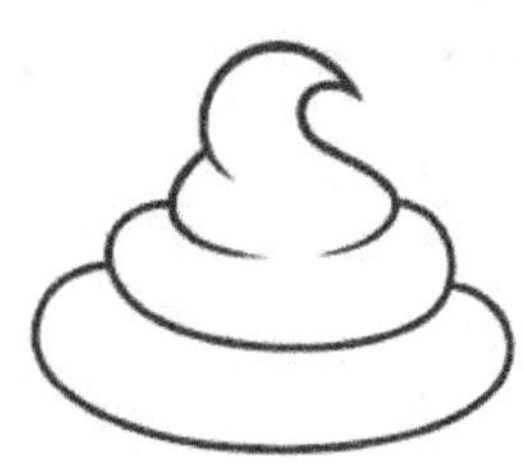

DOG

DAISY

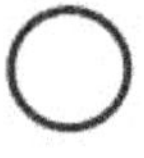

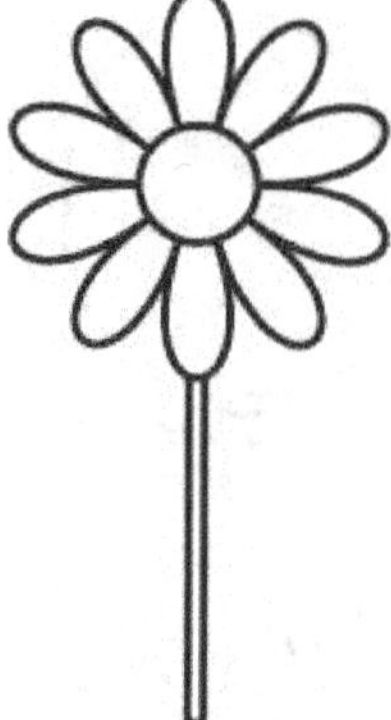

PLANETS

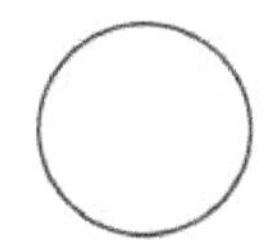
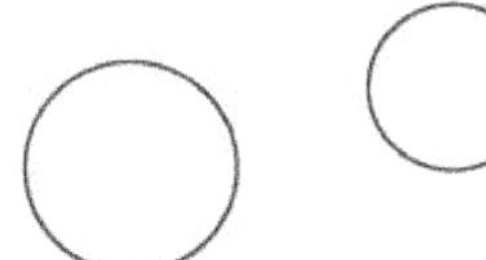
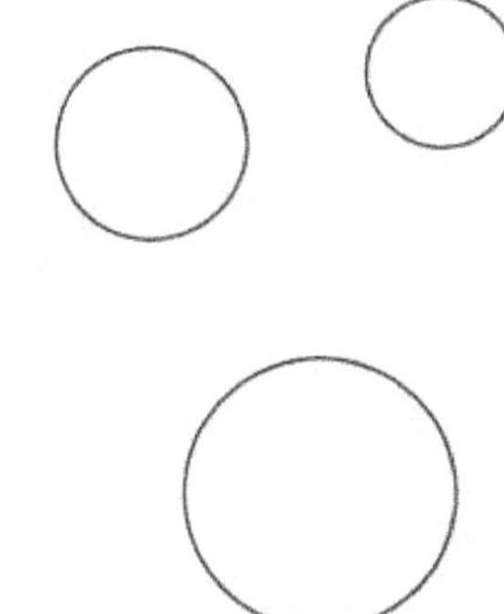
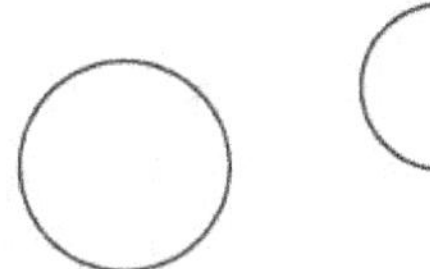
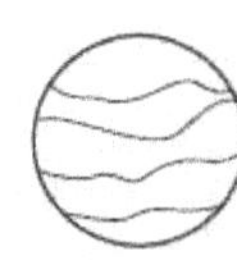
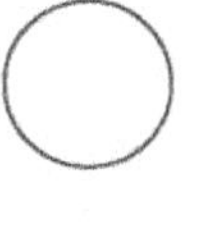
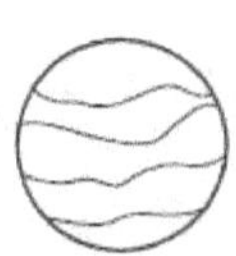
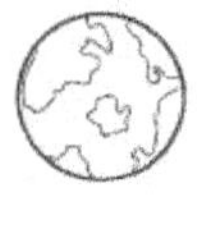
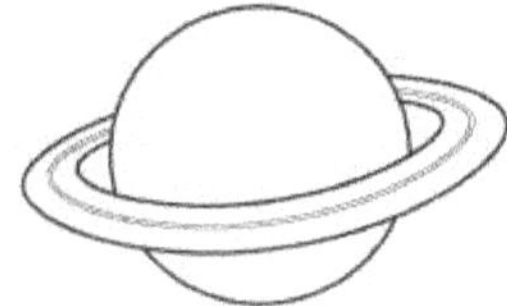
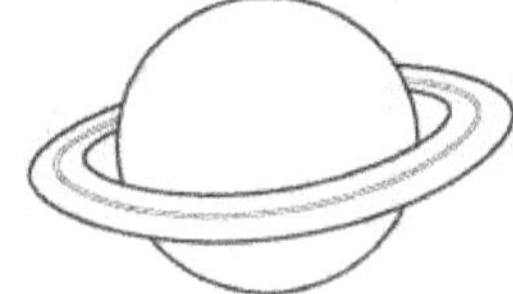
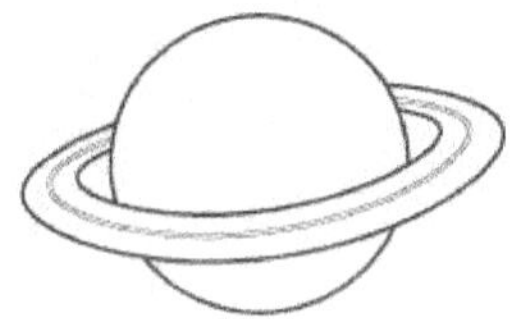
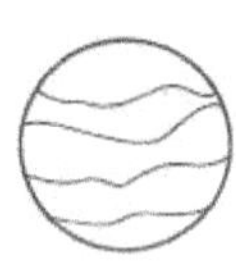
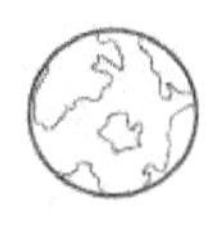
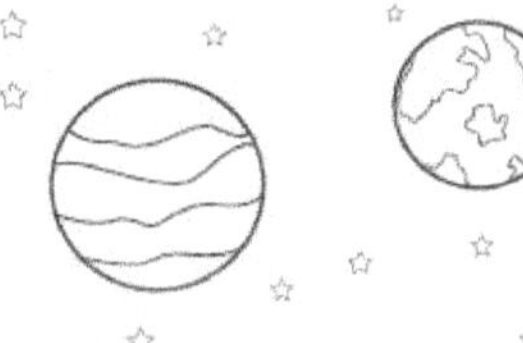
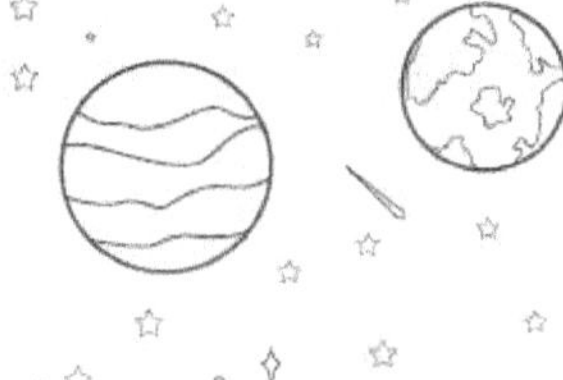
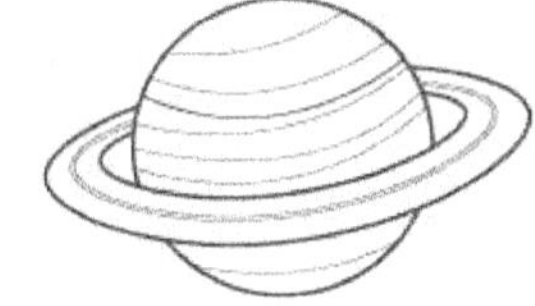
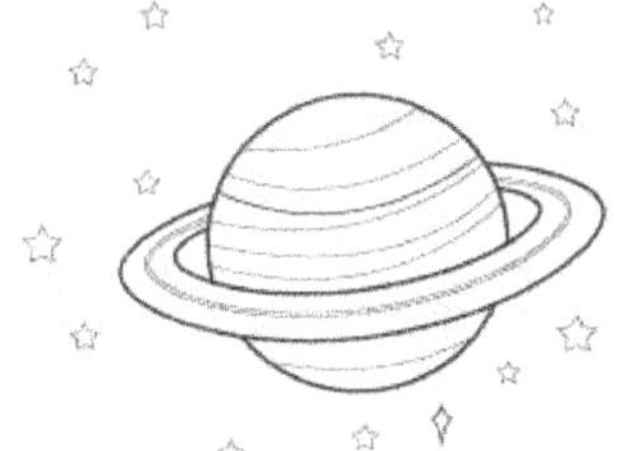
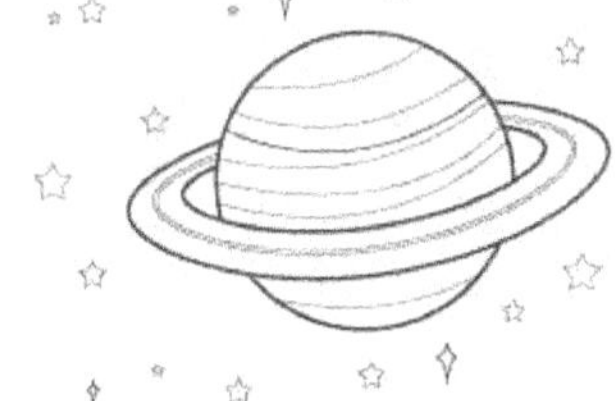
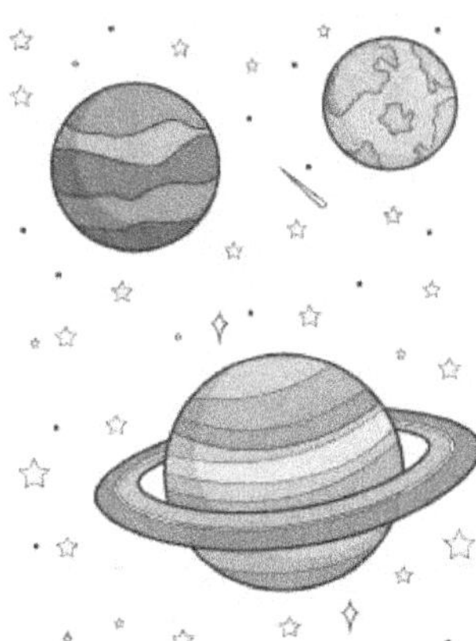

DRAGONS

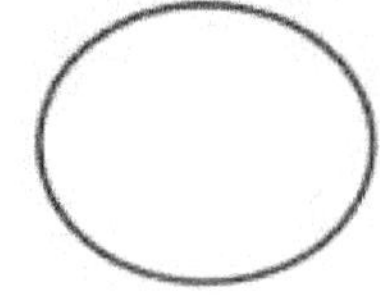 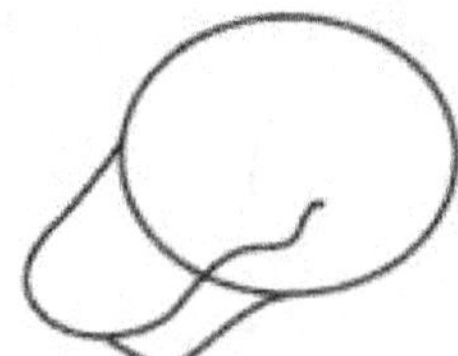 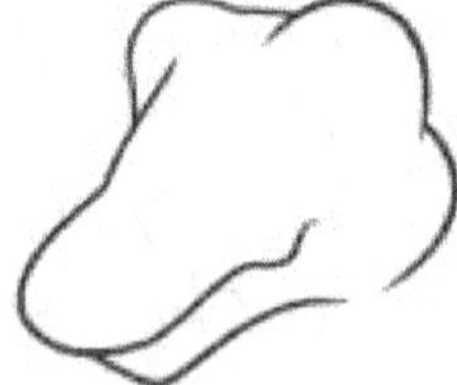

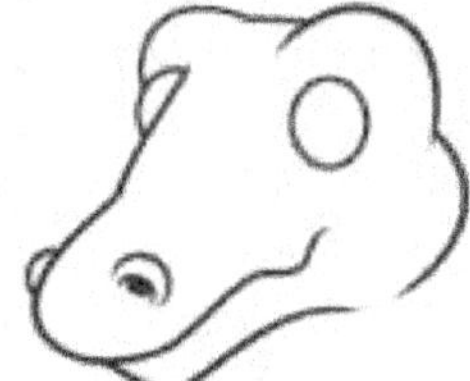 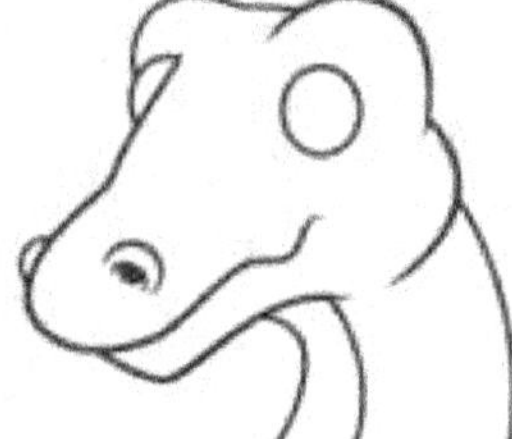 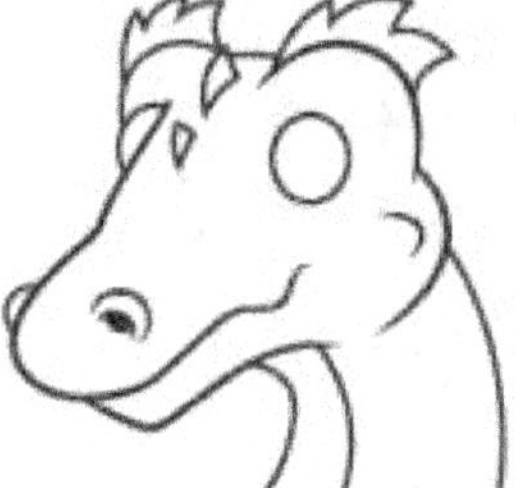

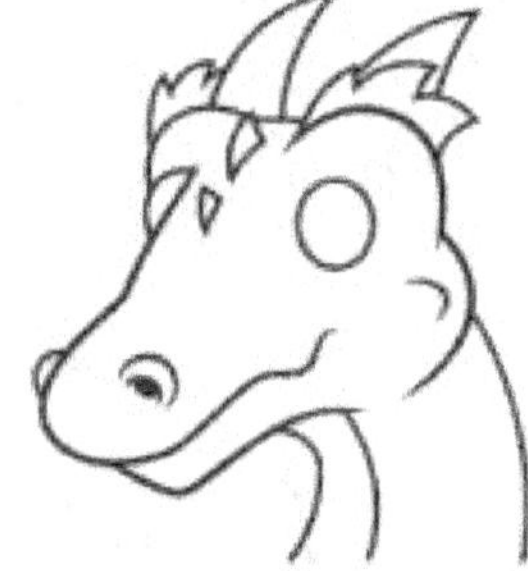 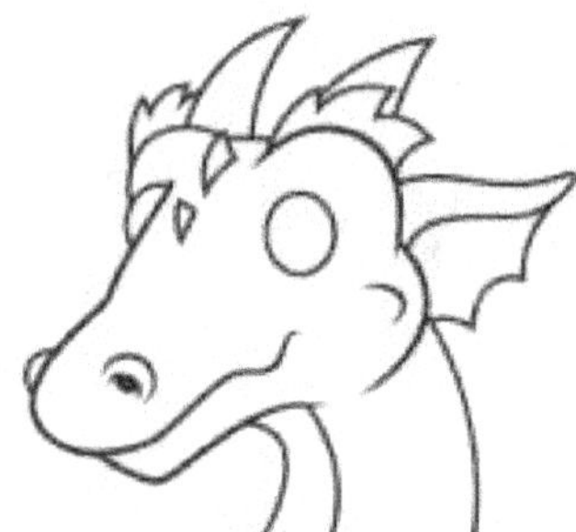 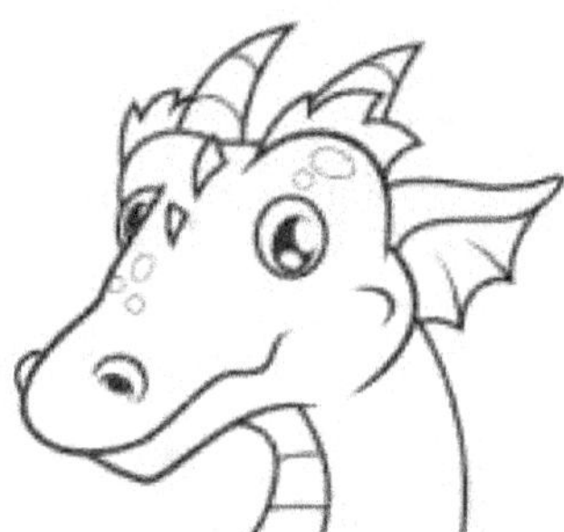

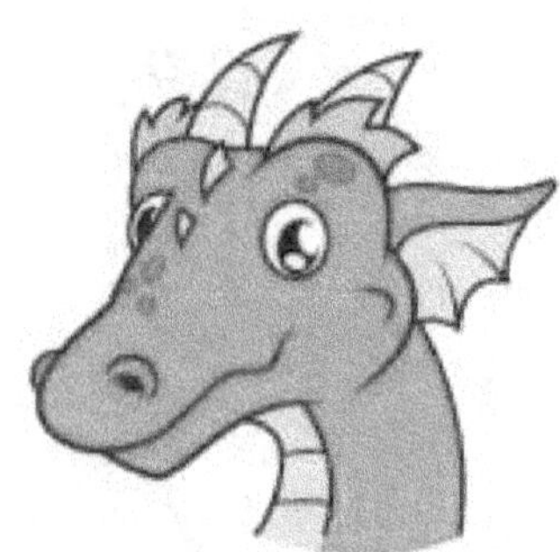

GHITAR

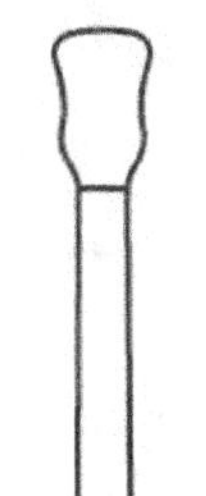

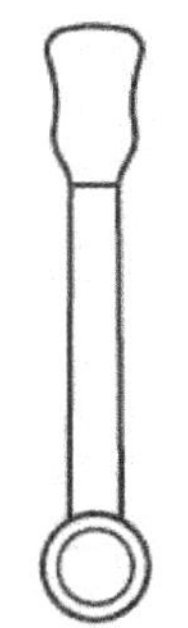

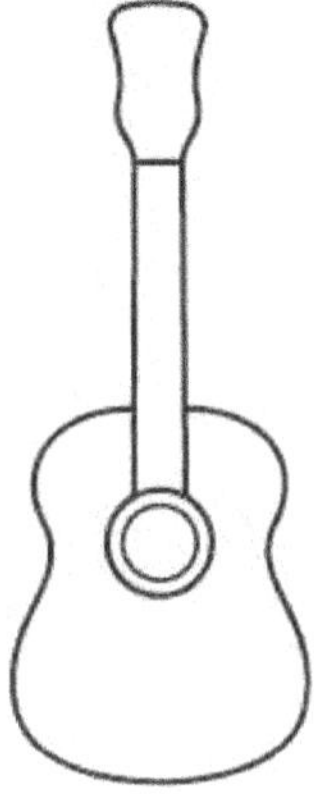

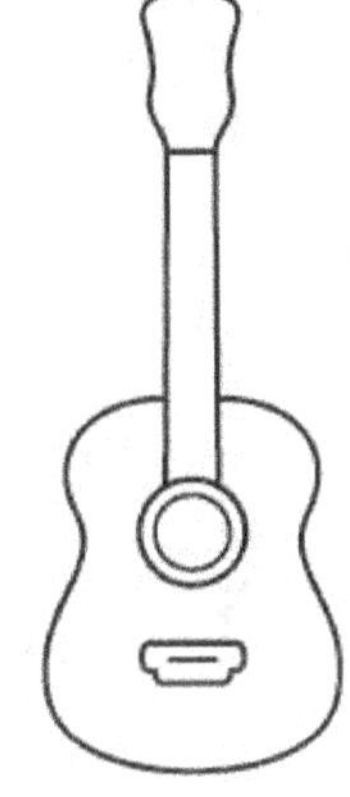

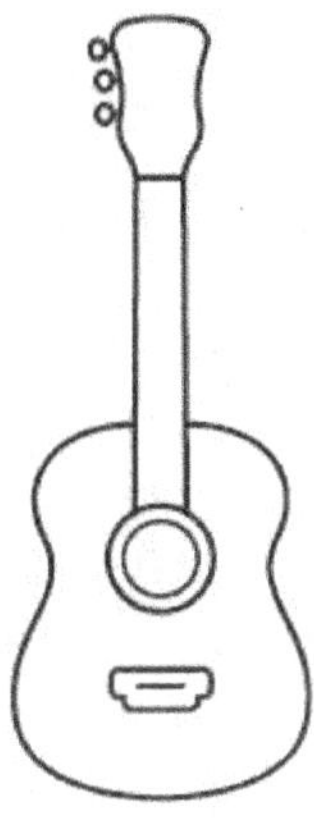

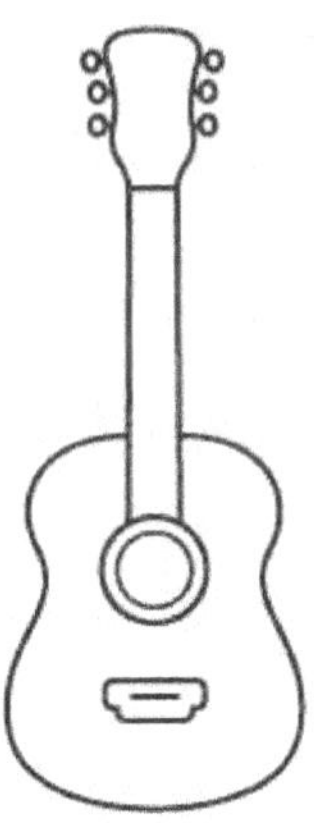

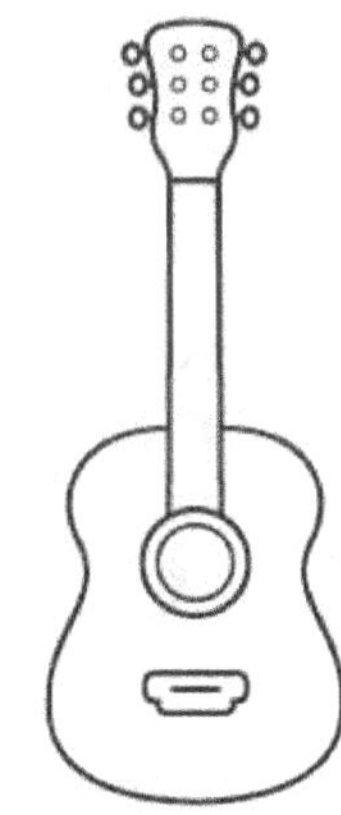

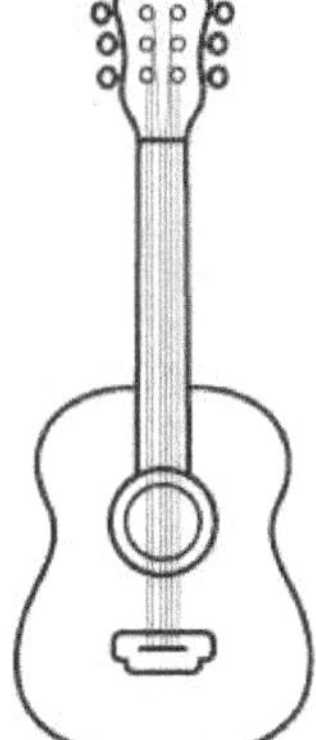

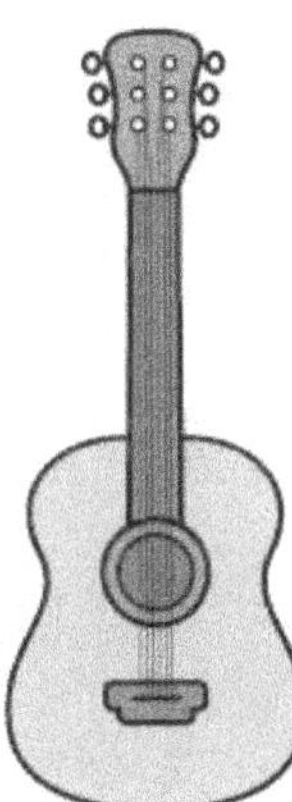

CHARMANDER

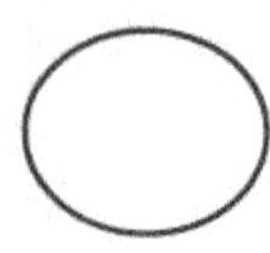 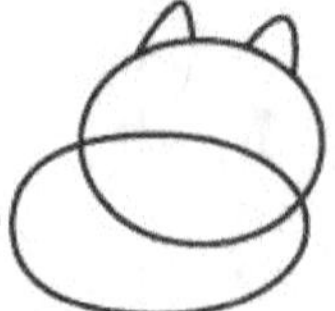 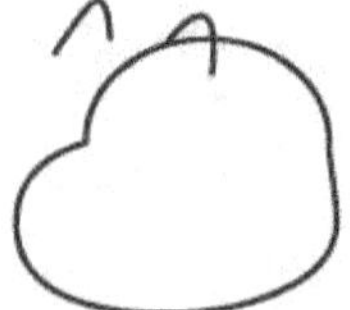

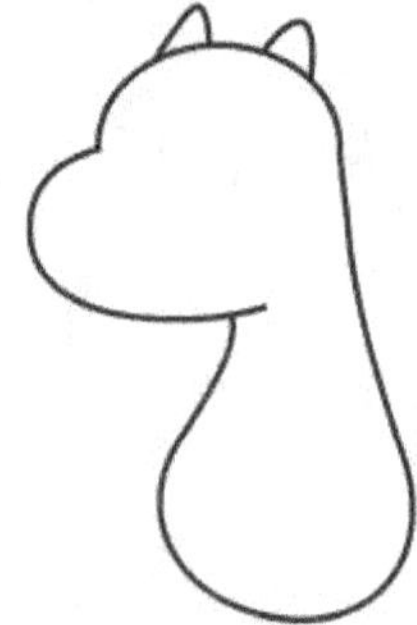 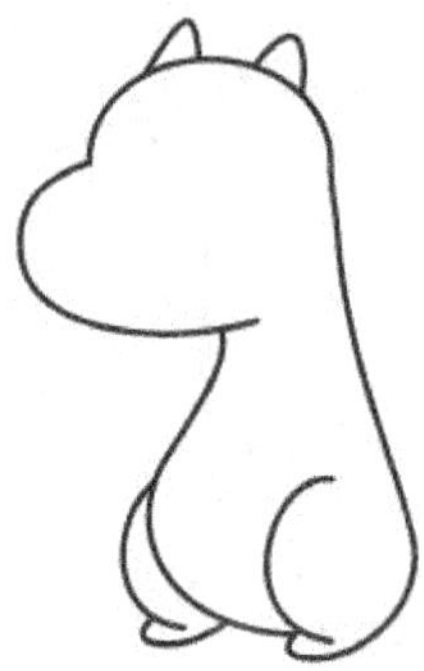 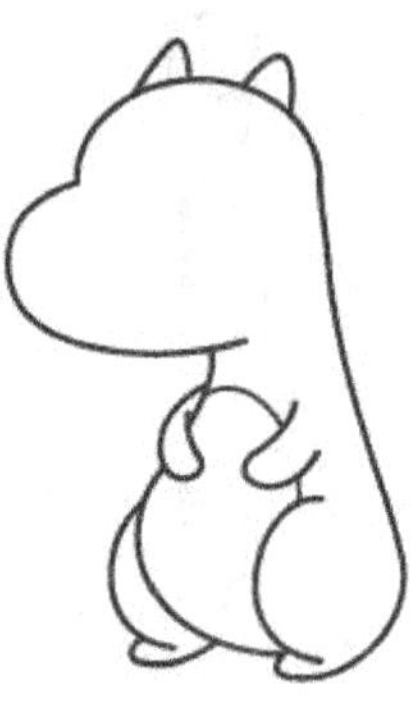

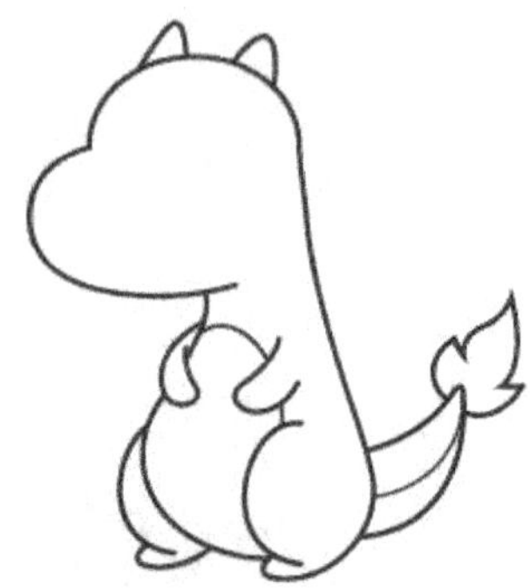 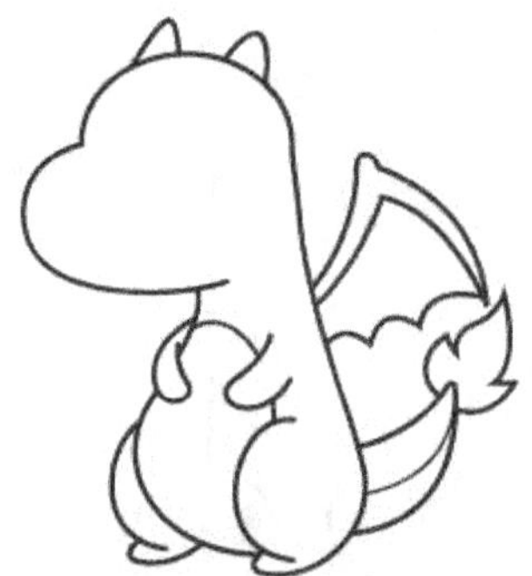 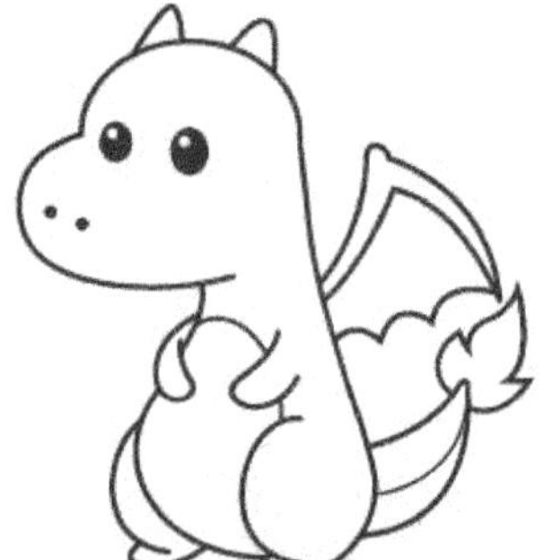

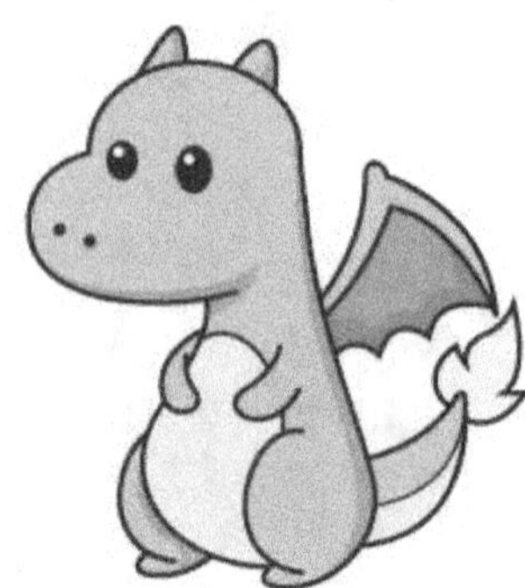

HAND

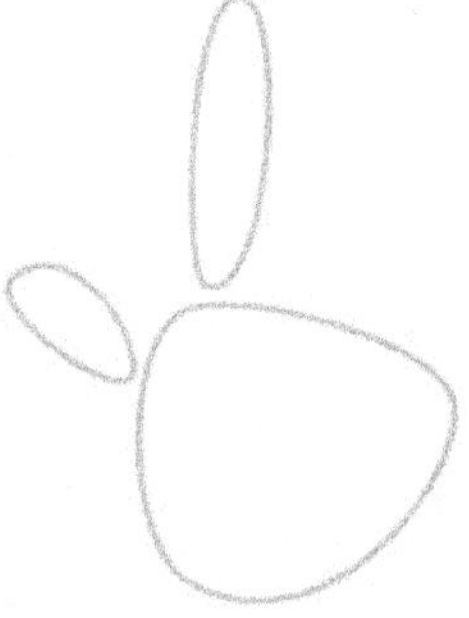
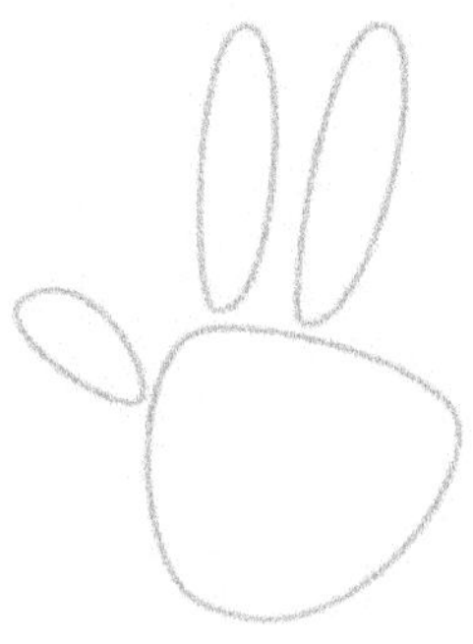
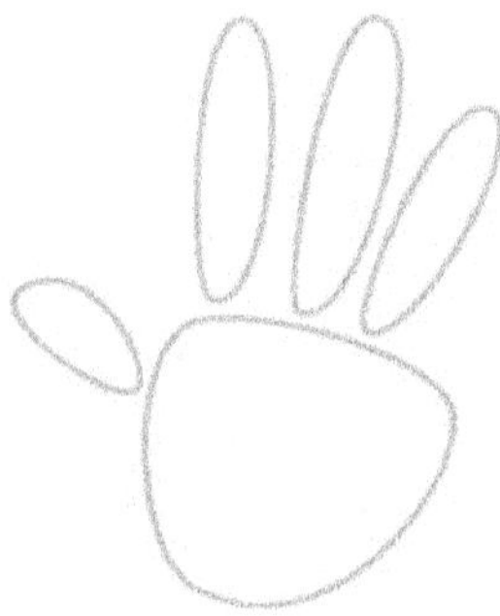
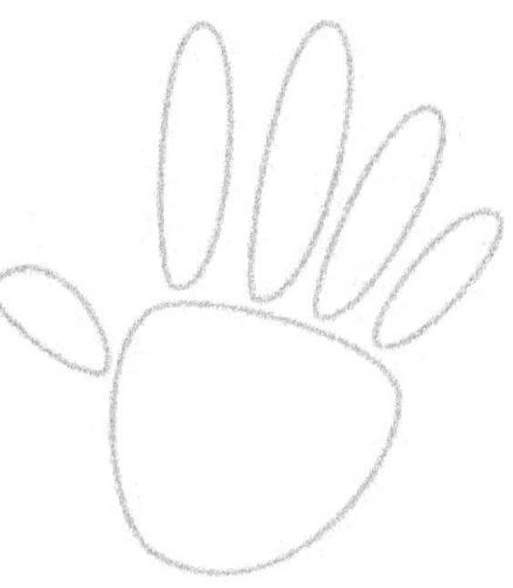
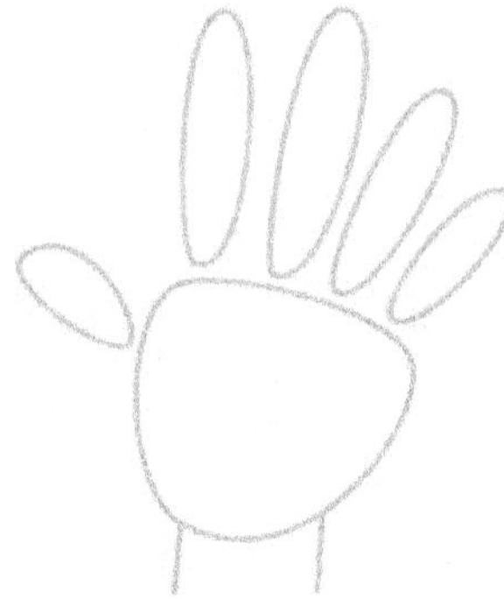
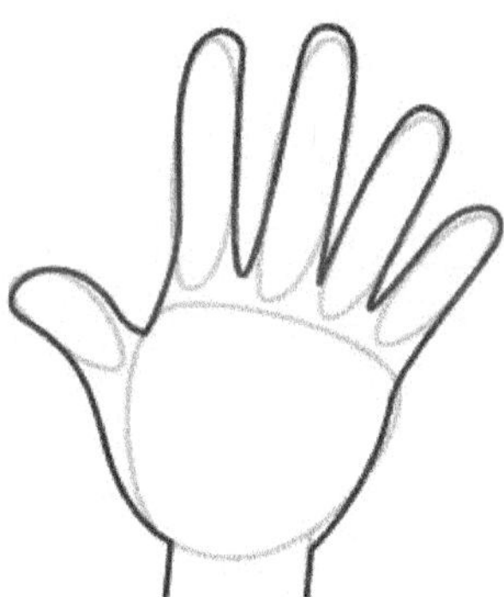
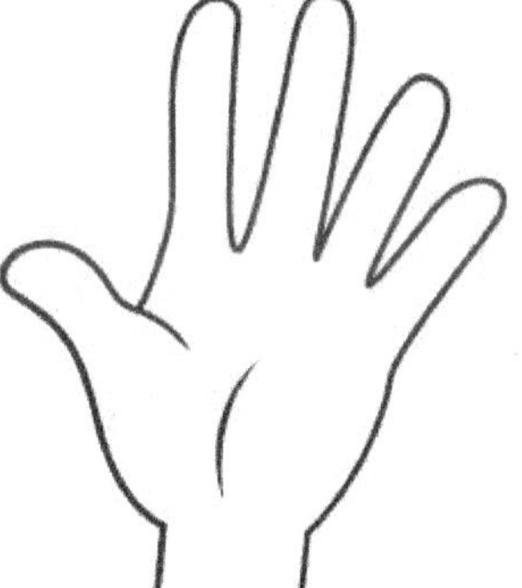
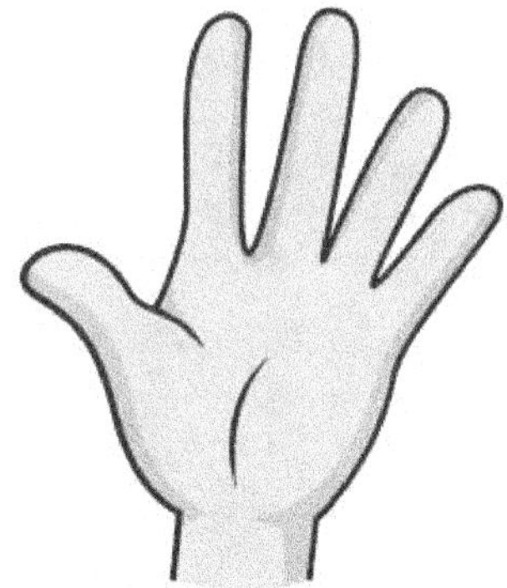

LIGHT PULP

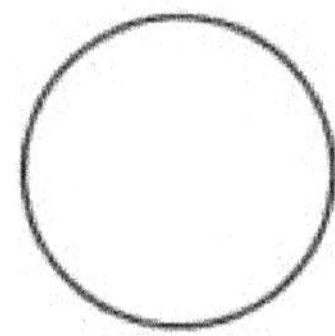
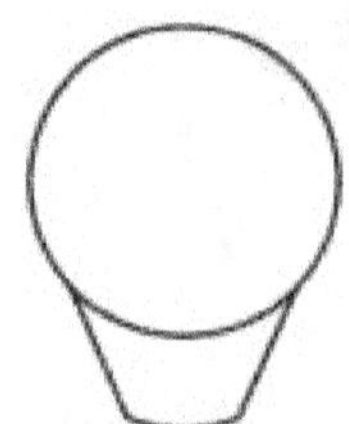
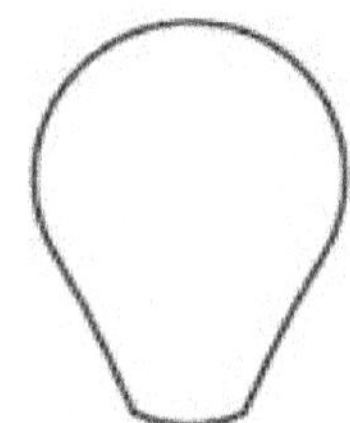
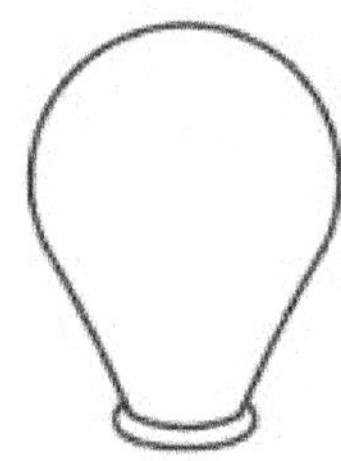
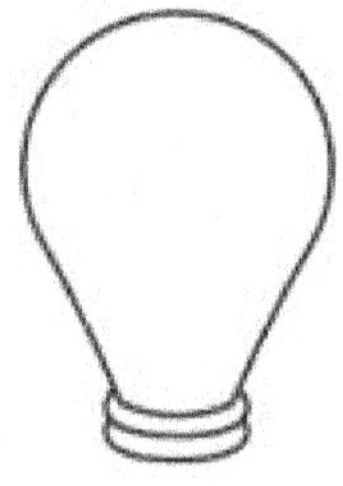
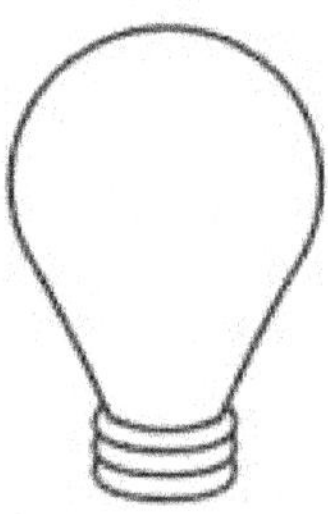
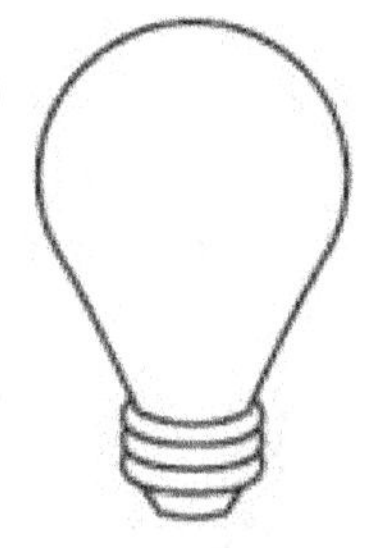

MOTORCYCLE

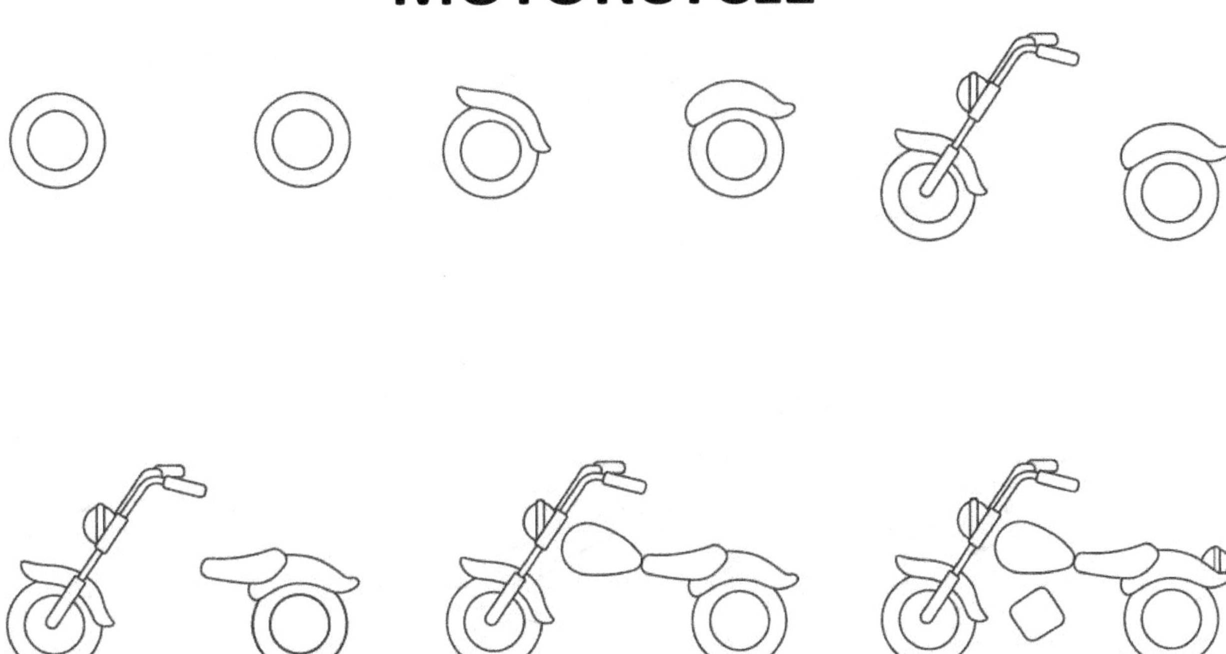
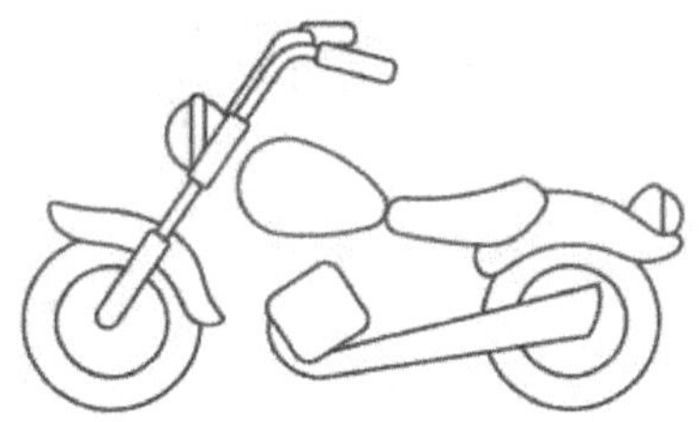
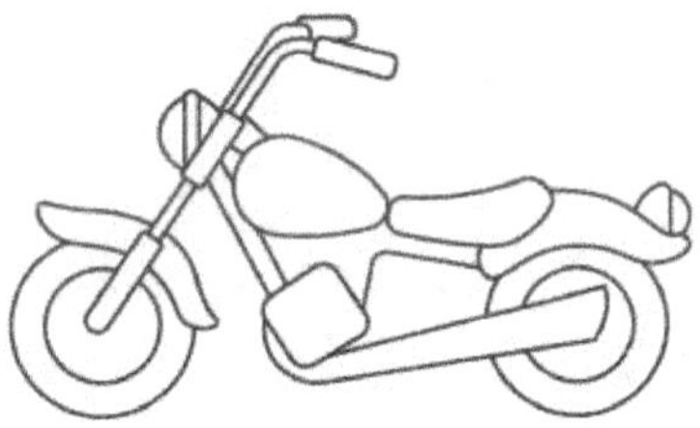
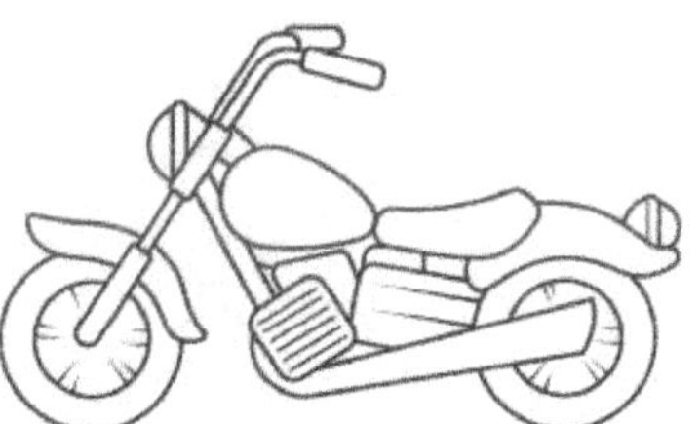
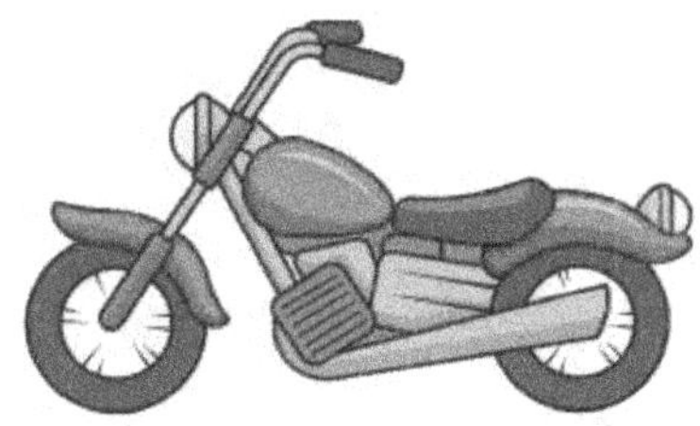

PAPER AIRPLANE

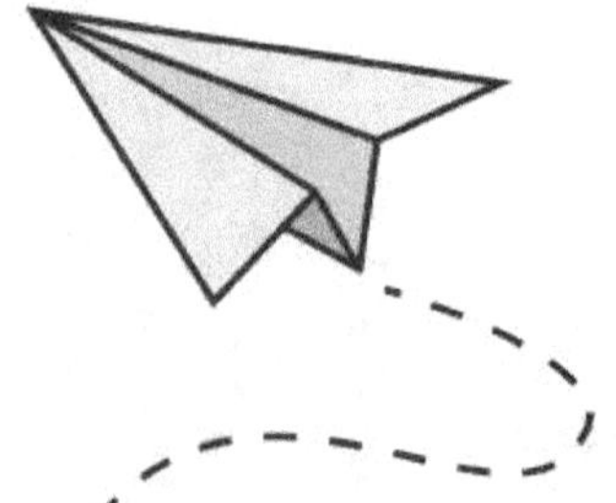

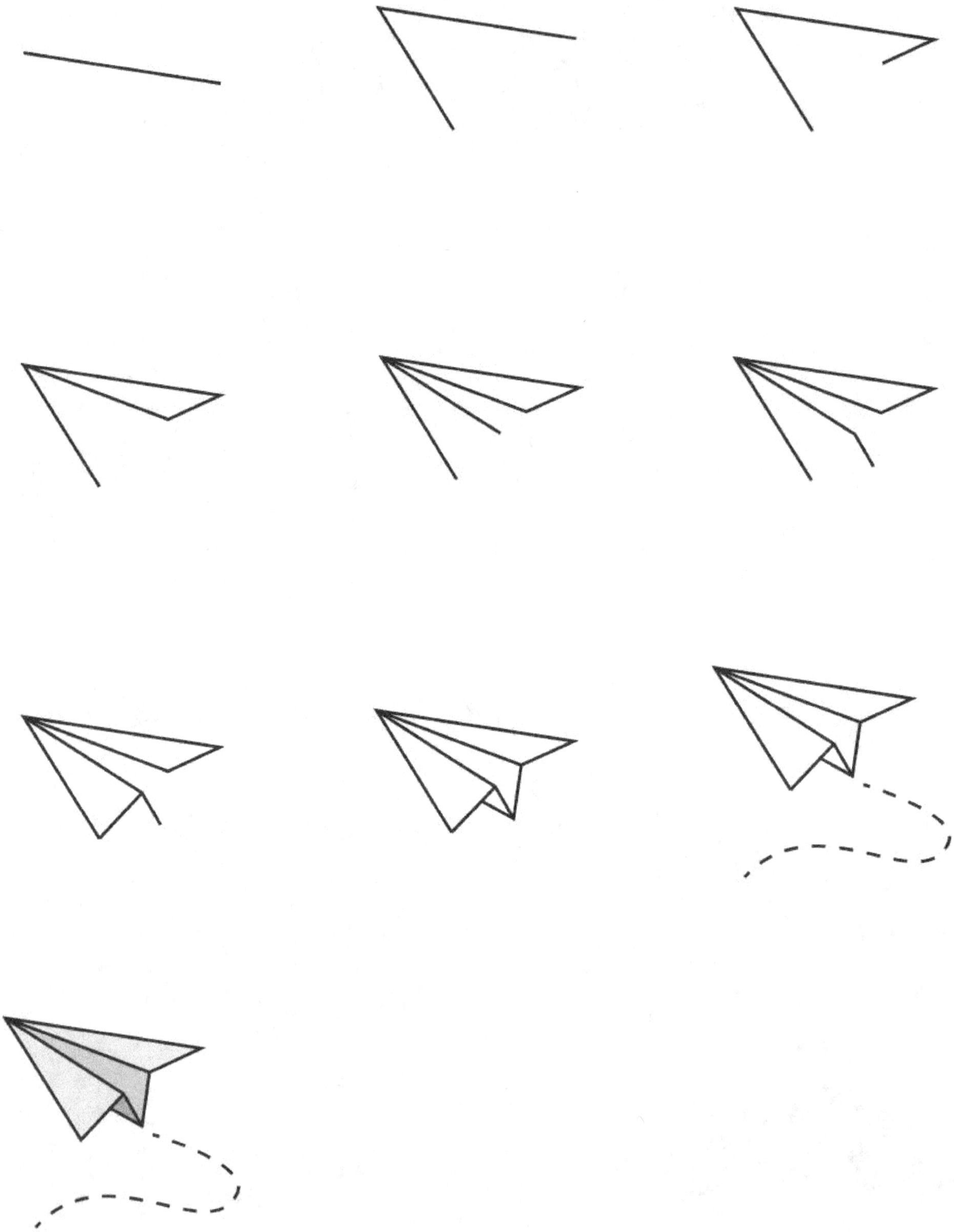

CAT

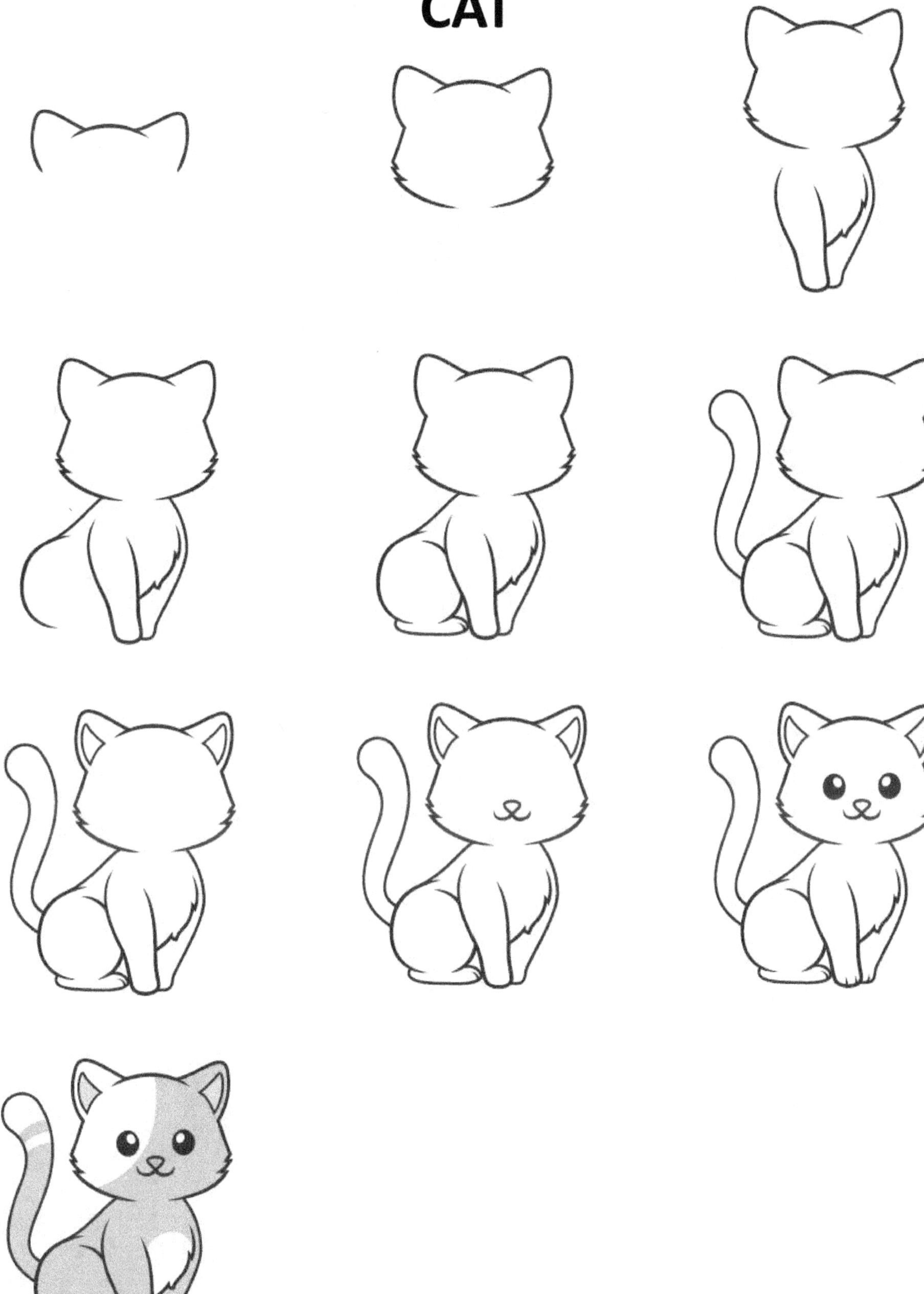

PENCIL

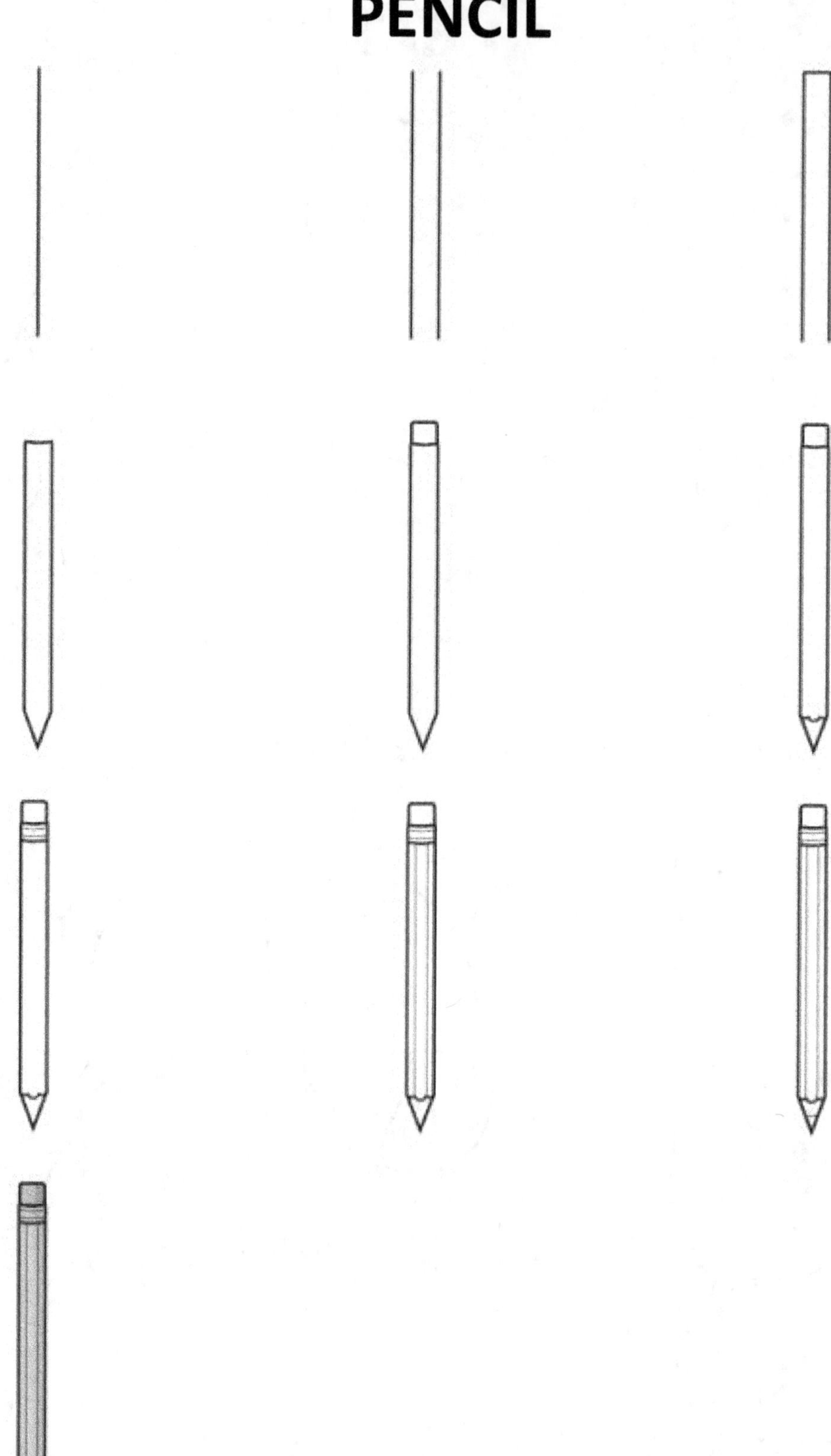

LIZARD

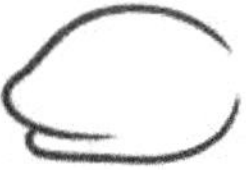 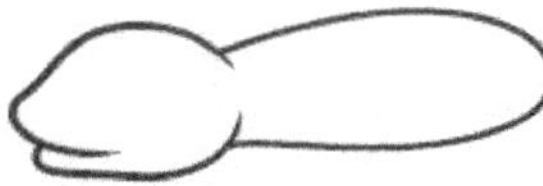

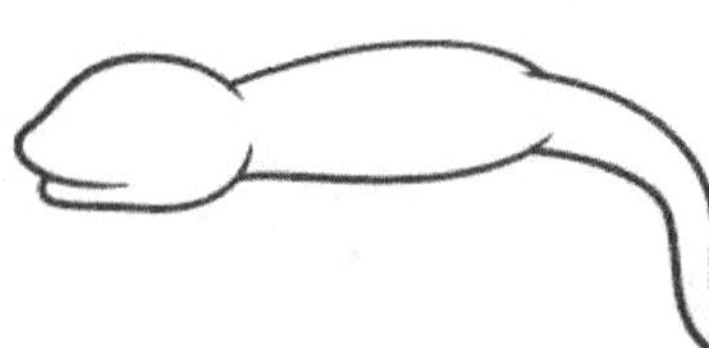 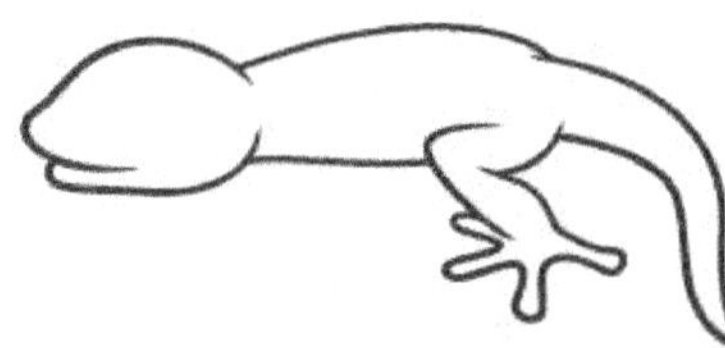 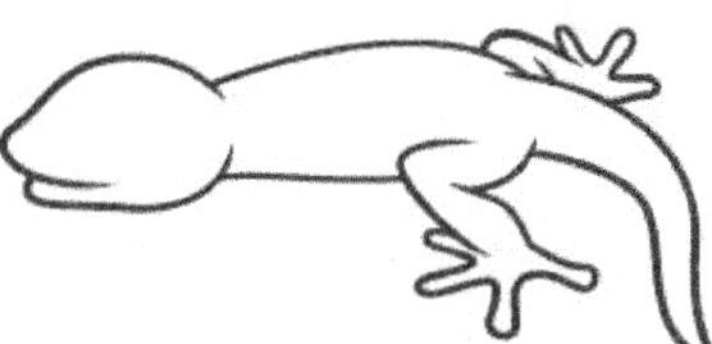

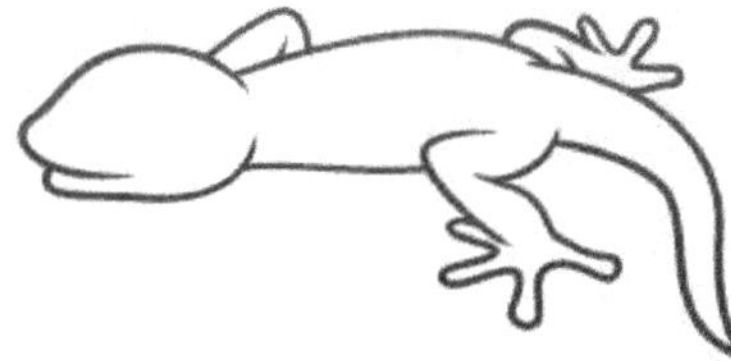 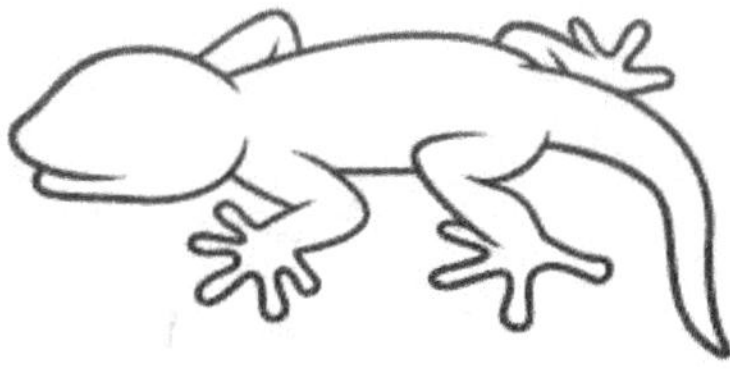 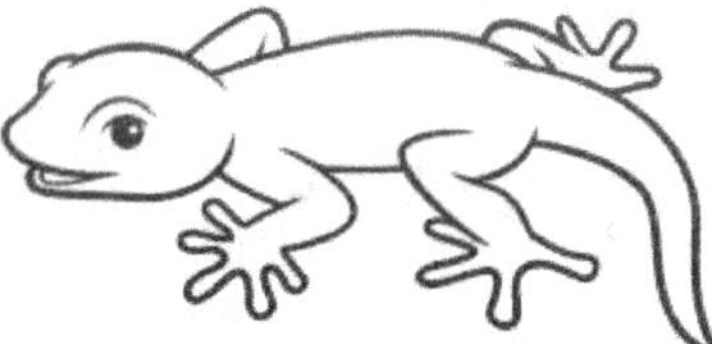

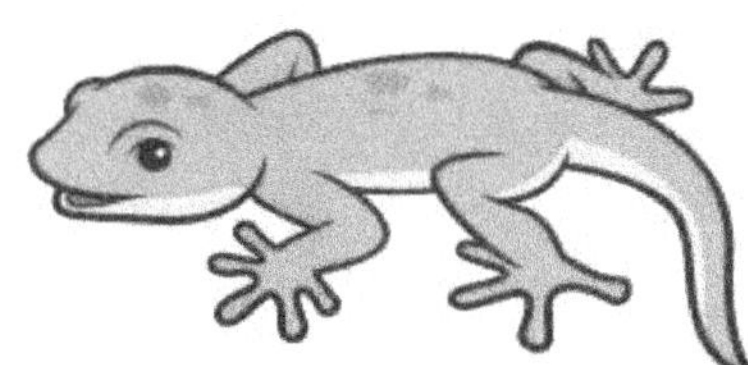

PHONE

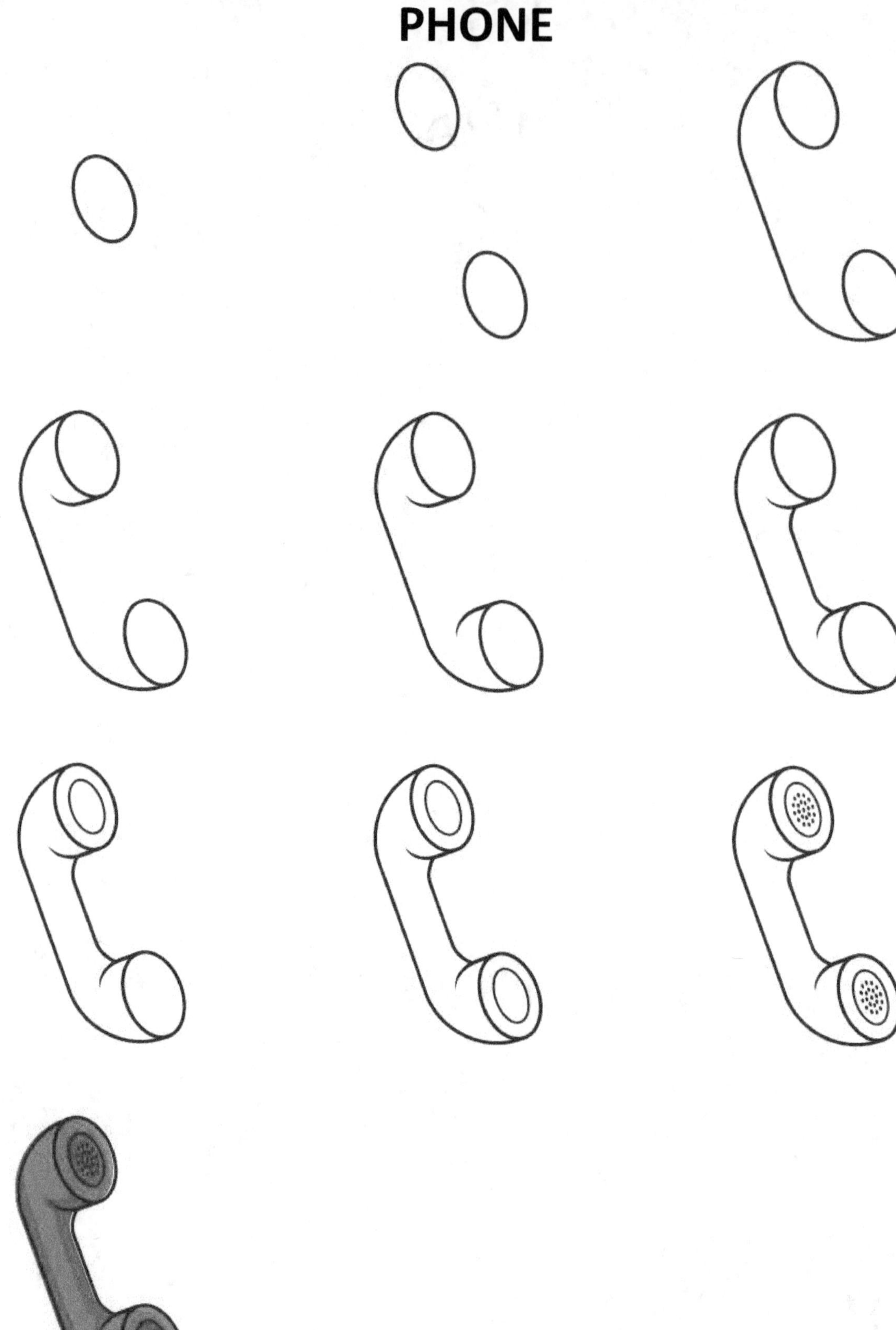

PEACOCK

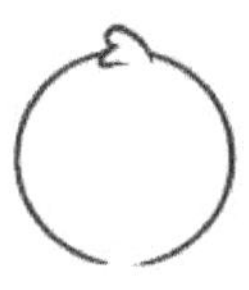 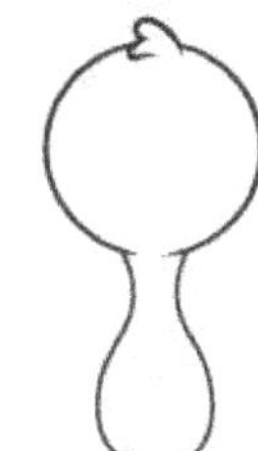 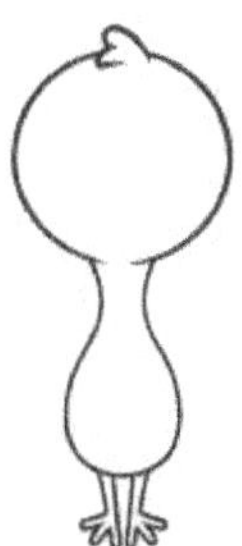

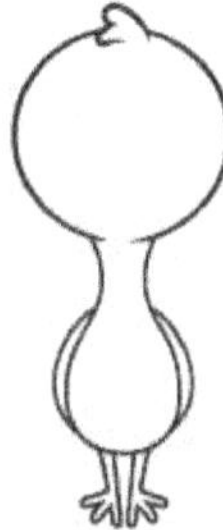 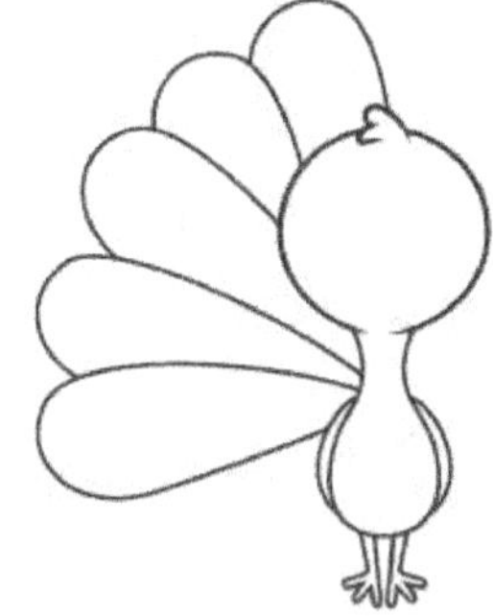 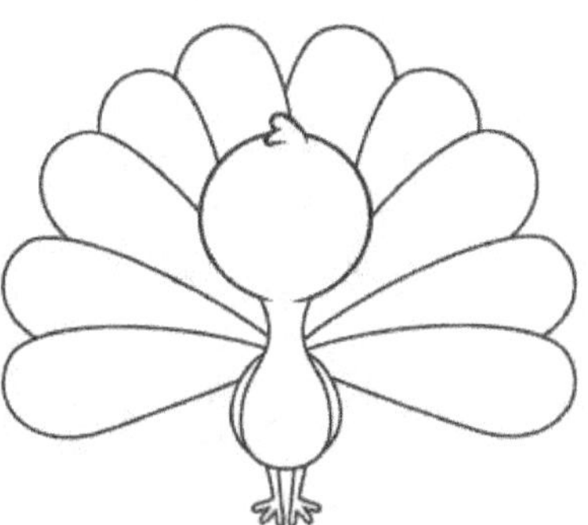

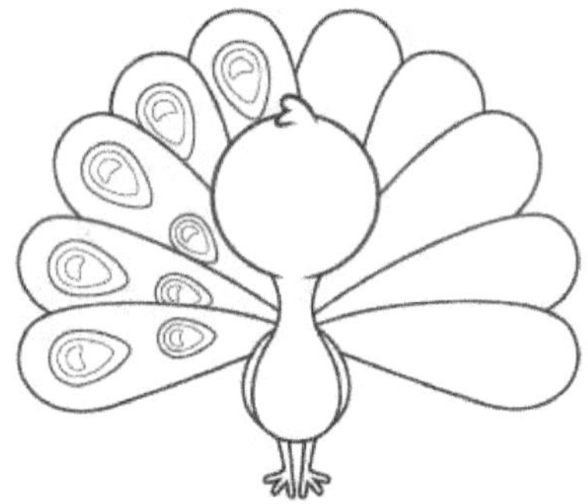 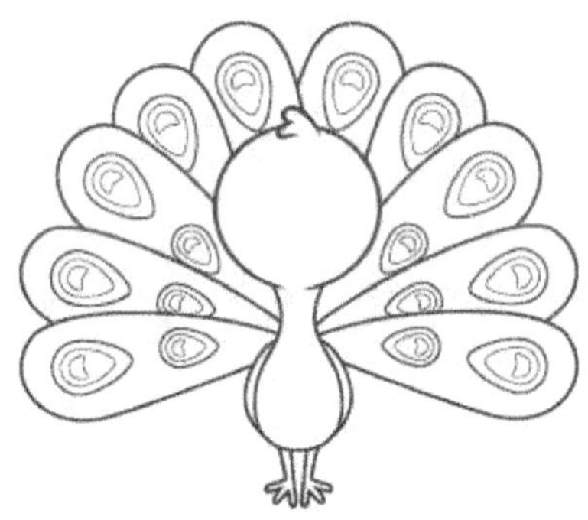 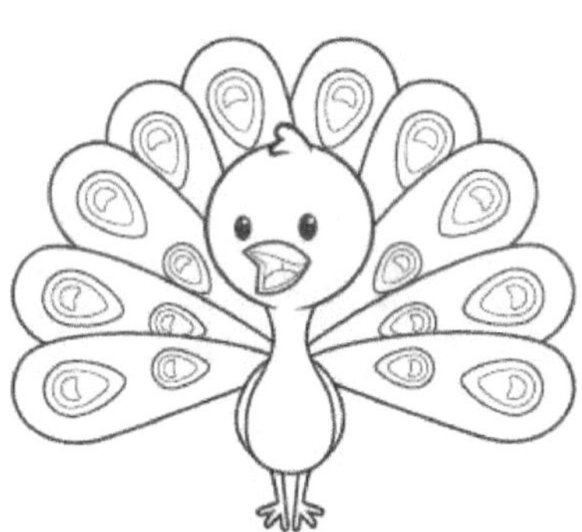

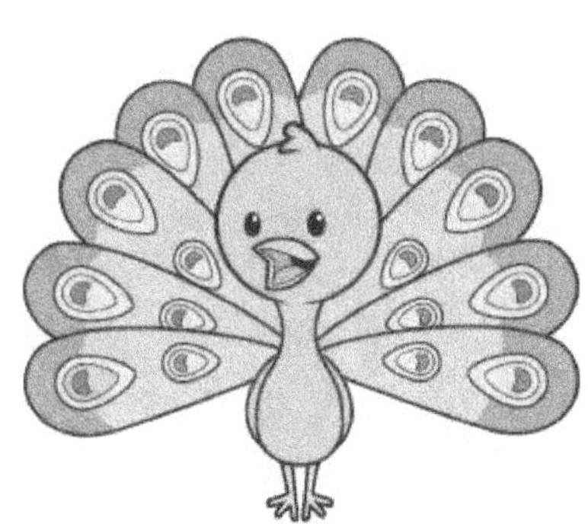

PYRAMID

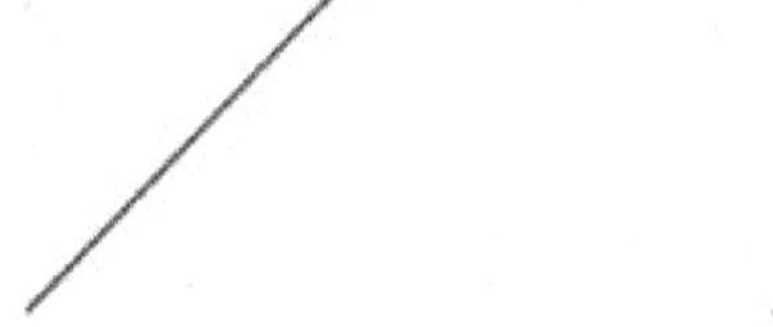 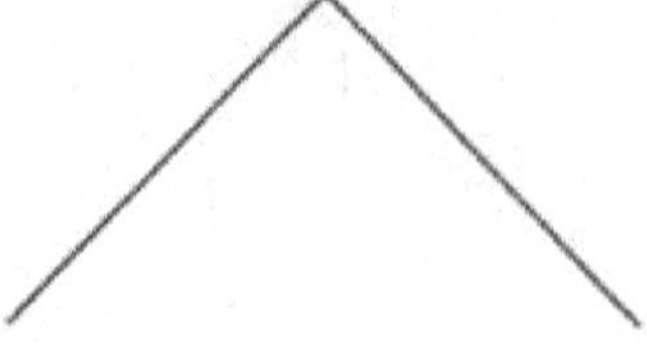 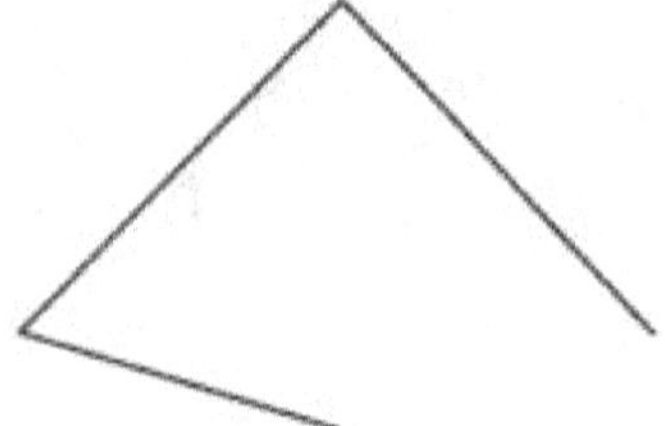

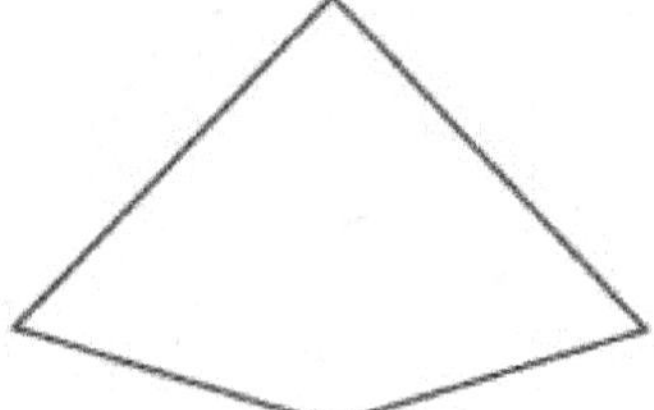 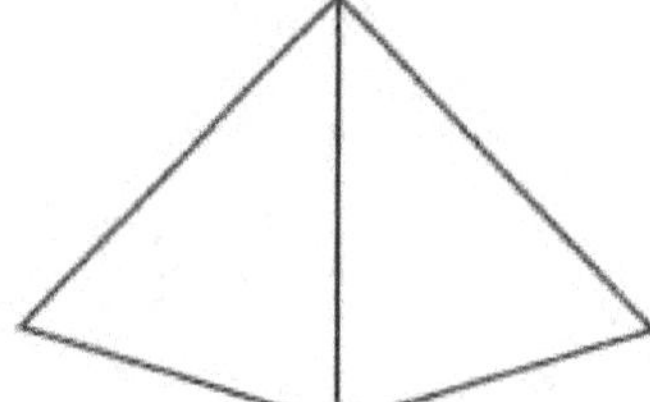 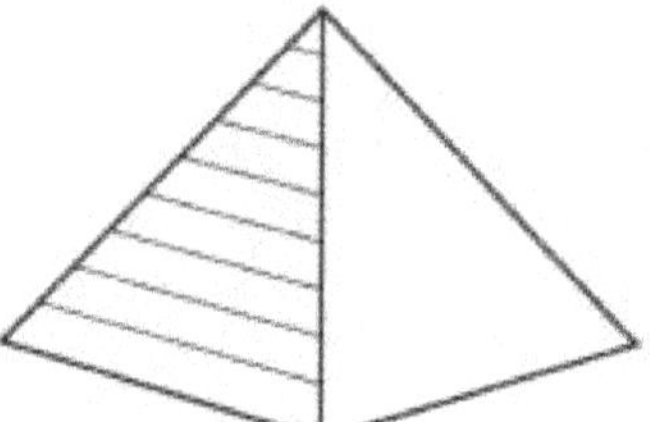

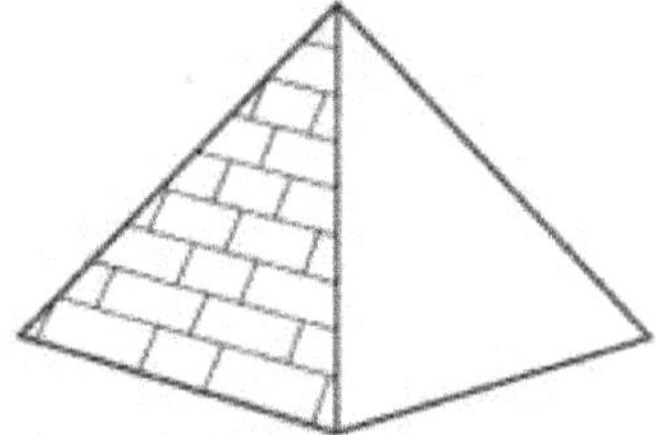 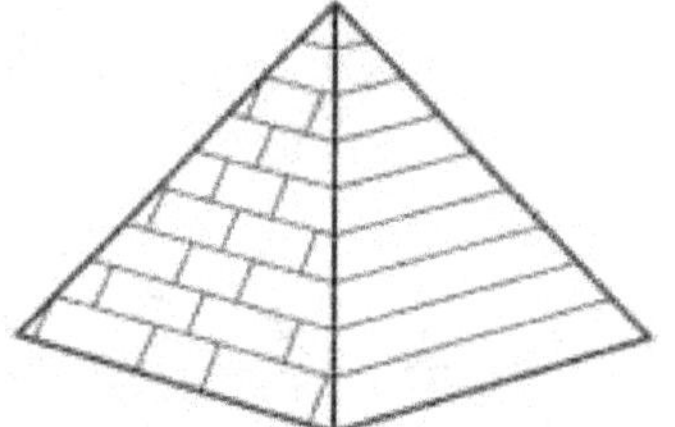 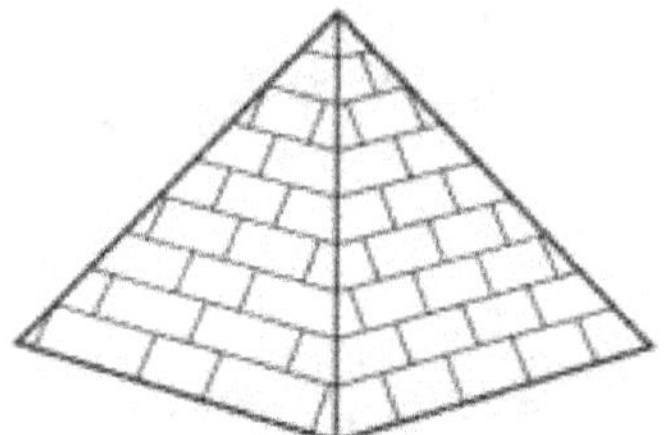

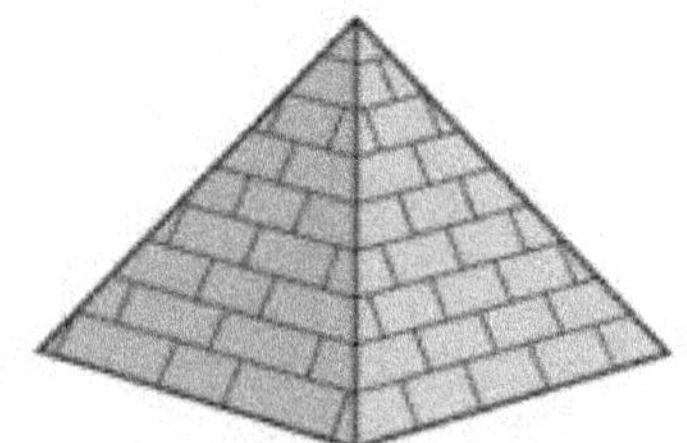

A PARROT

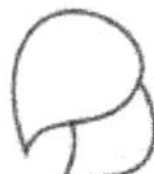
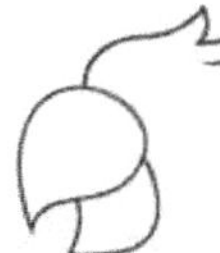

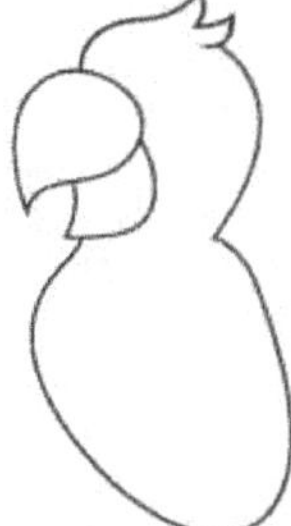
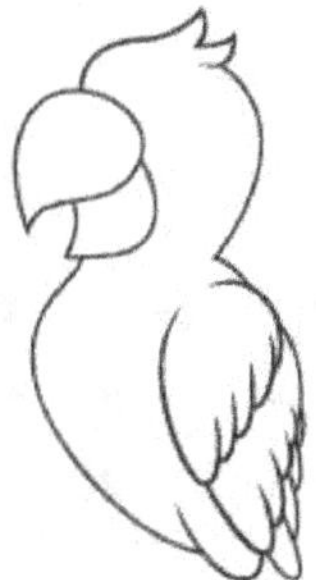
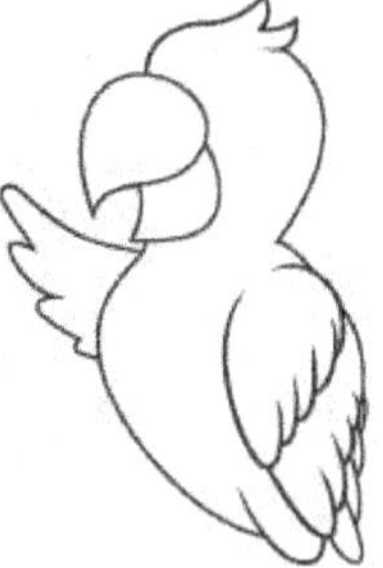

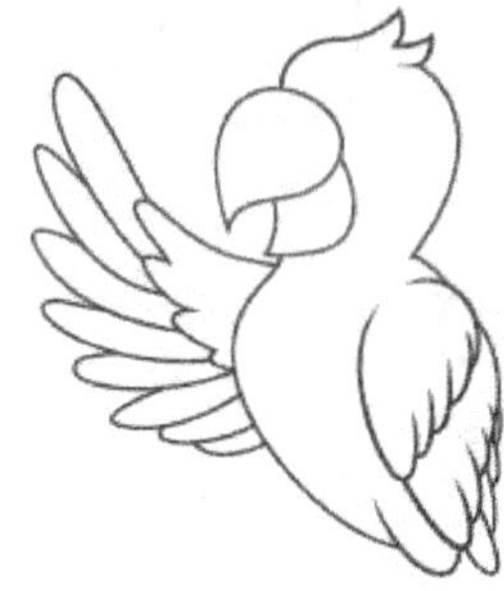
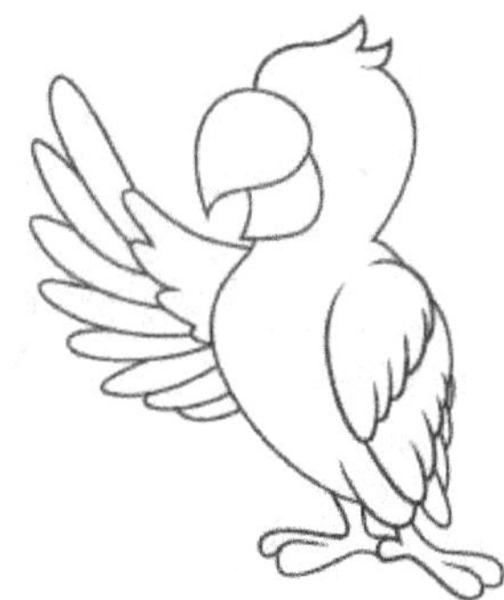
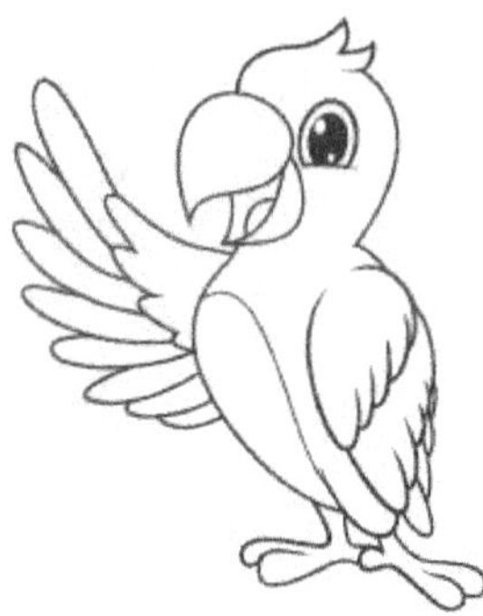

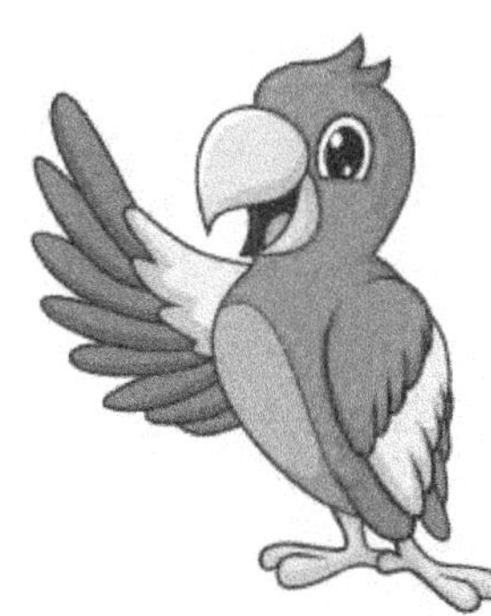

TRACTOR

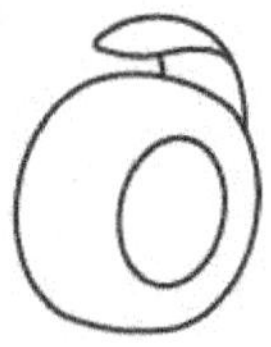
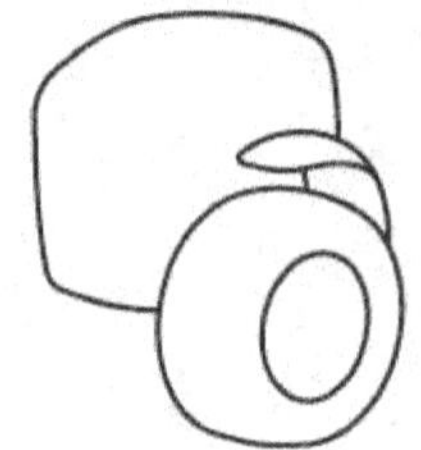
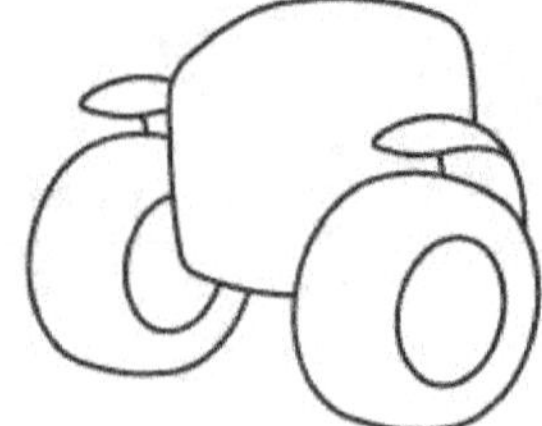
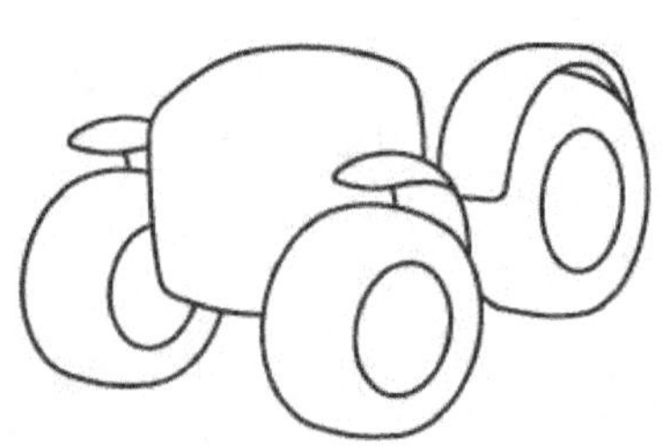
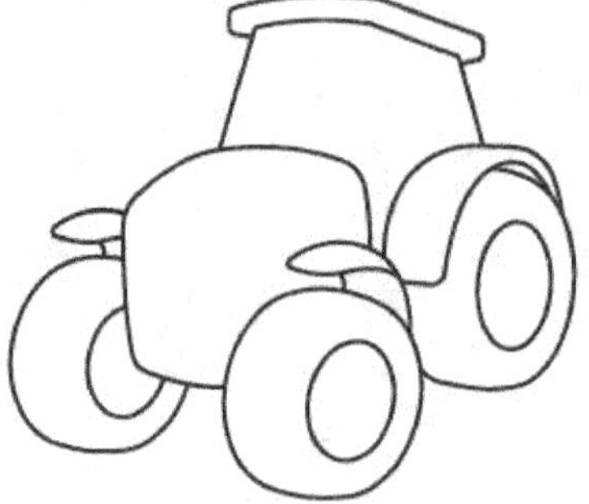
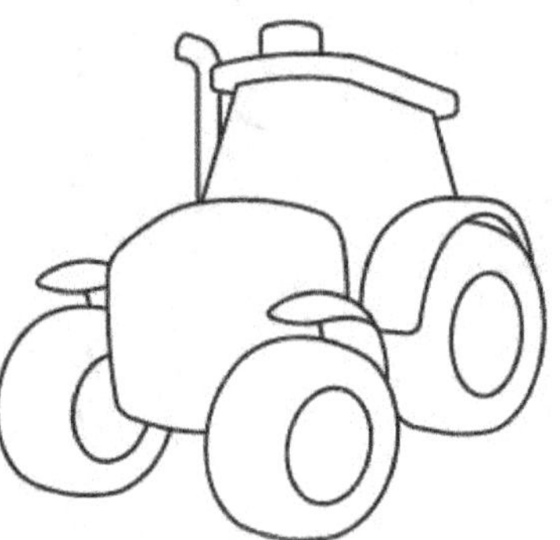
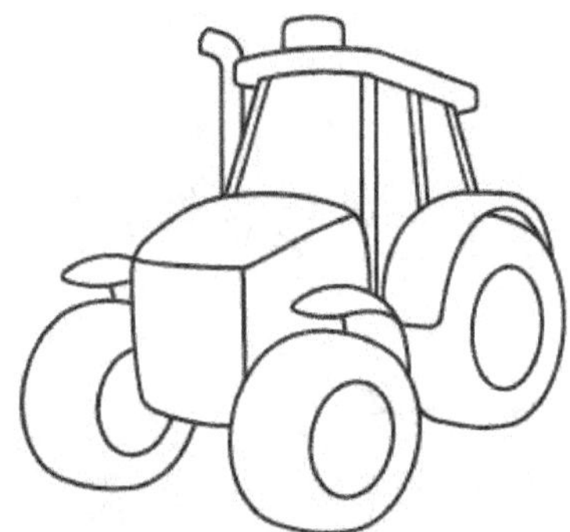
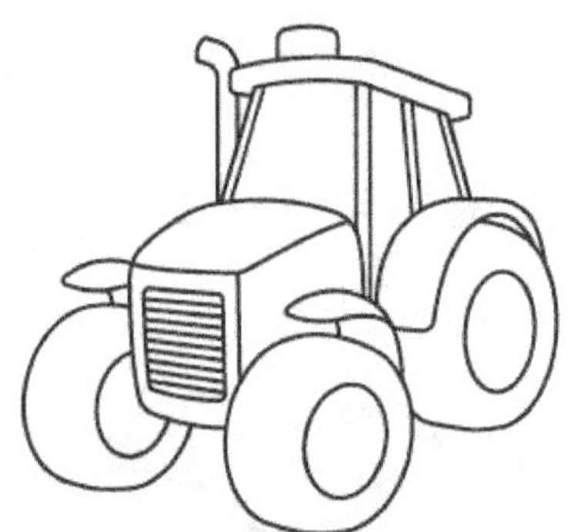
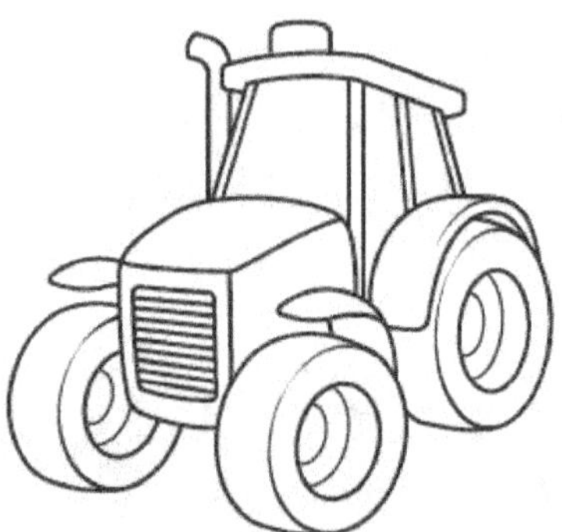
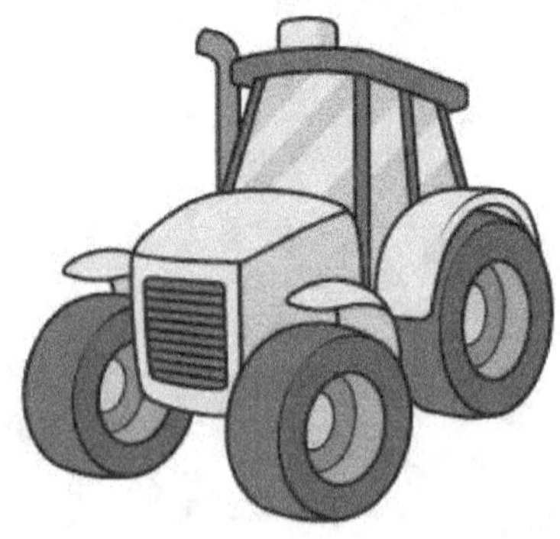

UMBRELLA

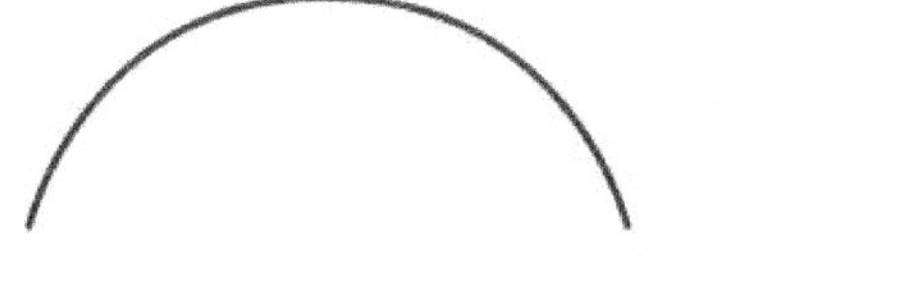
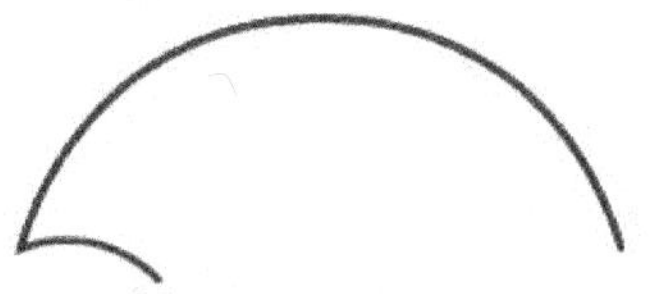
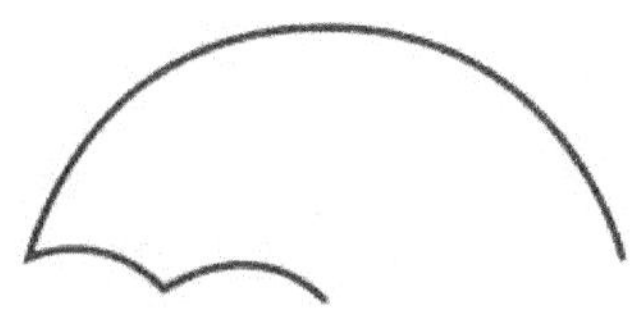

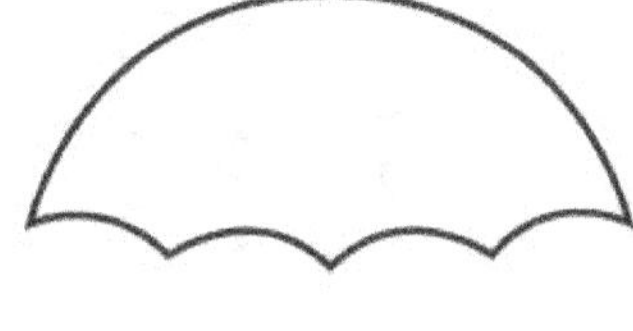
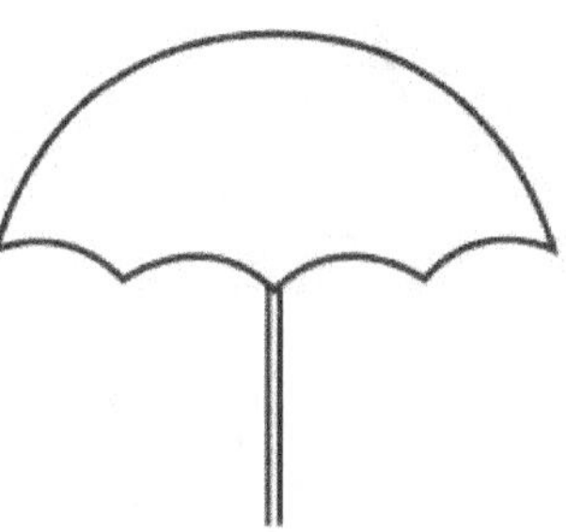
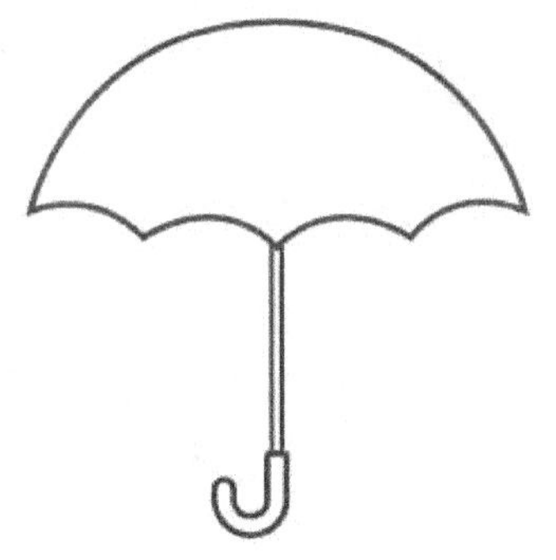
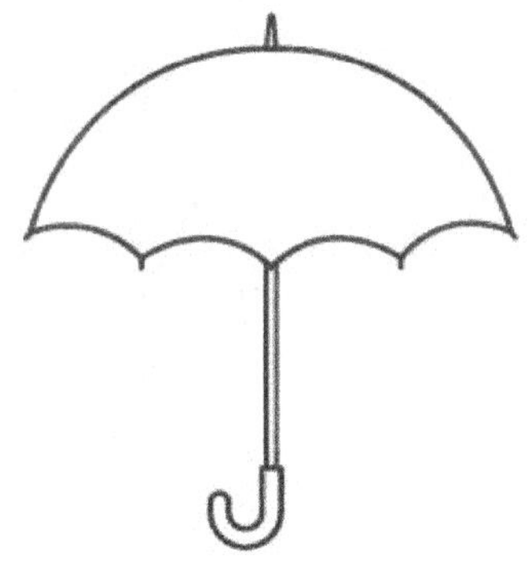
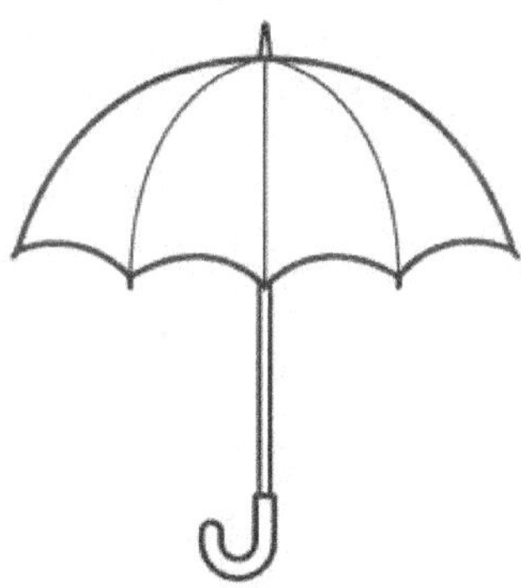
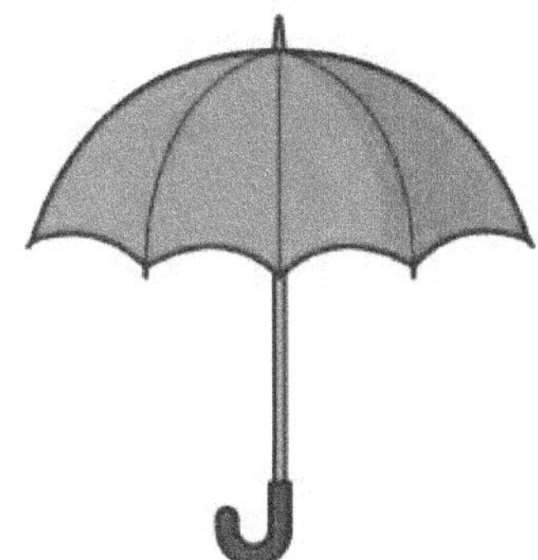

SNOPY

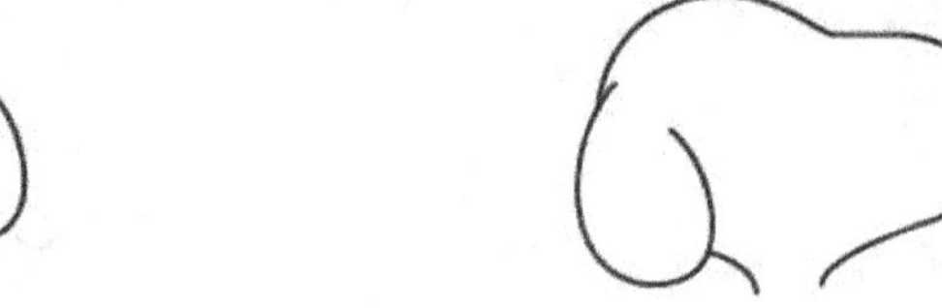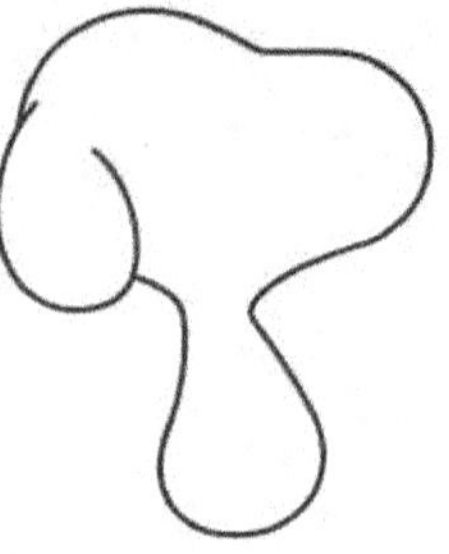

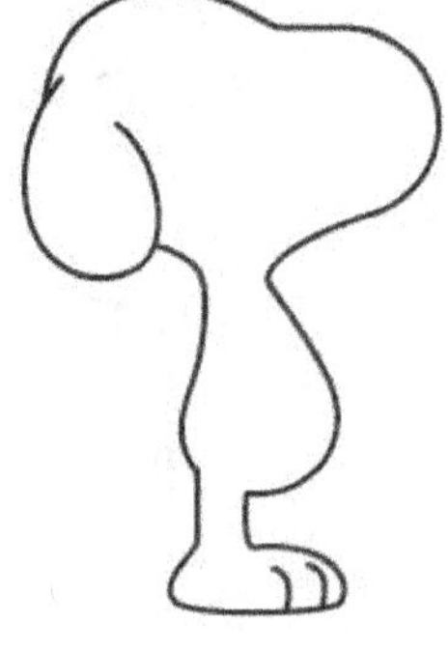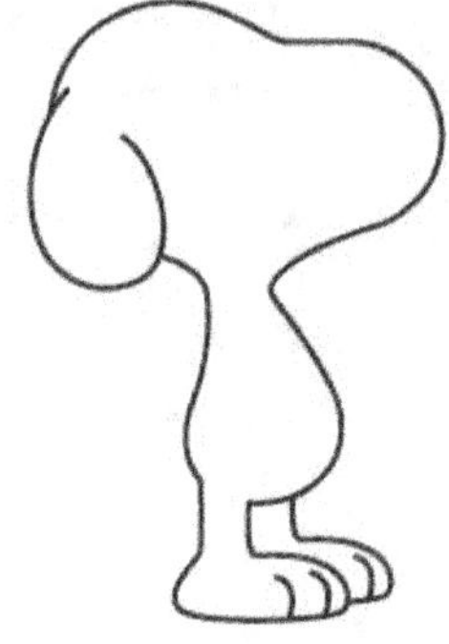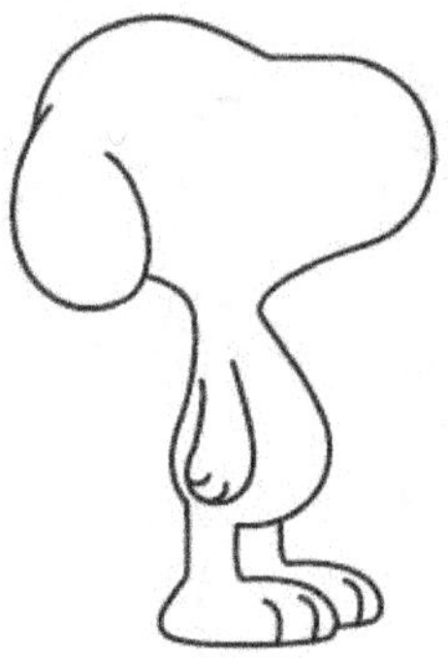

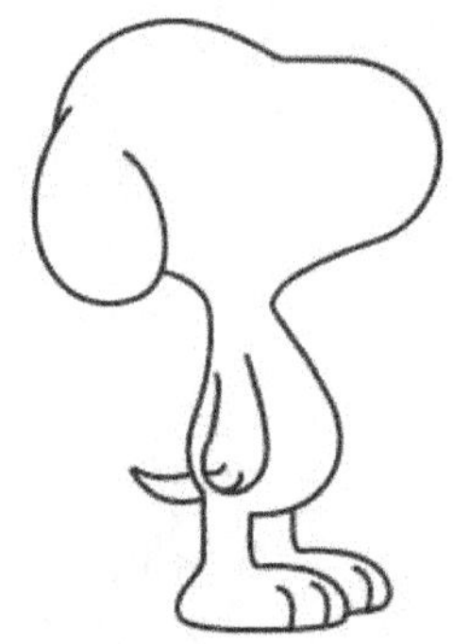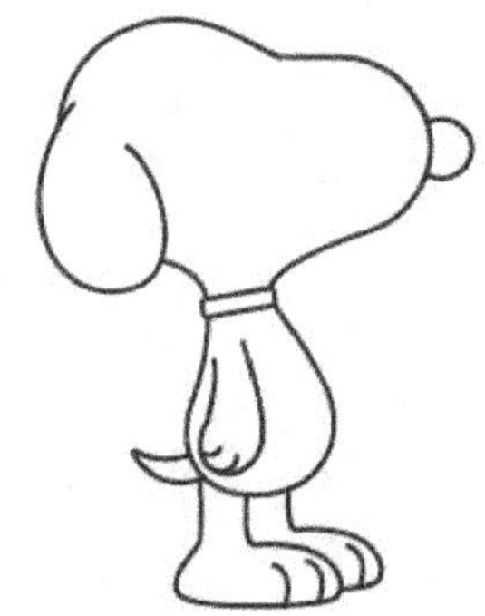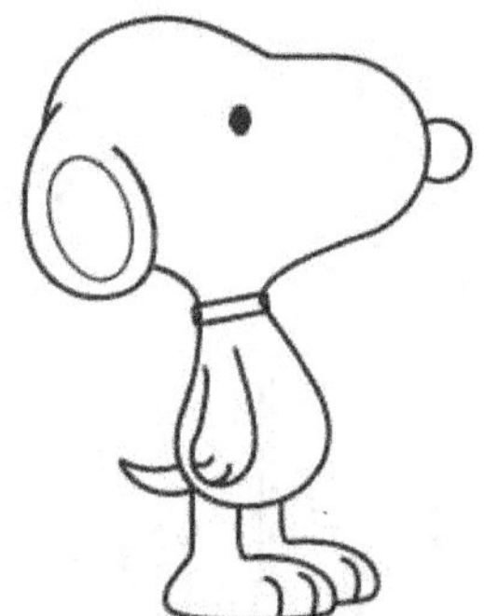

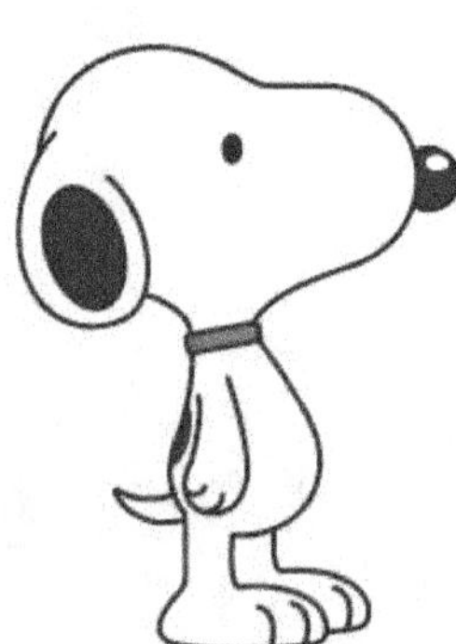

TURKEY

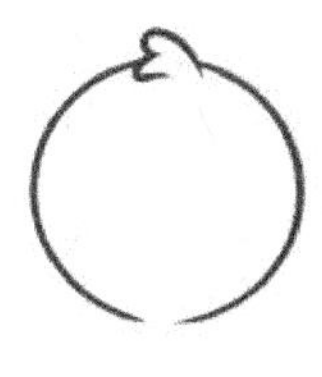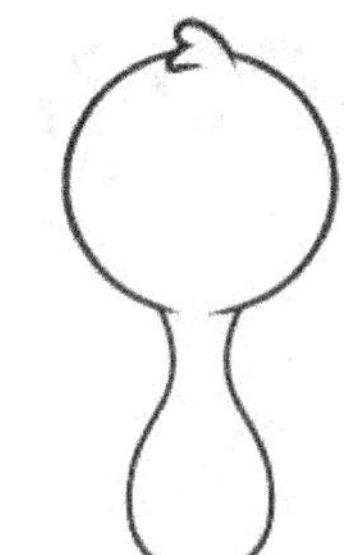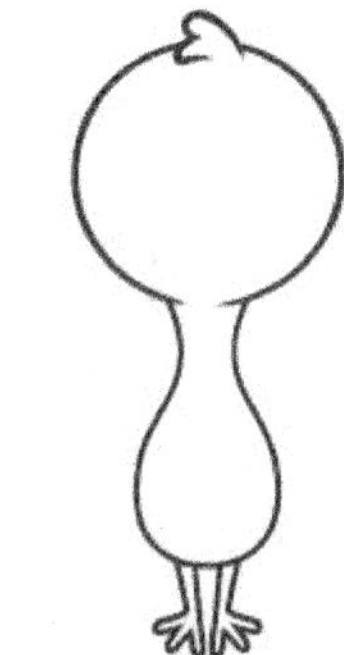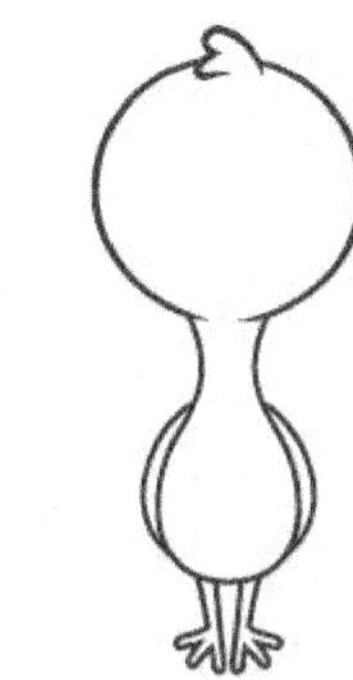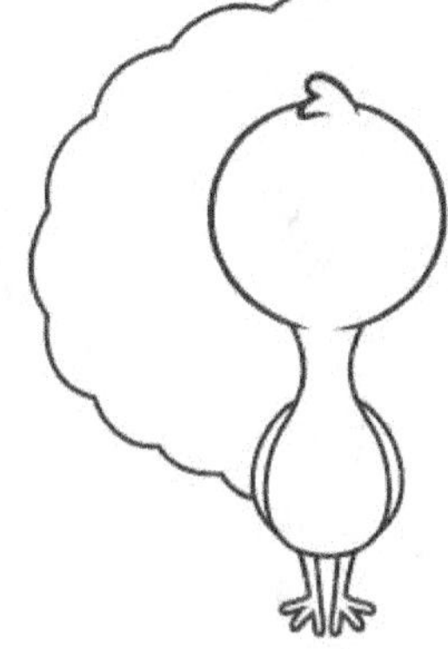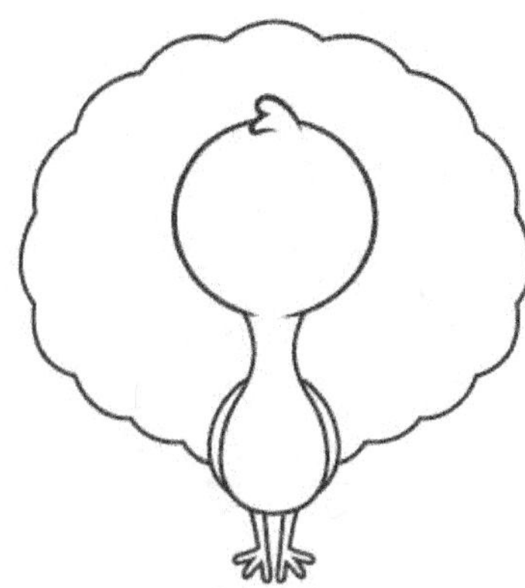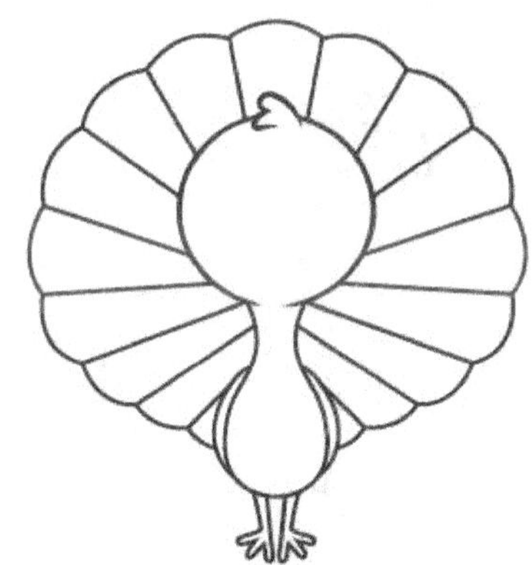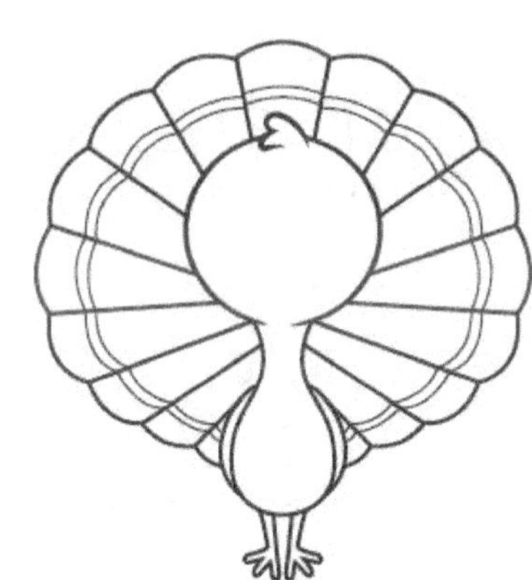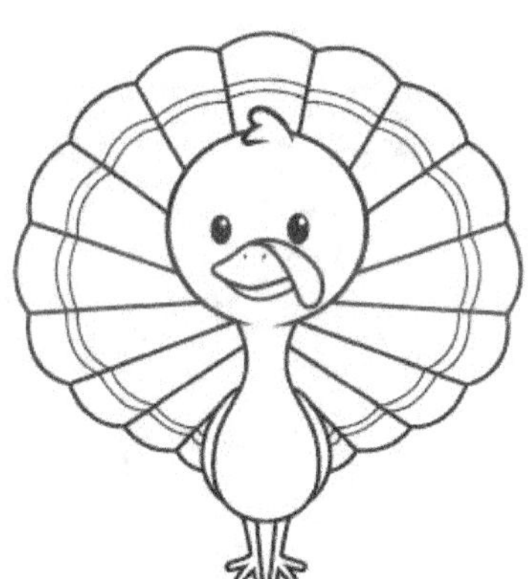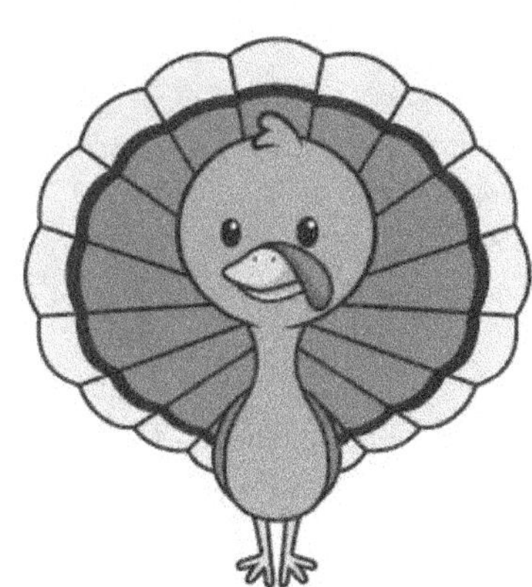

UNICORN

 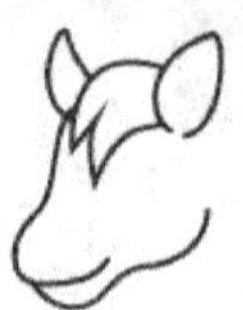 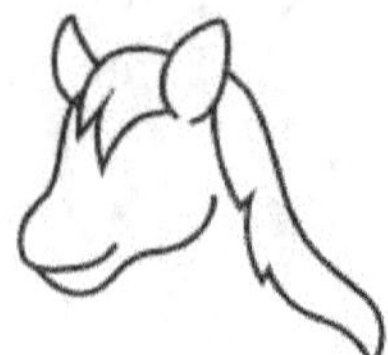

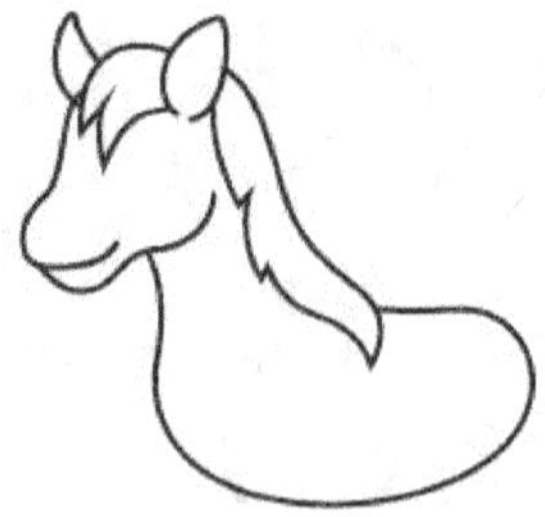 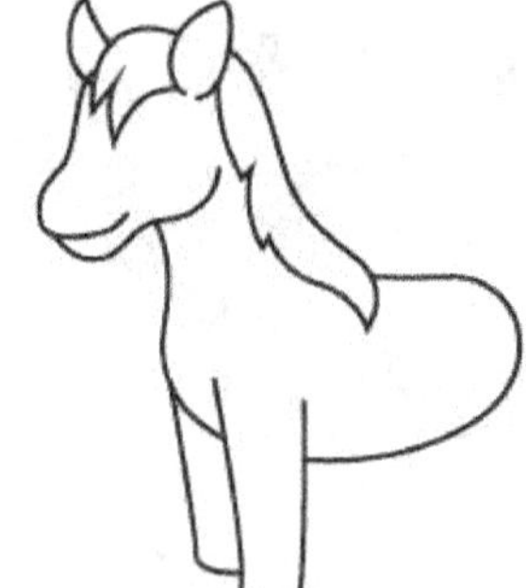 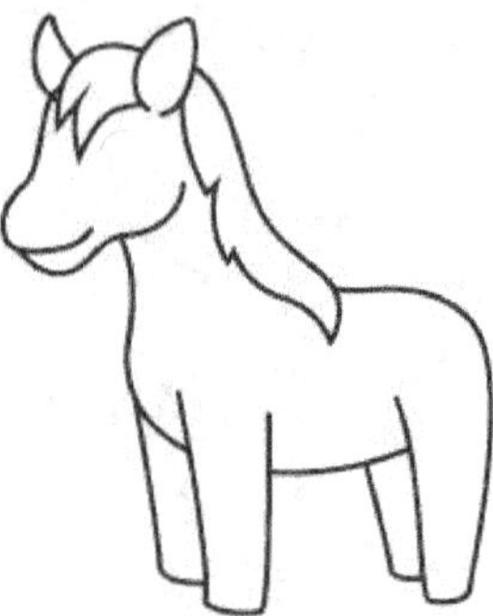

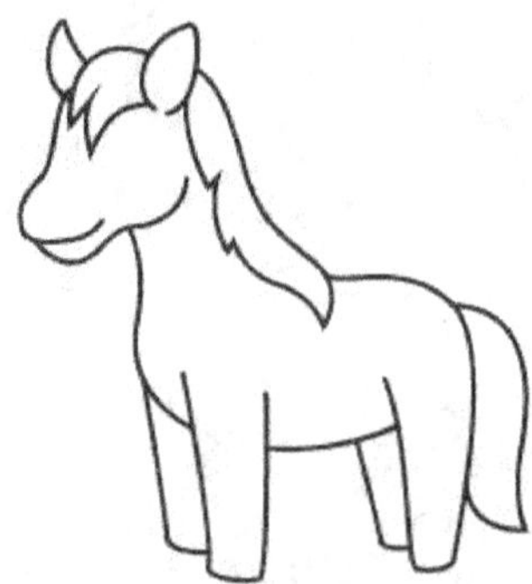 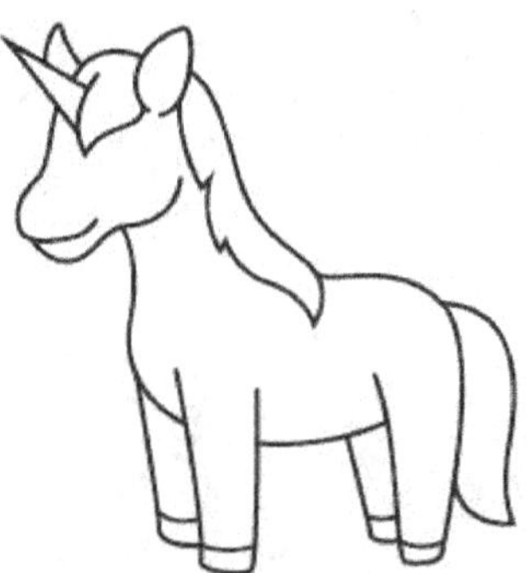 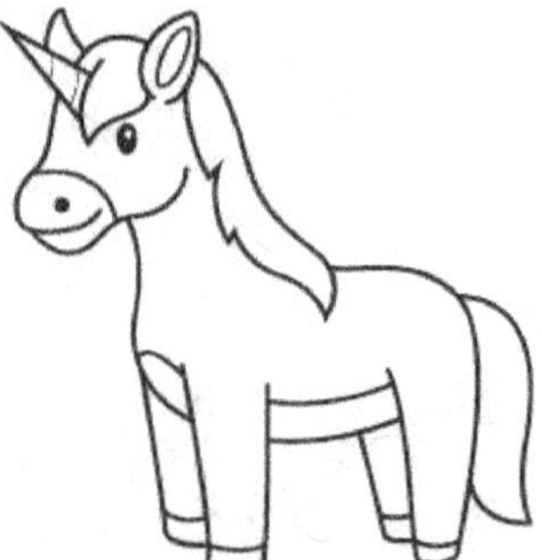

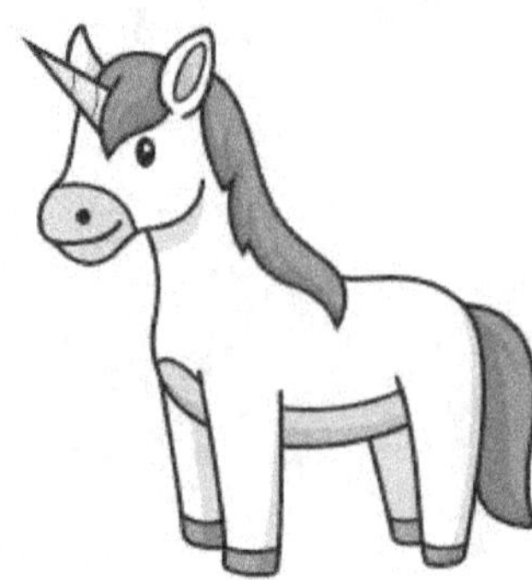

WATERMELON

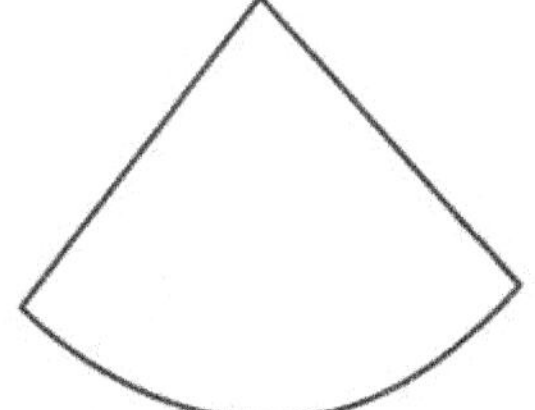 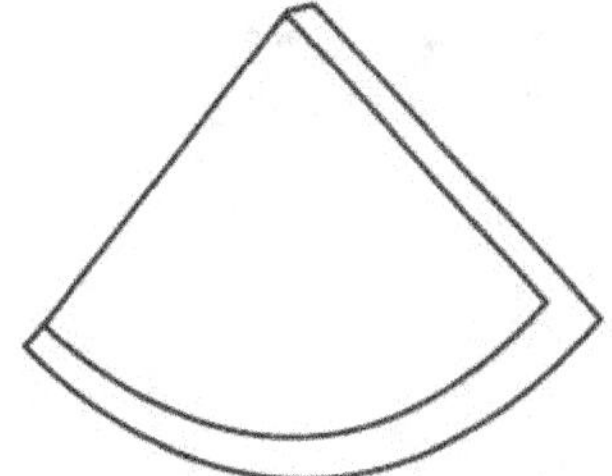 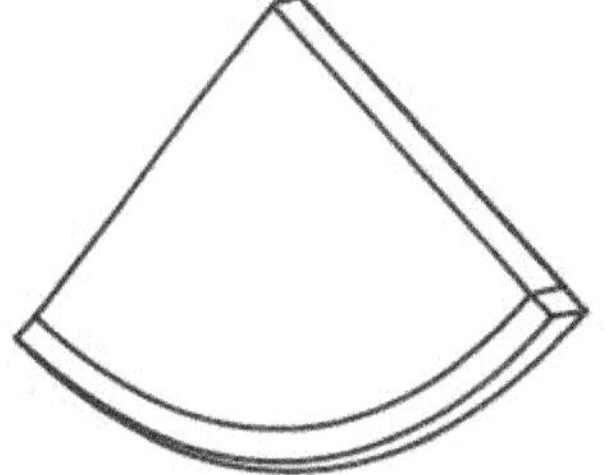

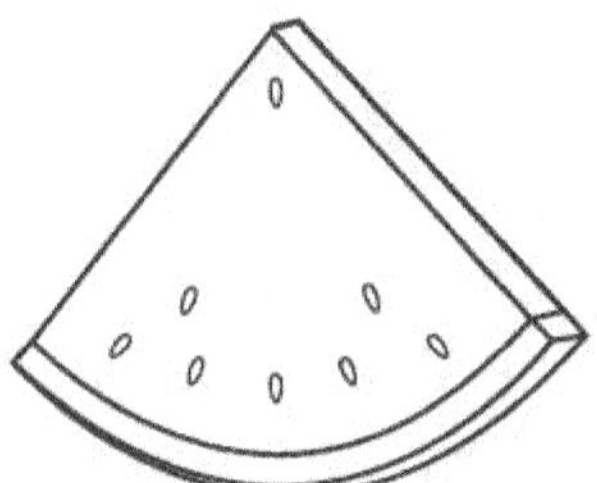 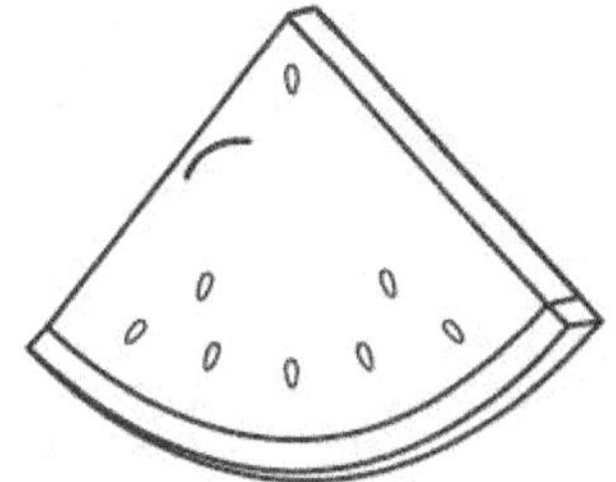 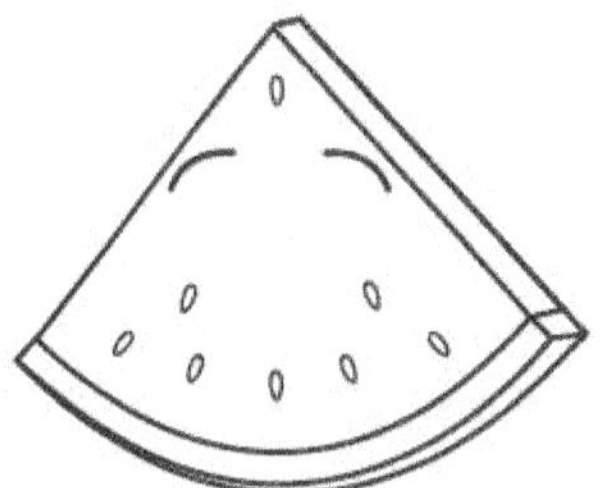

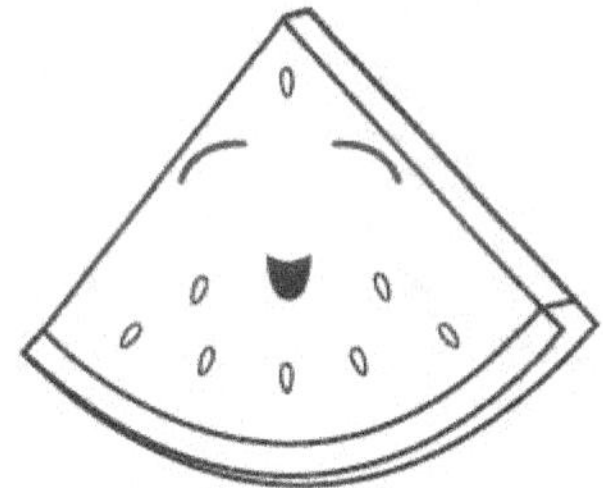 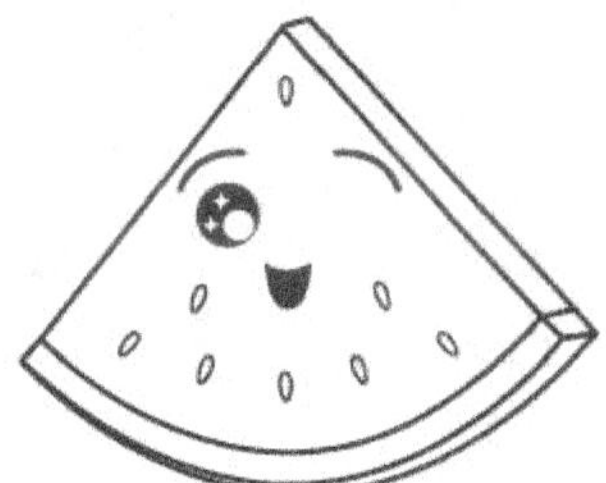 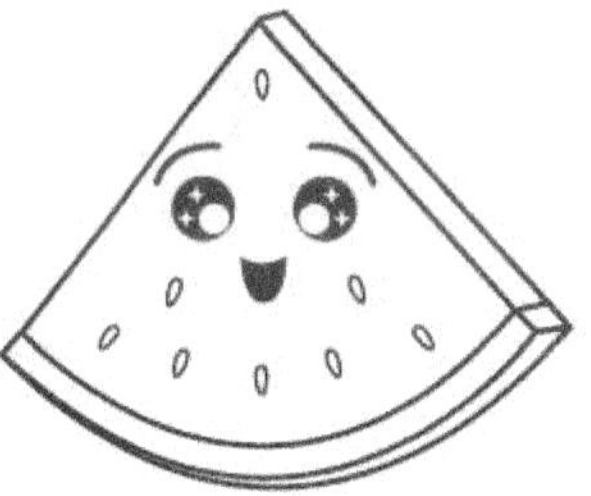

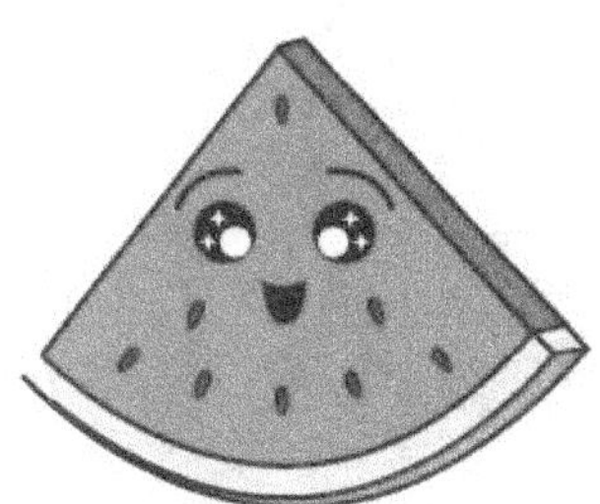

EARTH

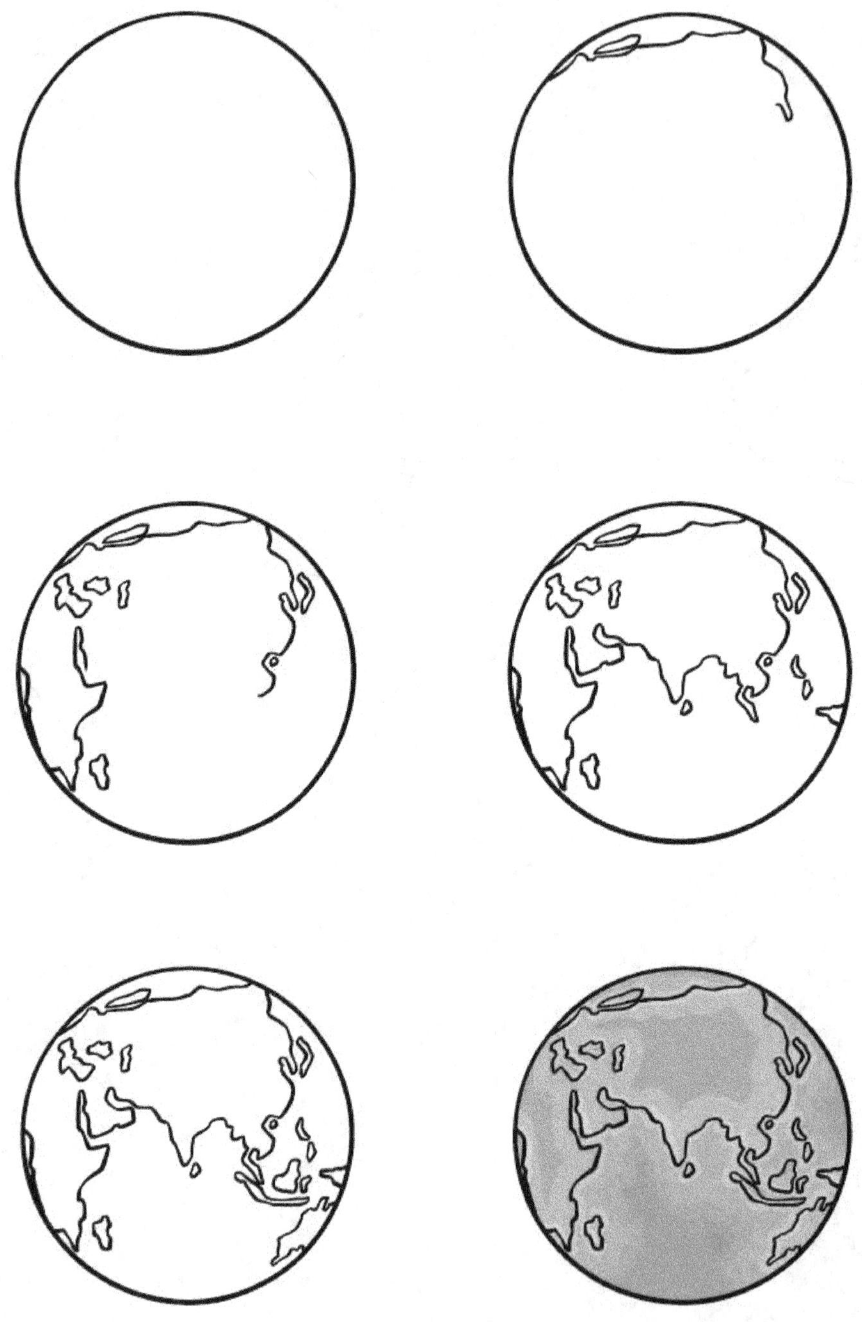

EASTER EGG

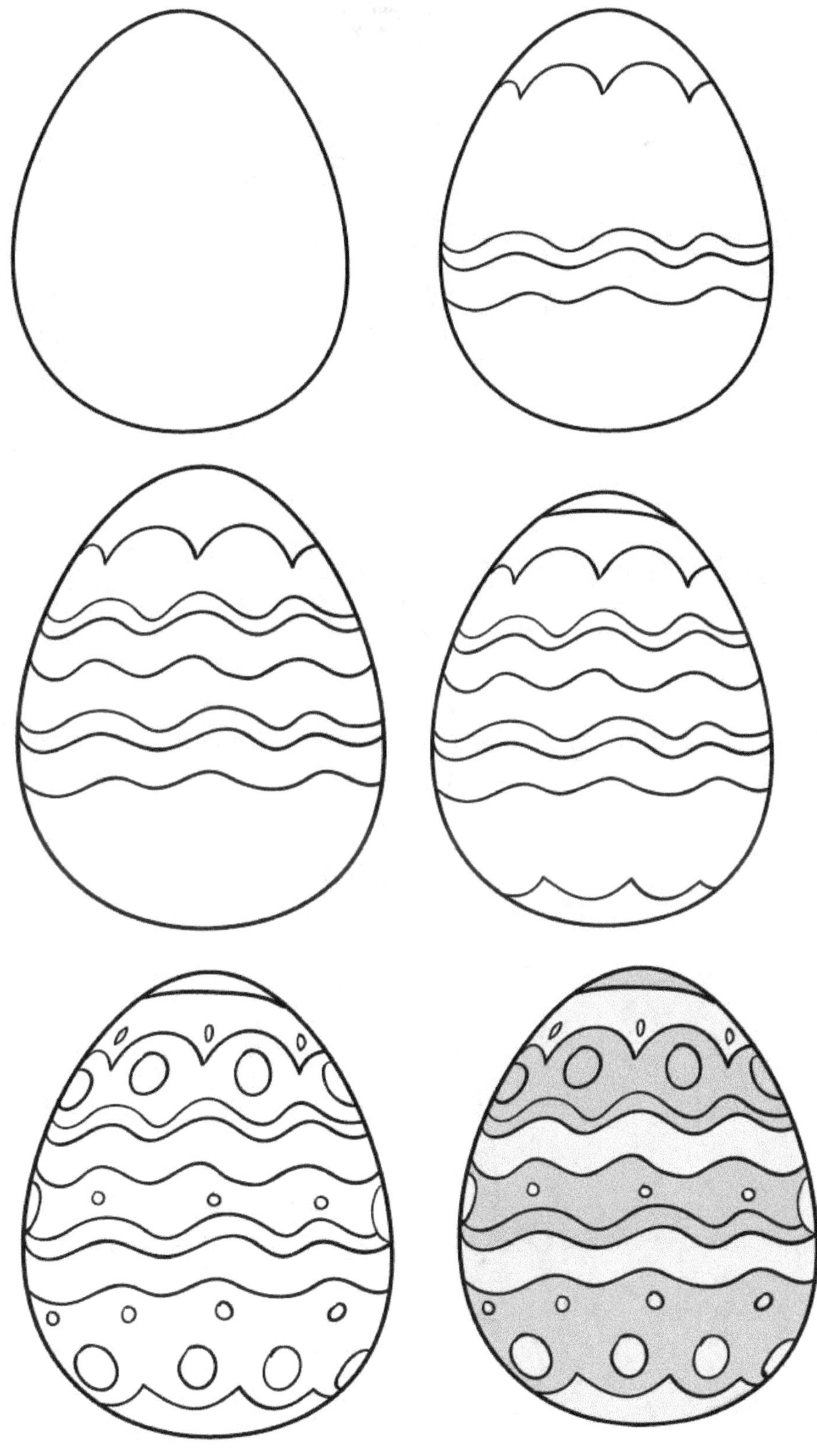

EGG

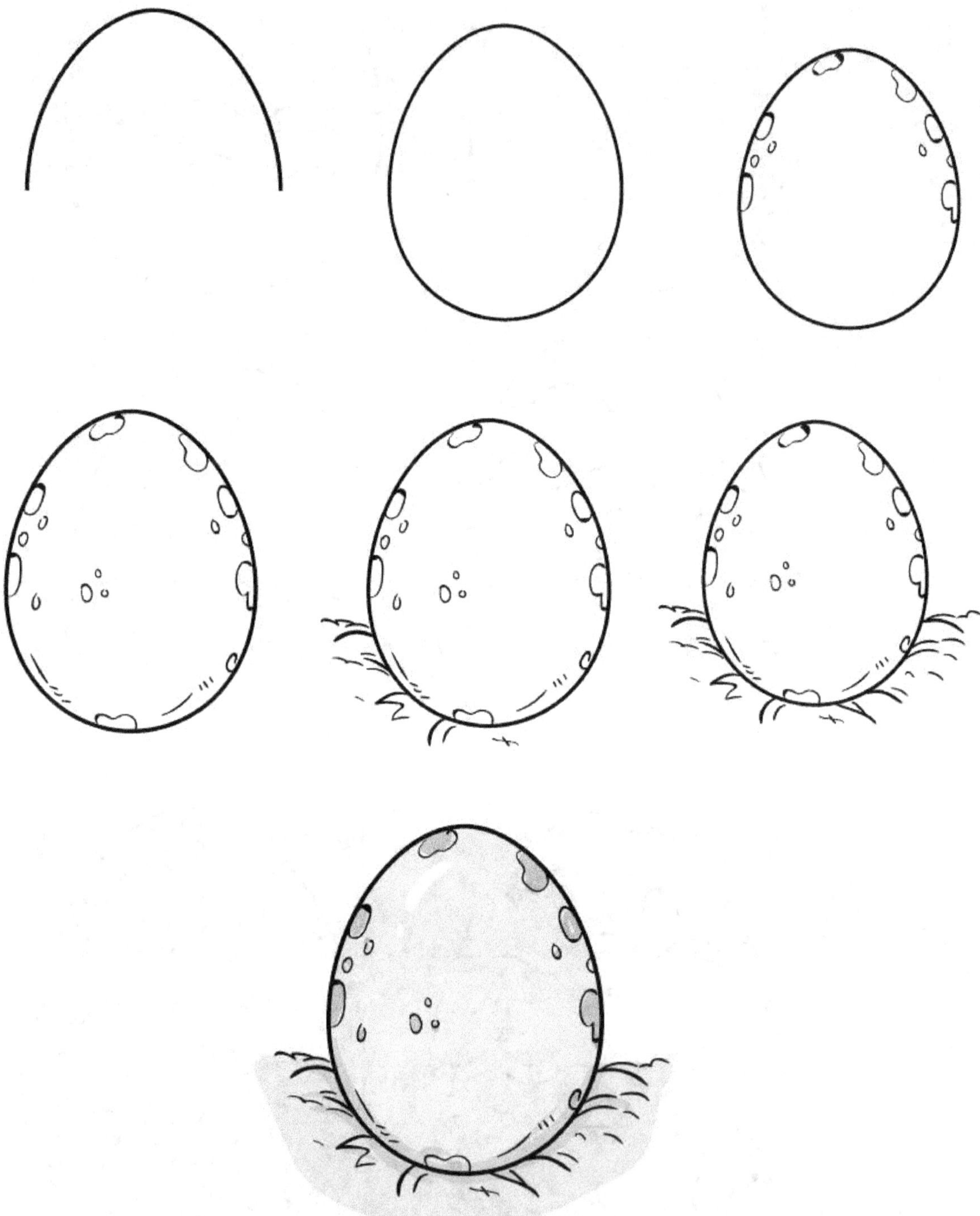

FLAG

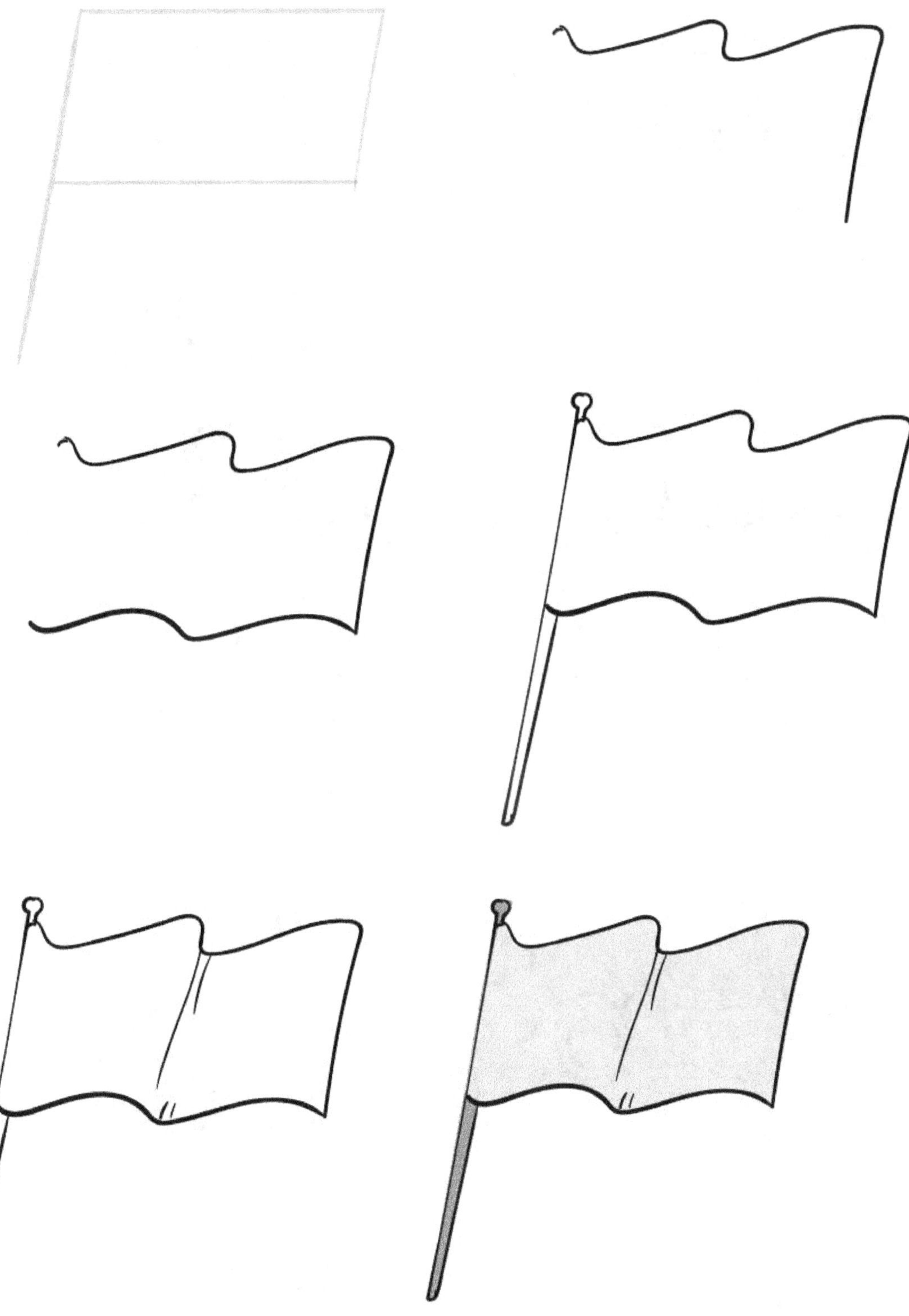

FOXY

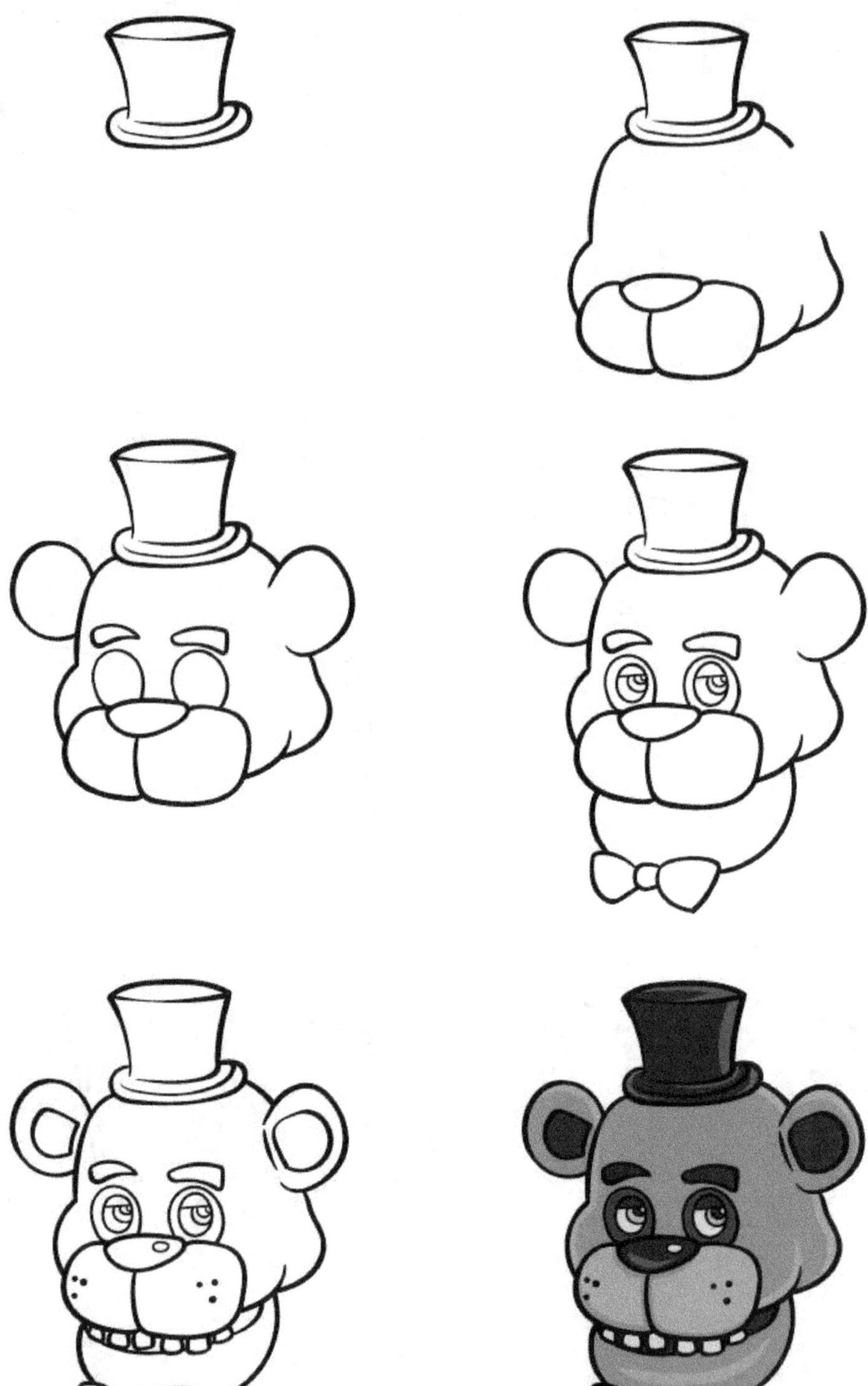

FLAMINGO

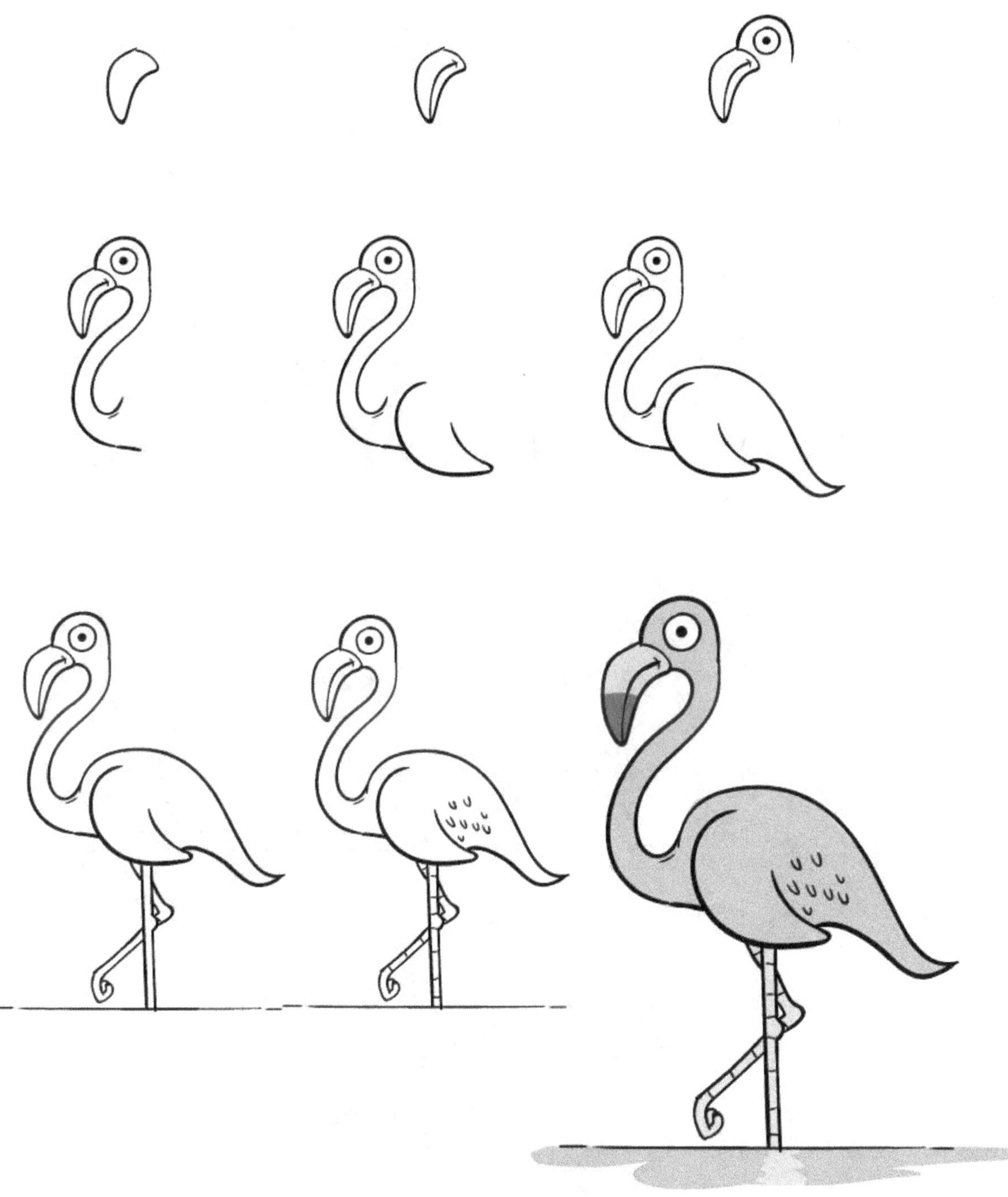

FRUITS

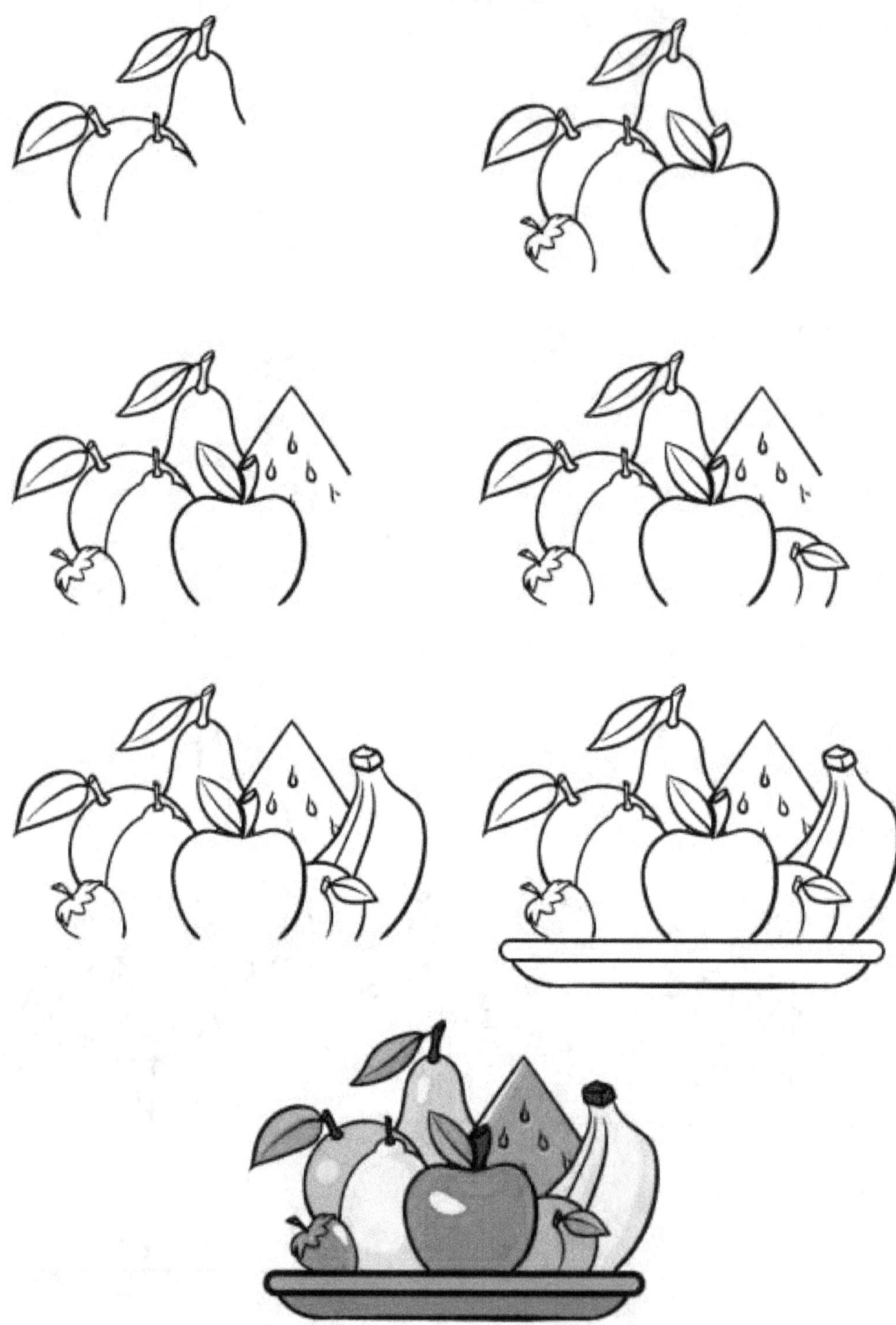

FURRY

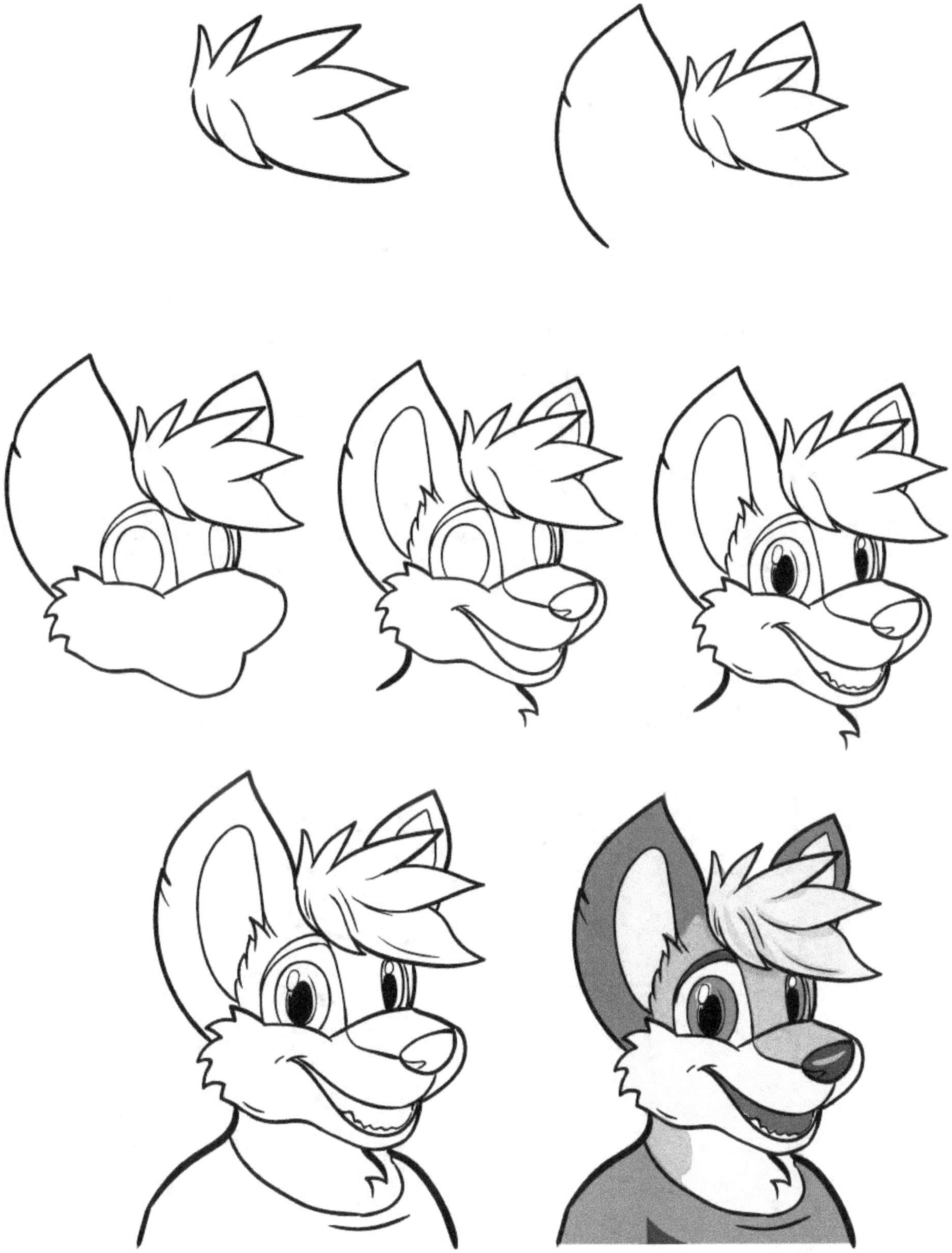

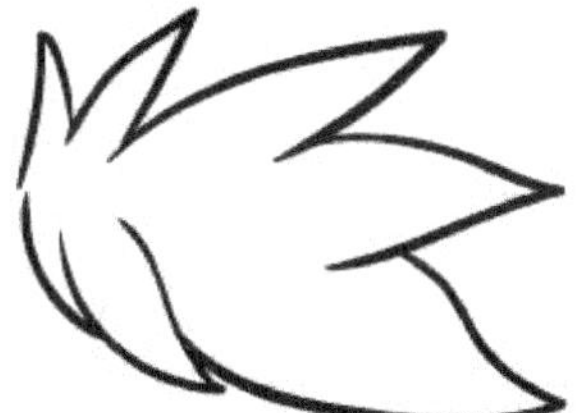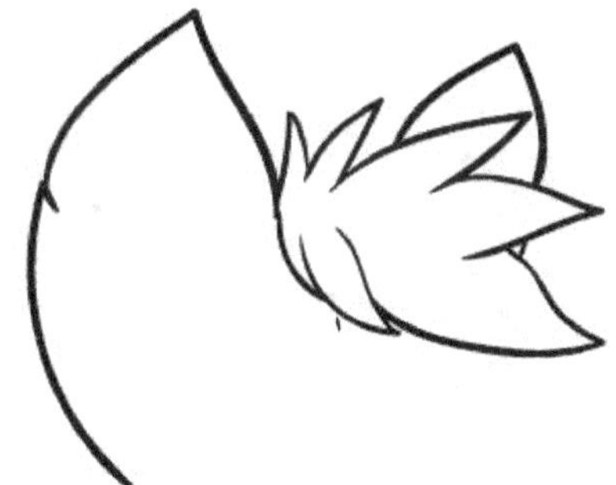

HAT

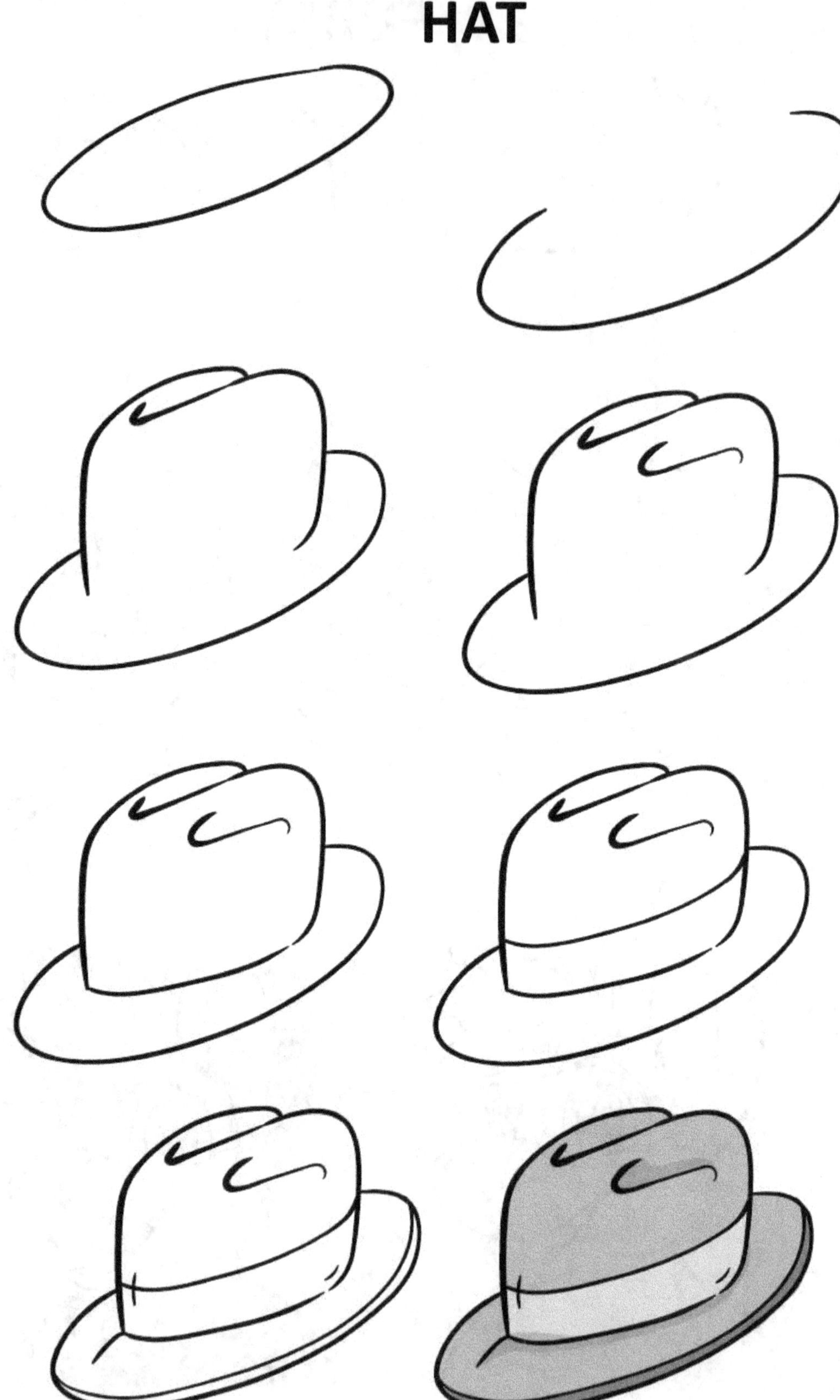

HOT AIR BALLOON

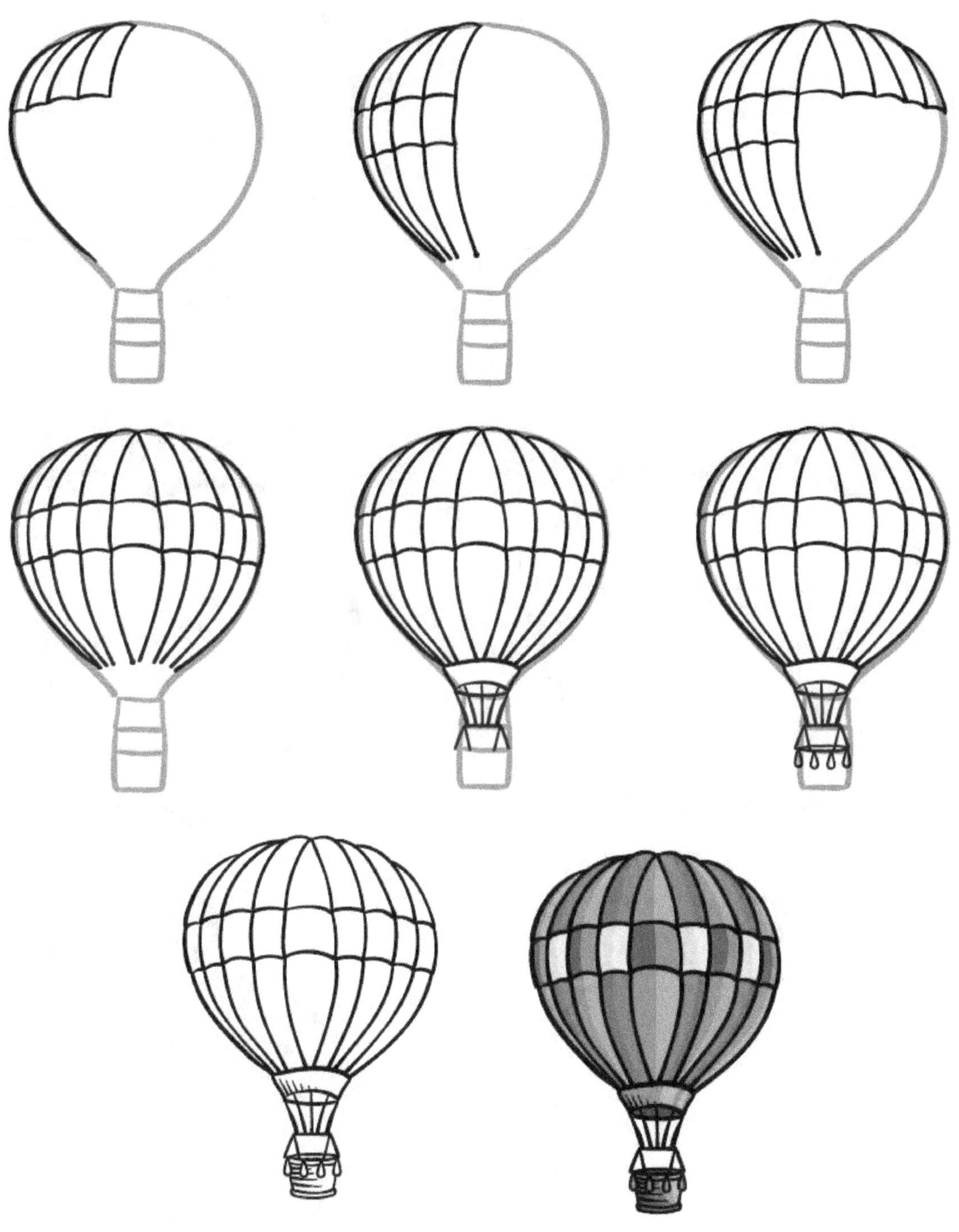

APPLE

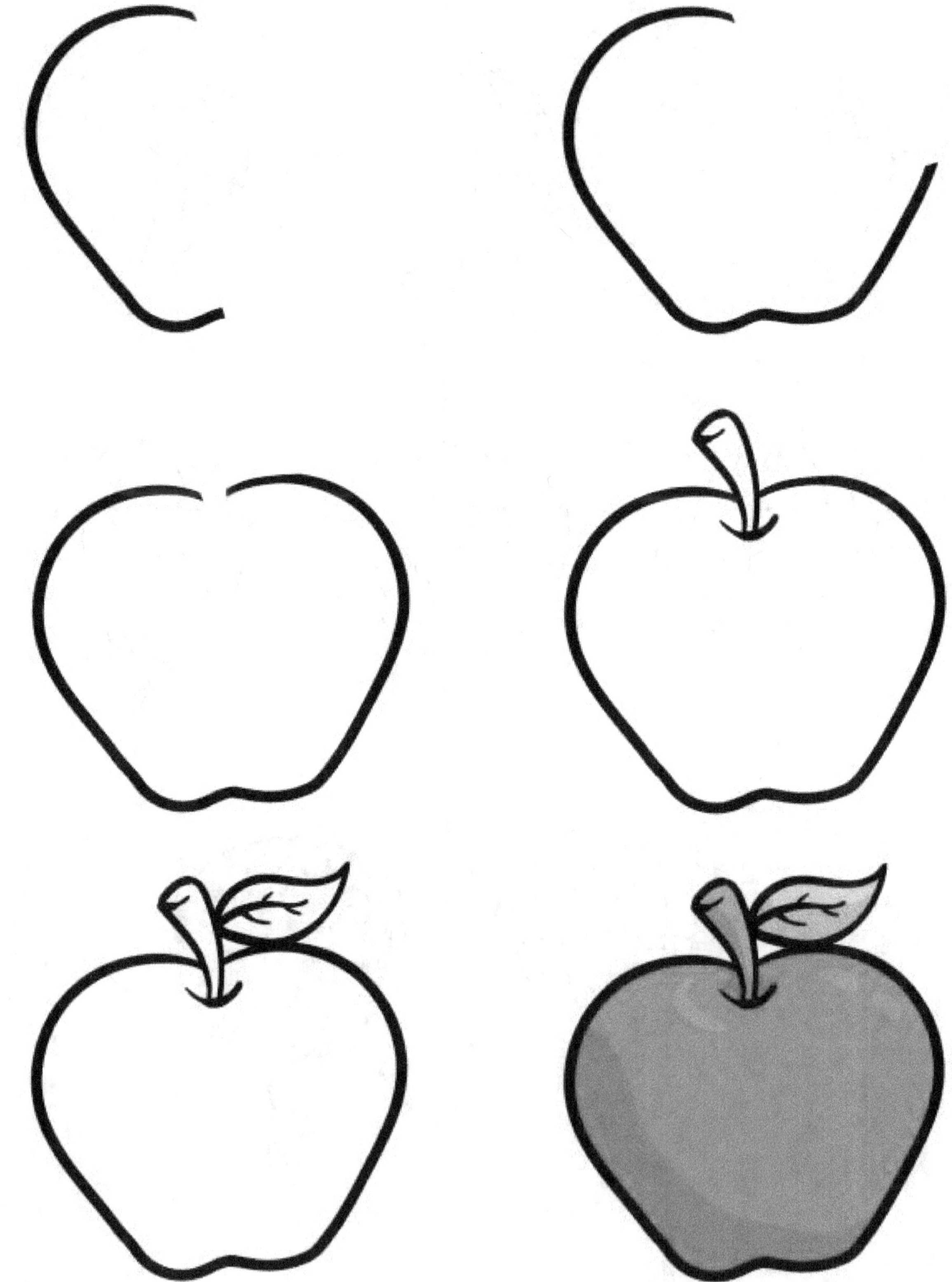

BANANA

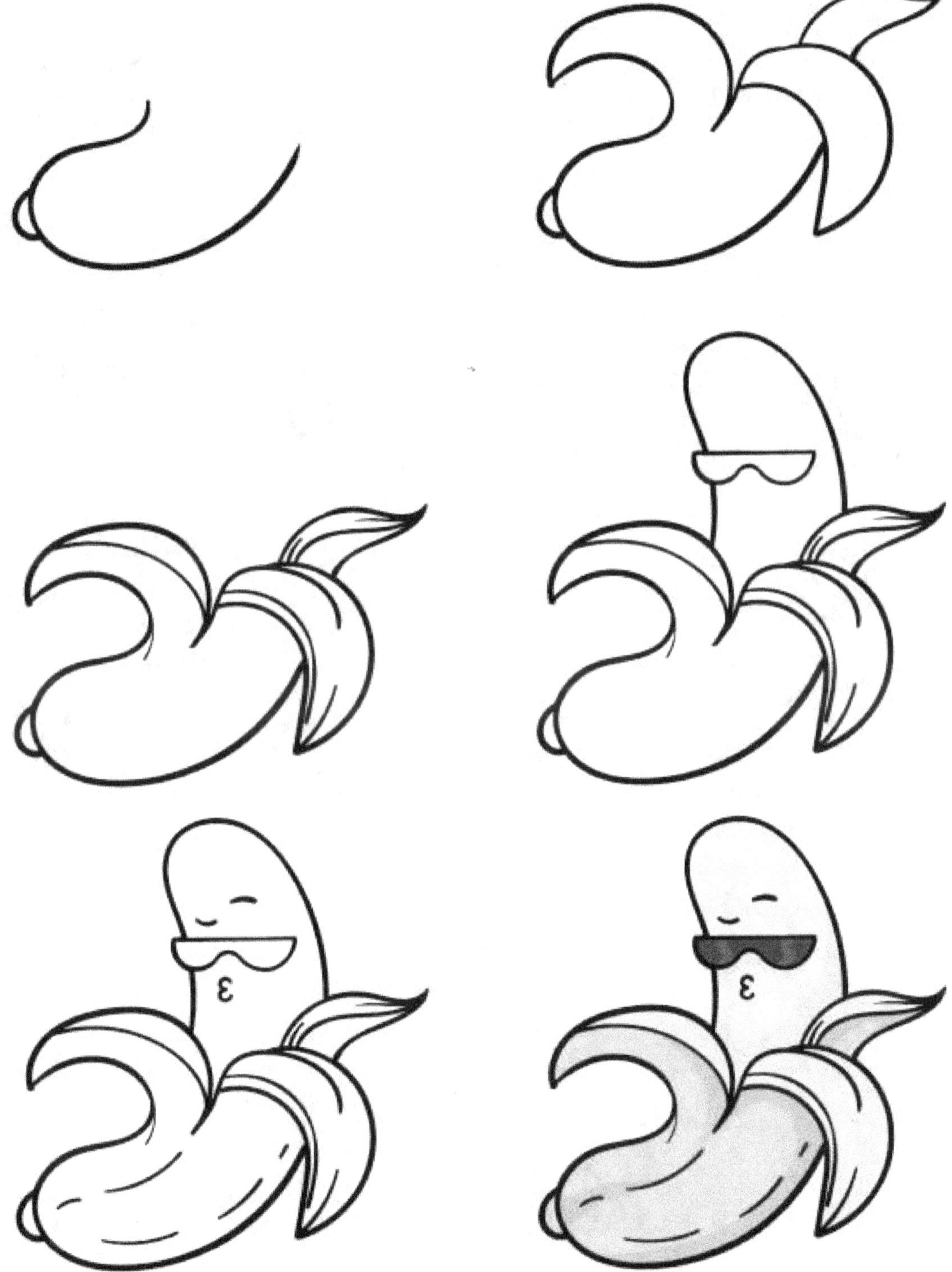

BIKE

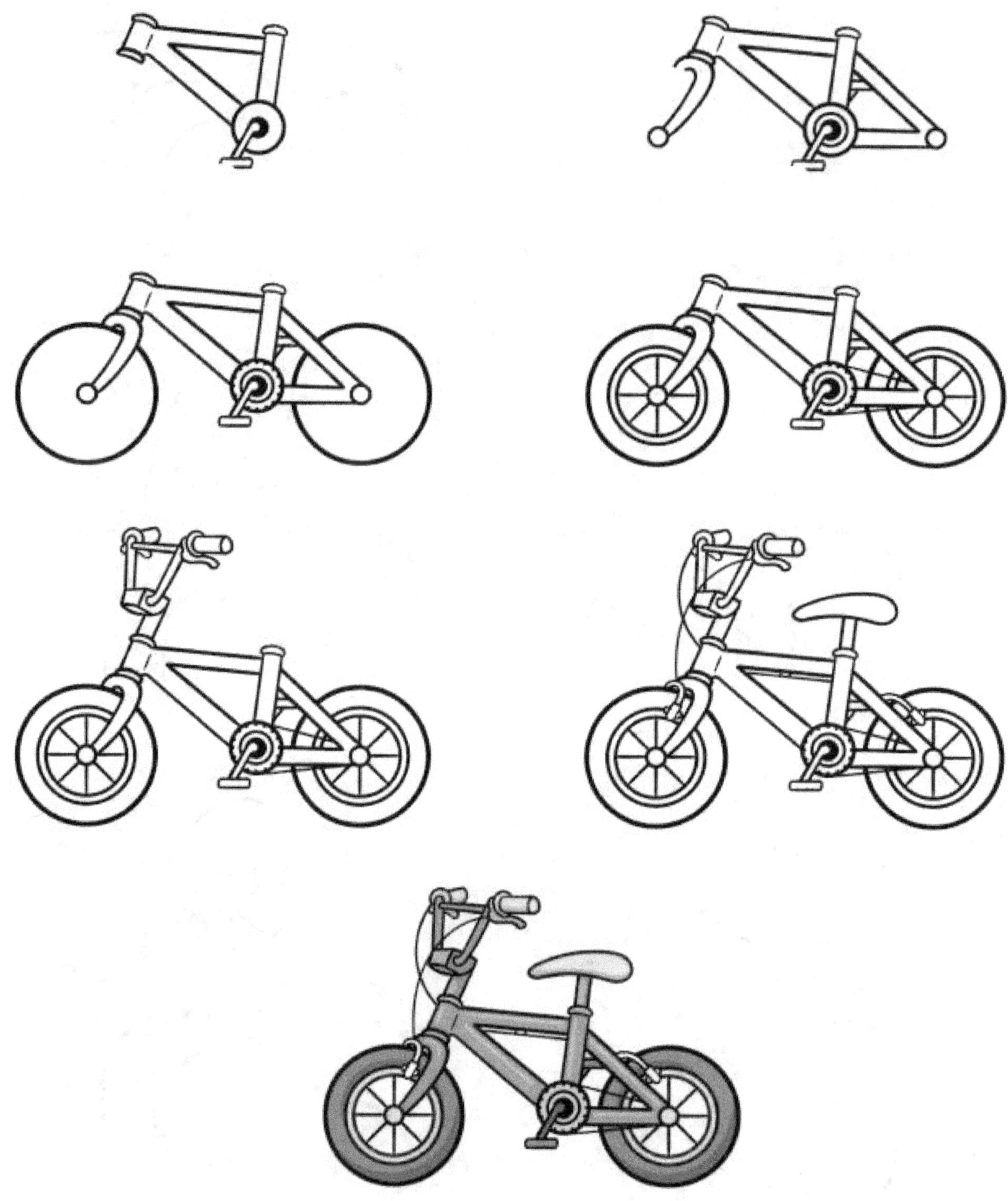

BOAT

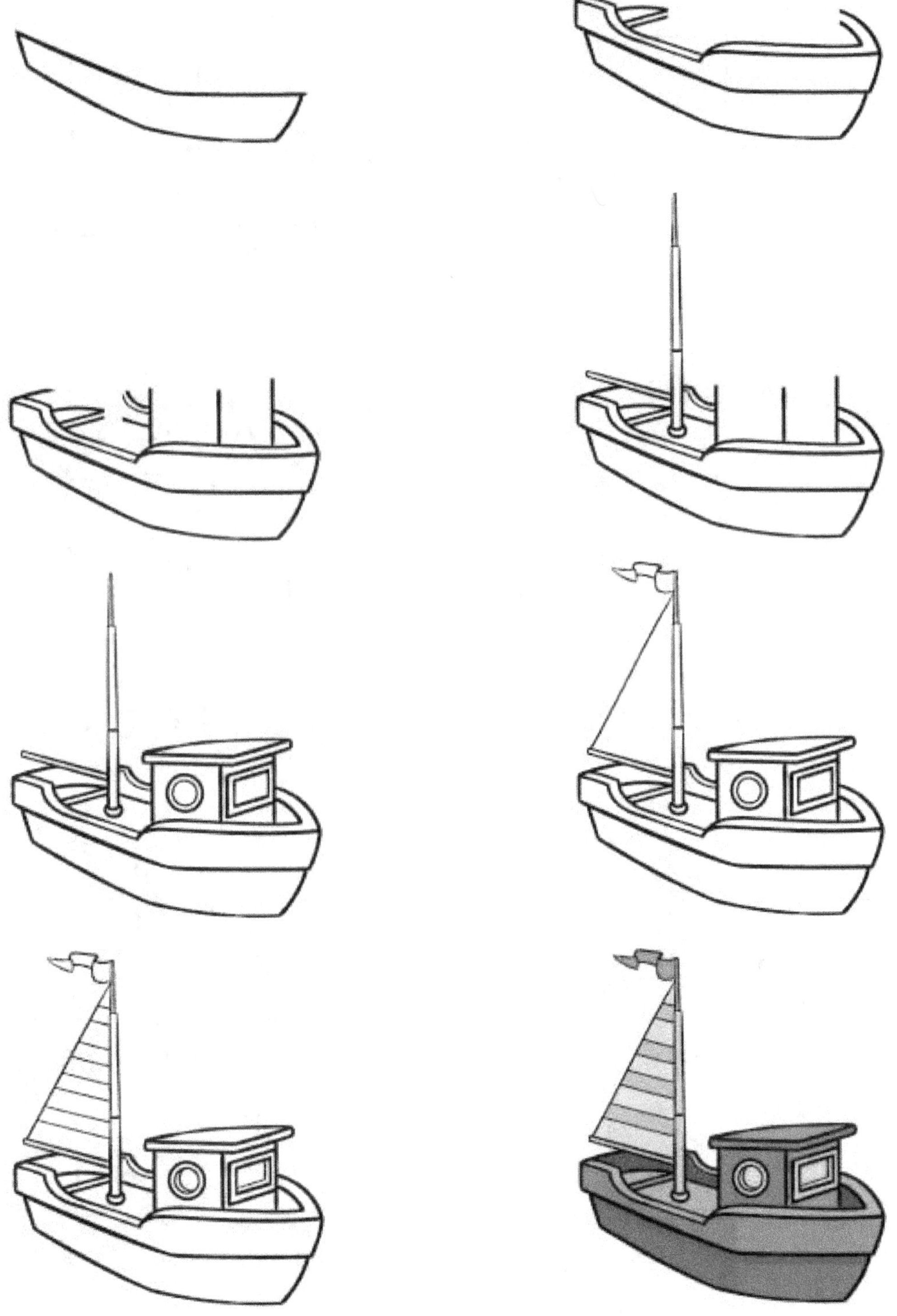

CASTLE

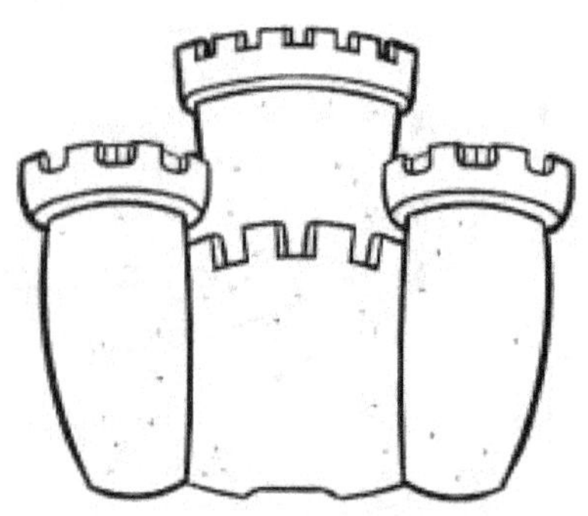

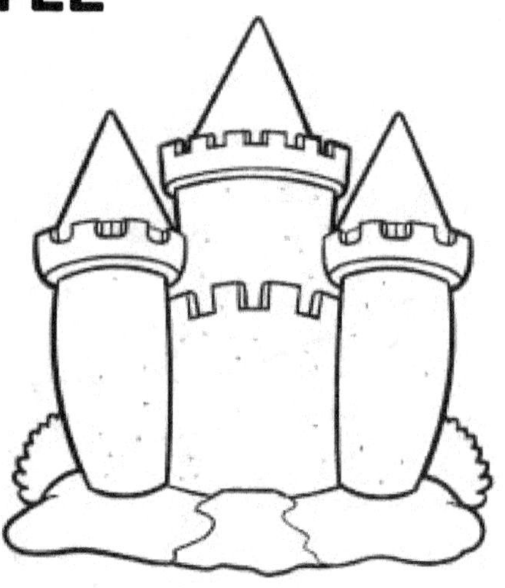

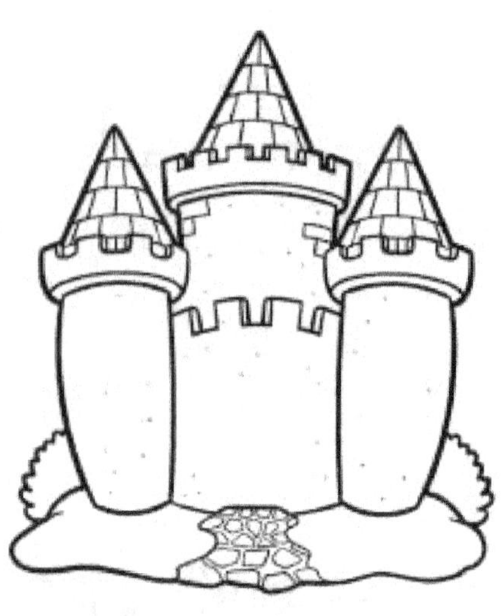

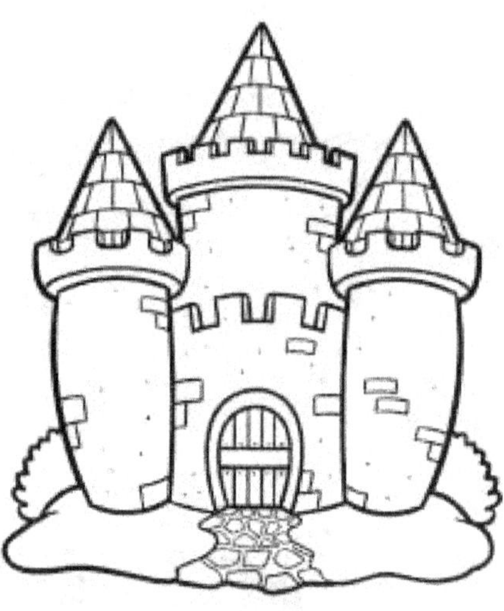

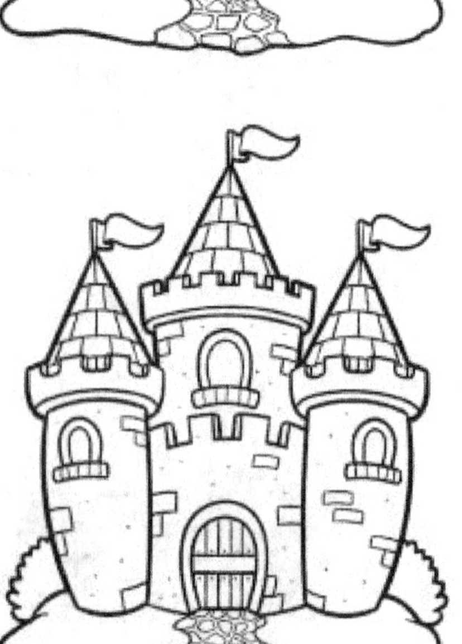

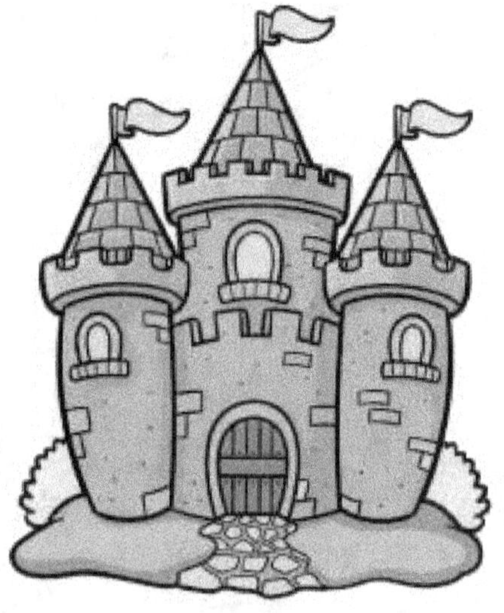

COMPUTER

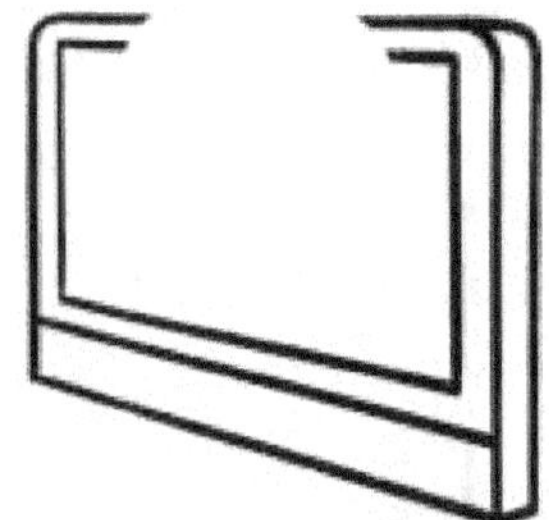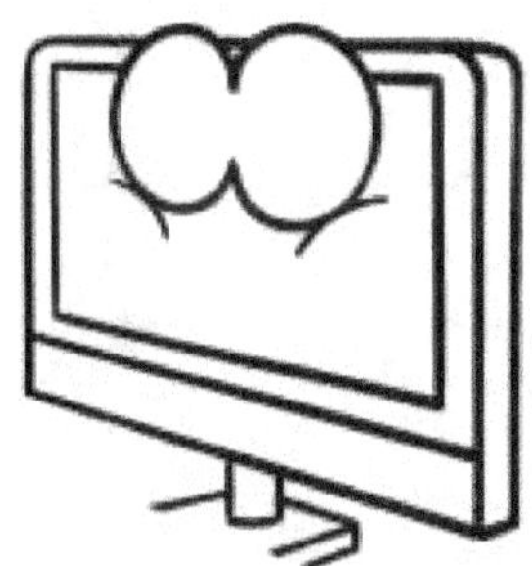
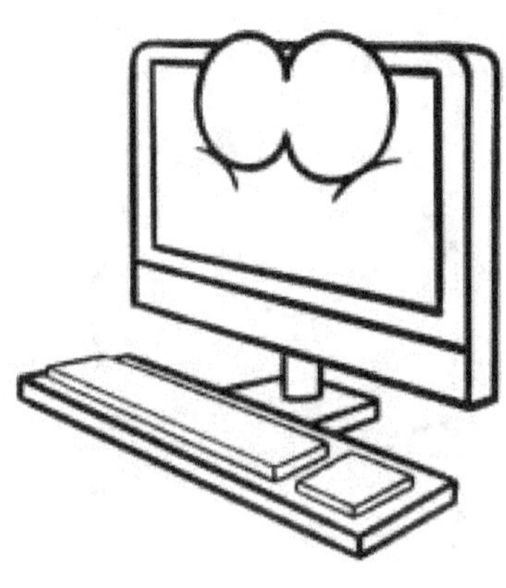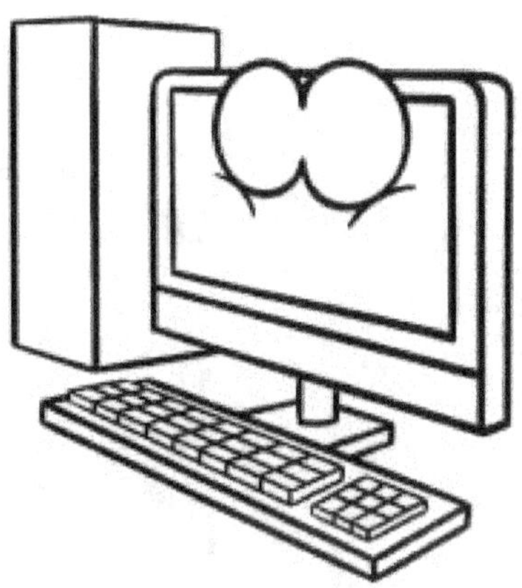
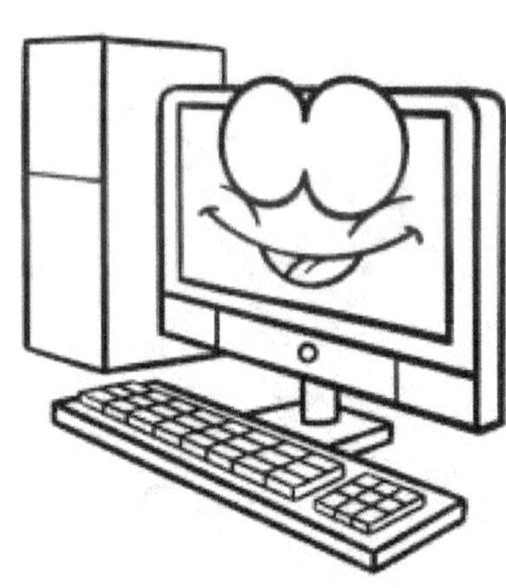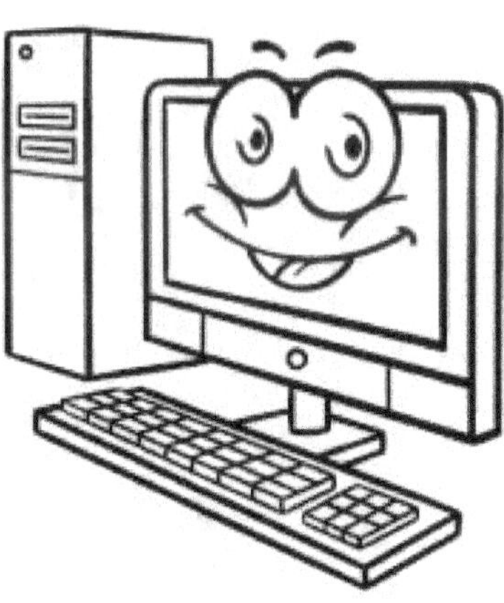
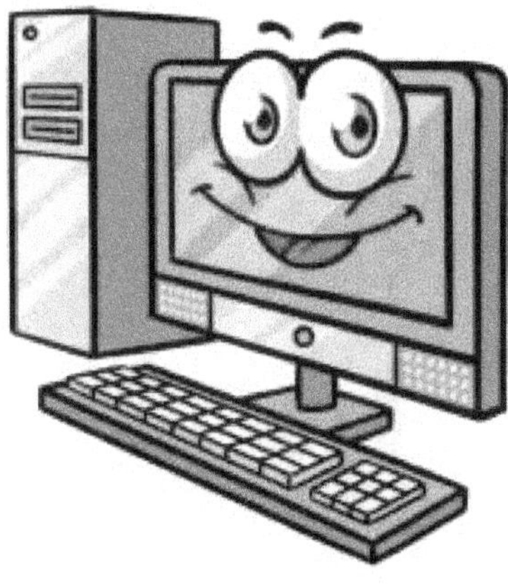

ICE CREAM

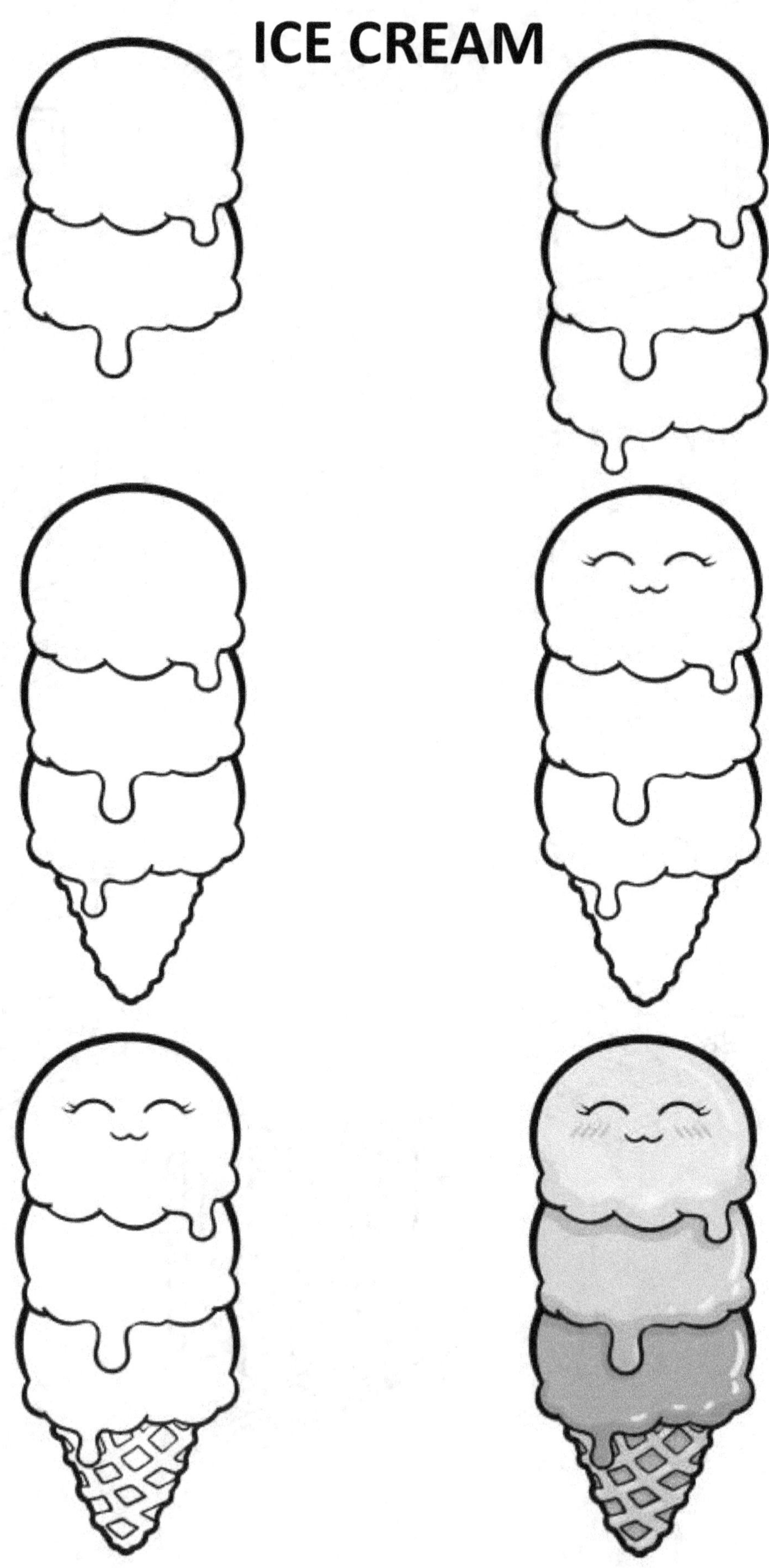

NURSE

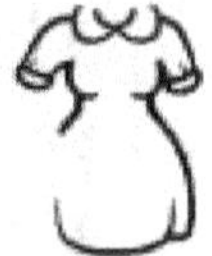
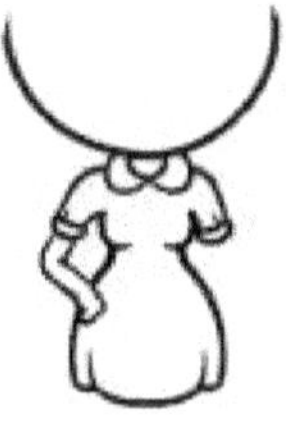
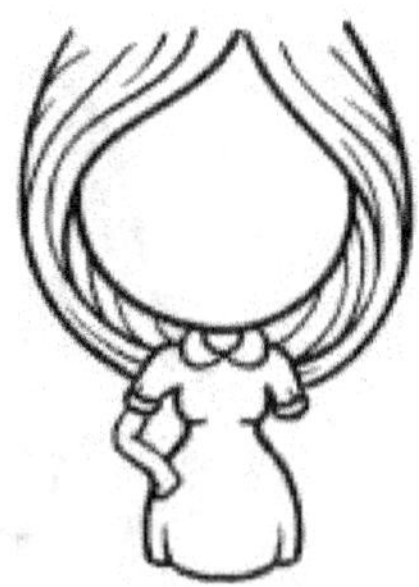
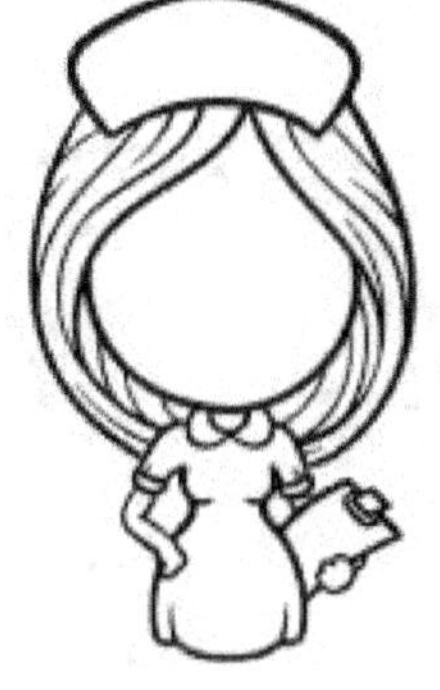
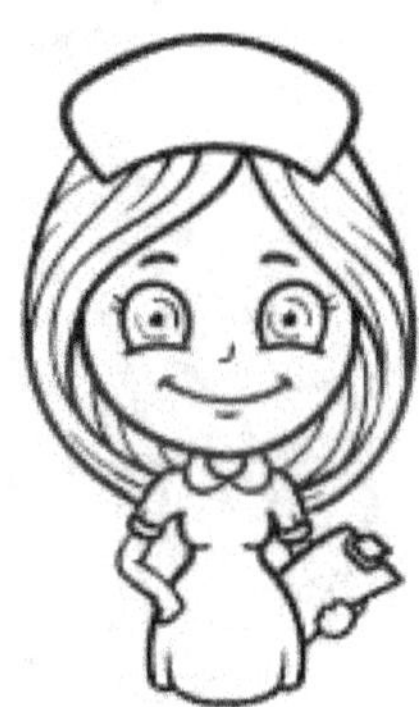
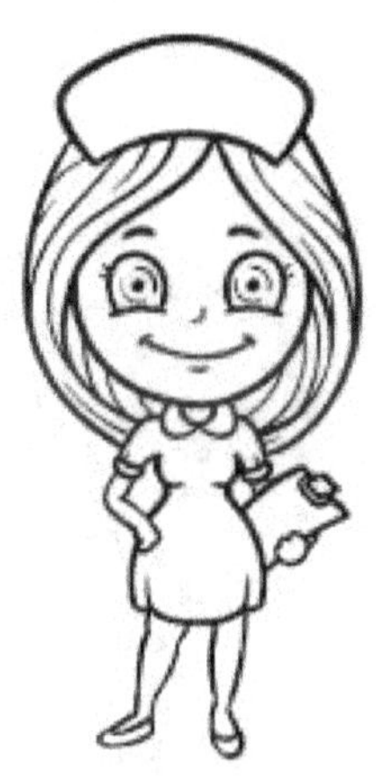
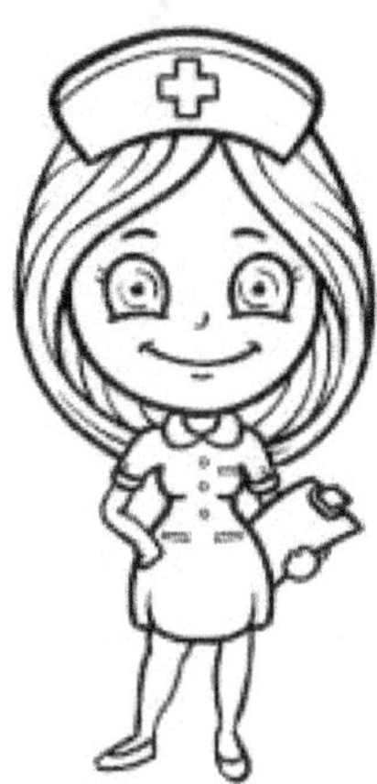
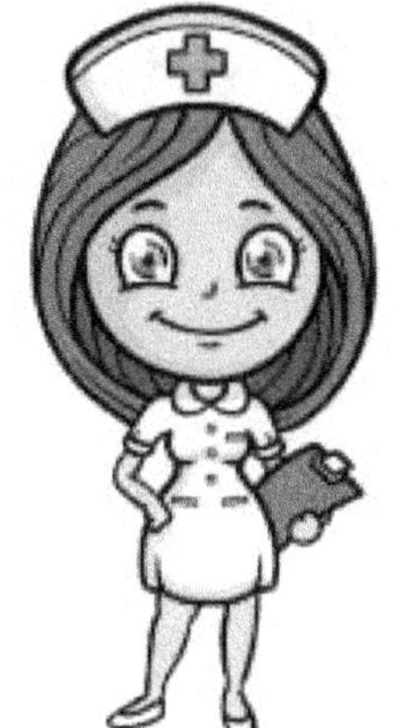

PHONE

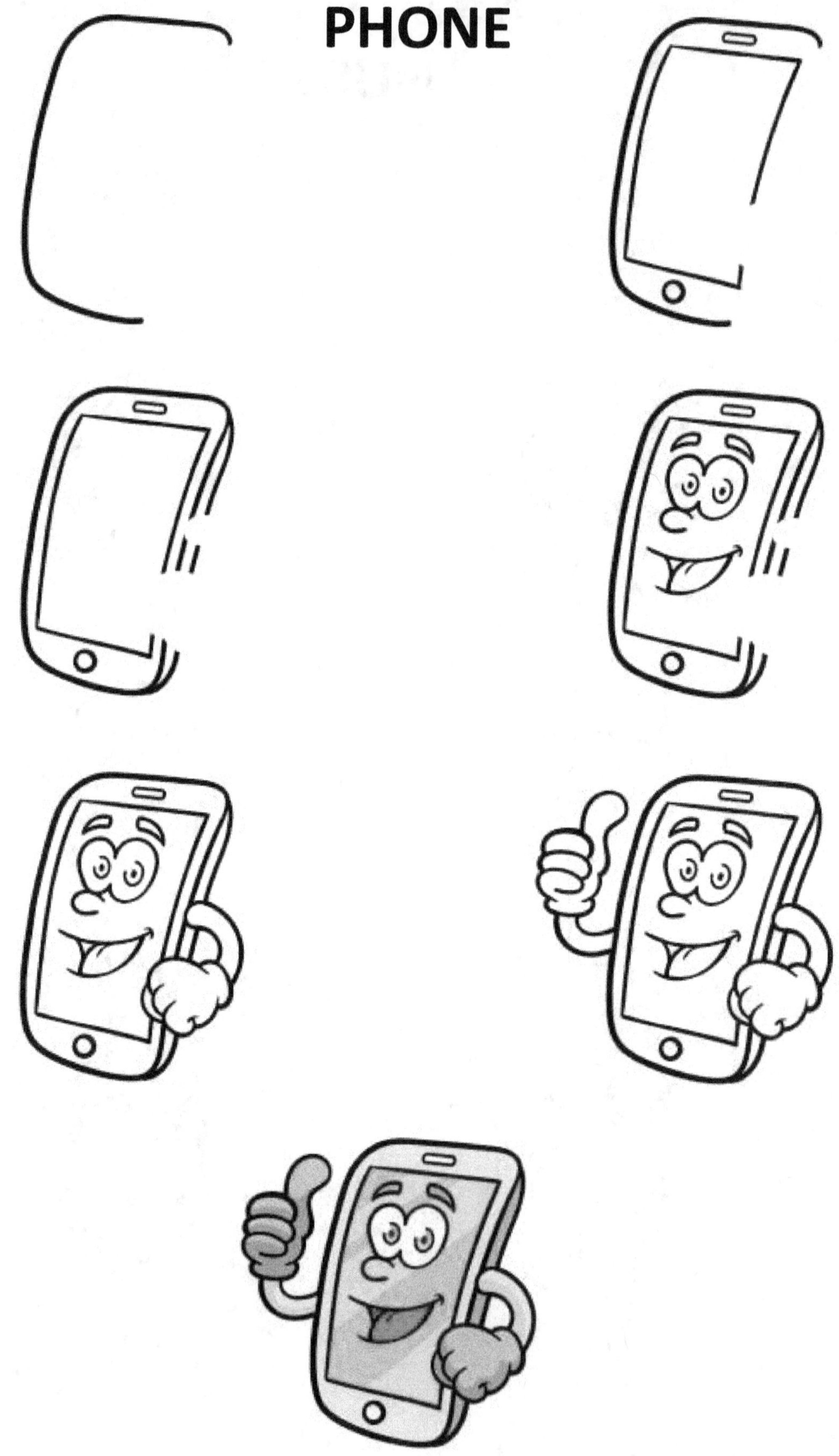

PLANT

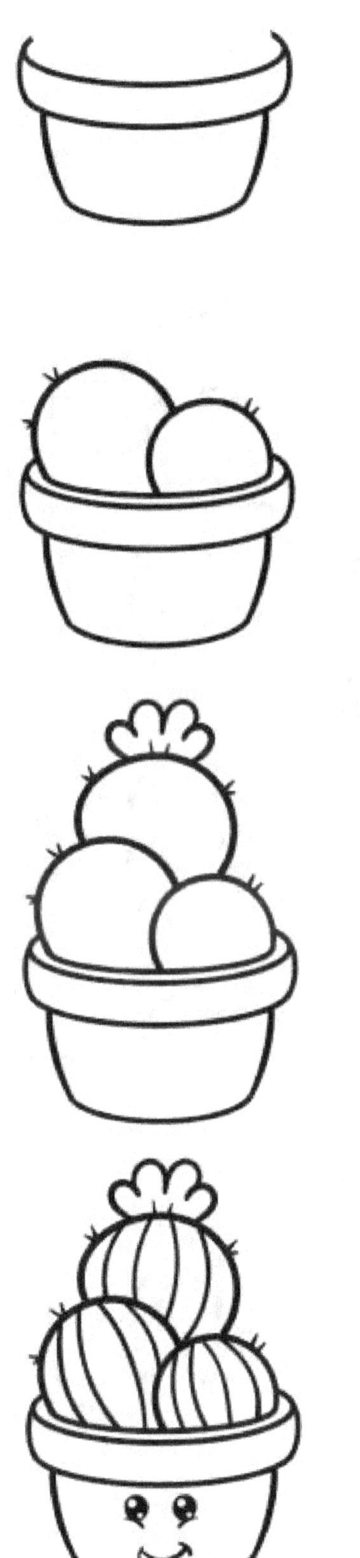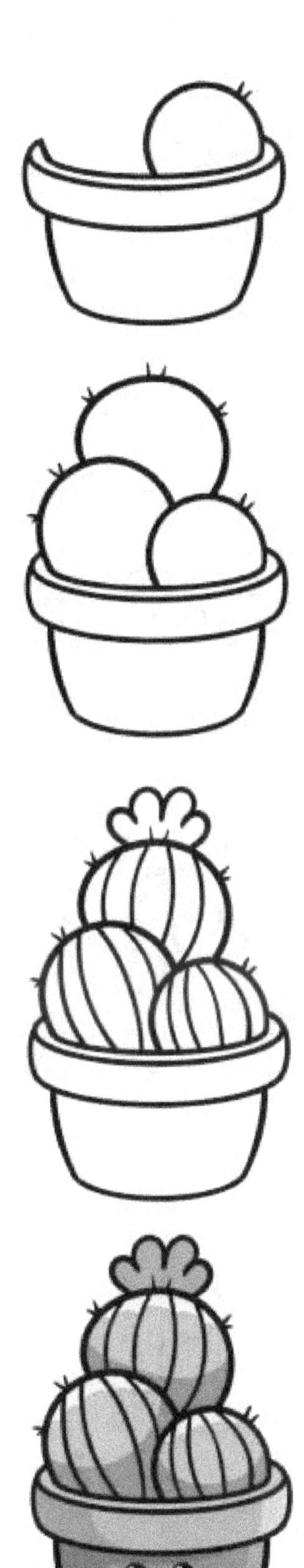

POLAN BEAR

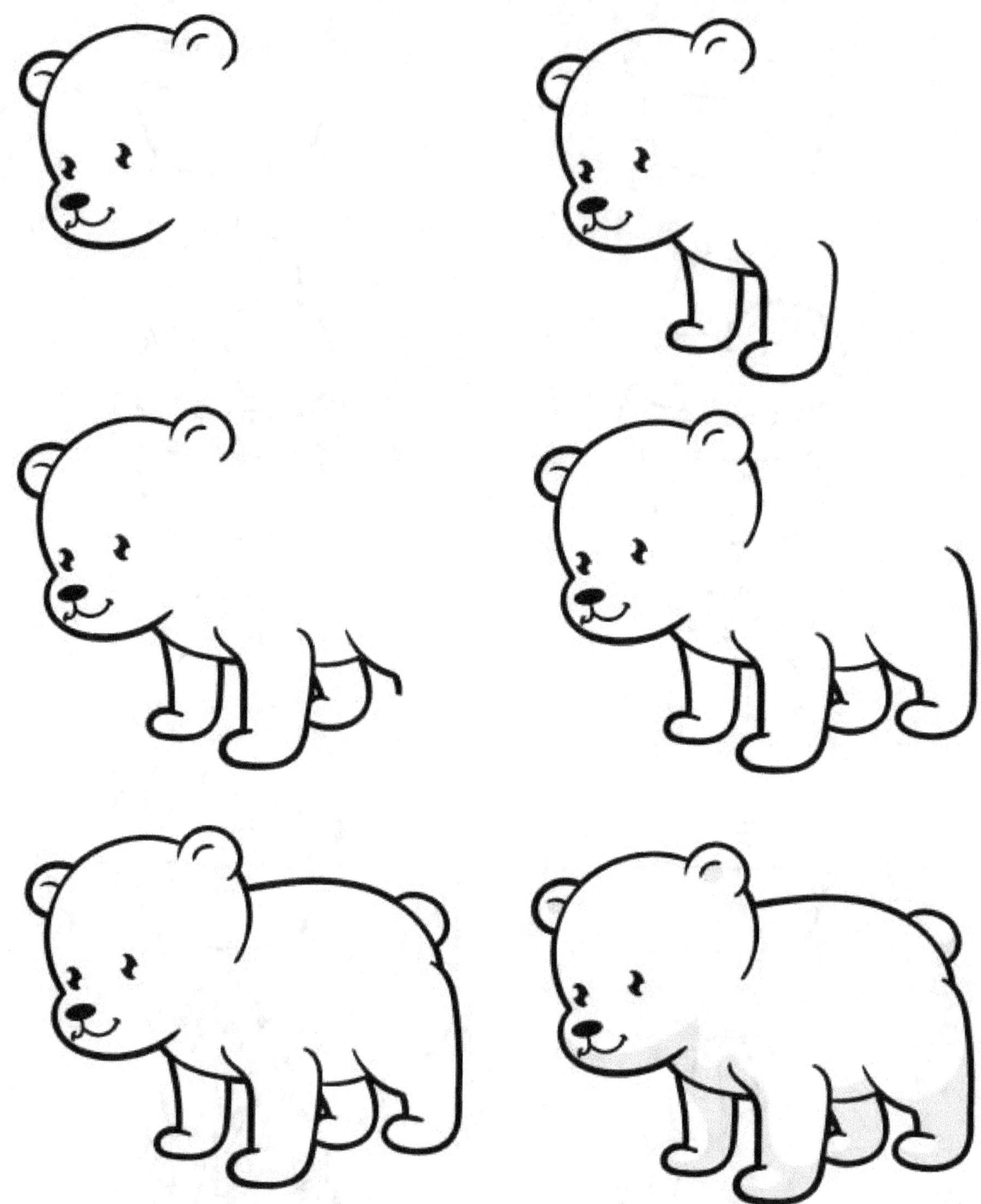

REINDER

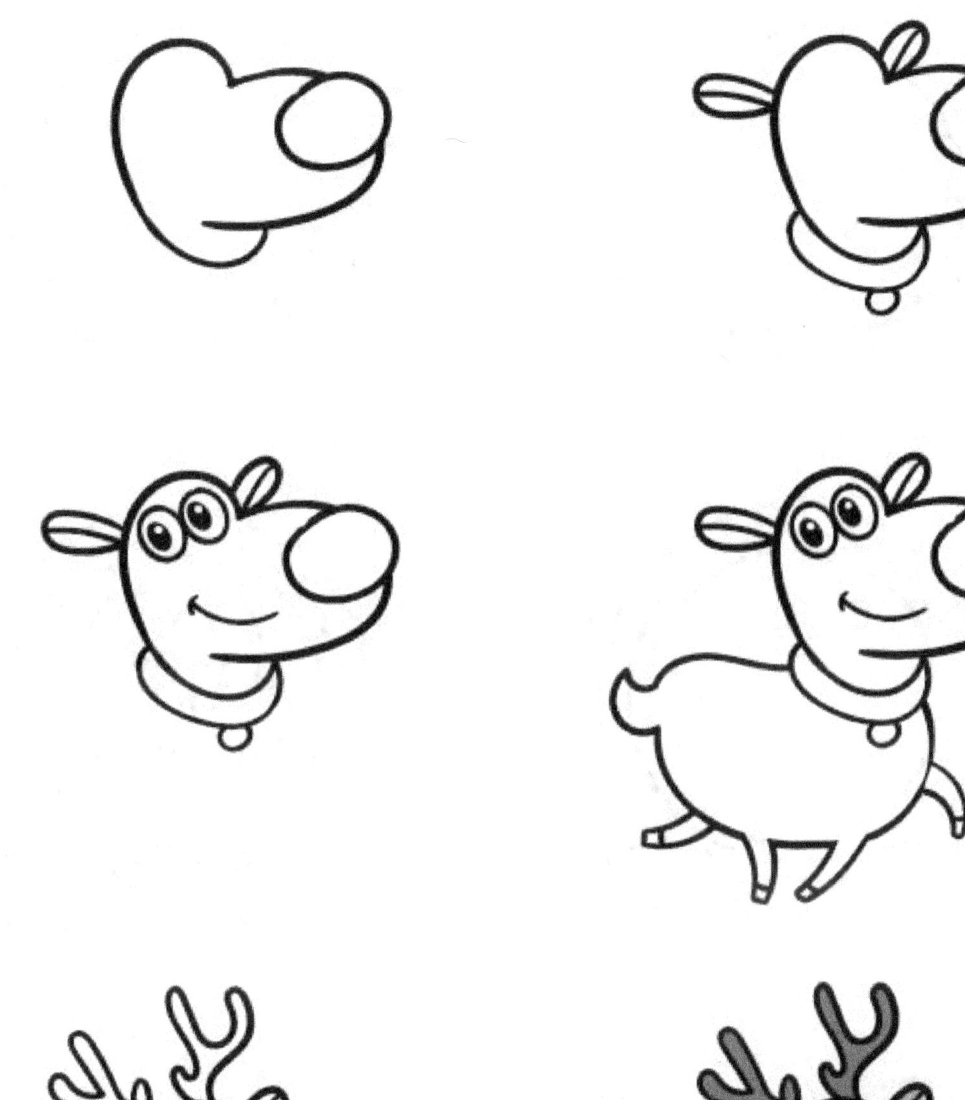

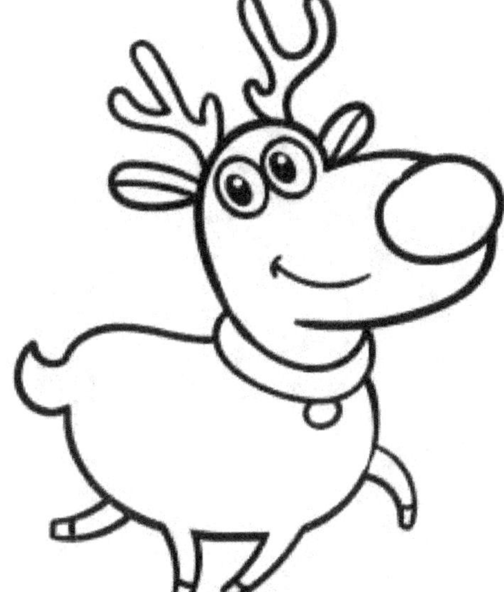

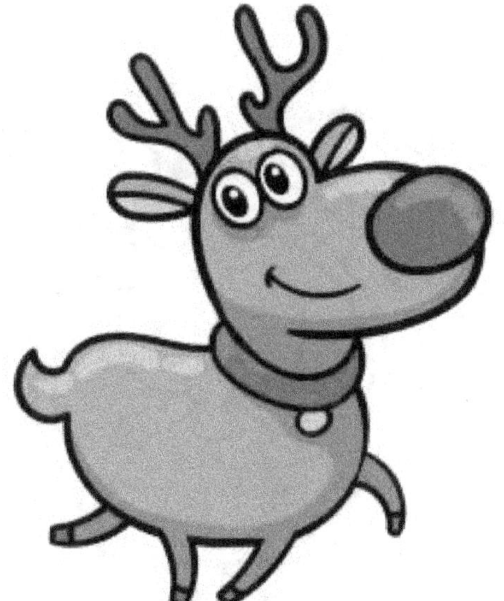

CLOCK

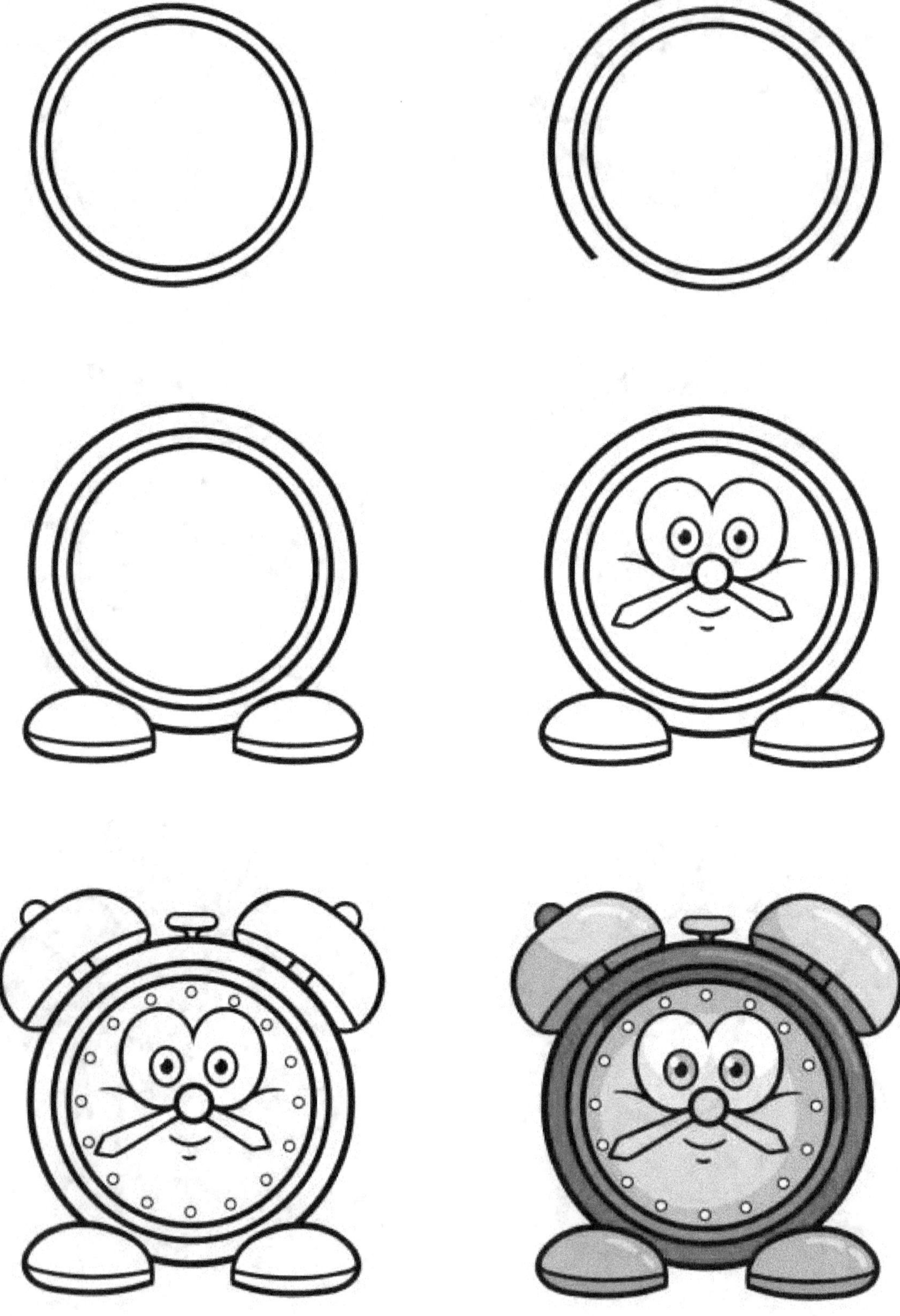

CAT

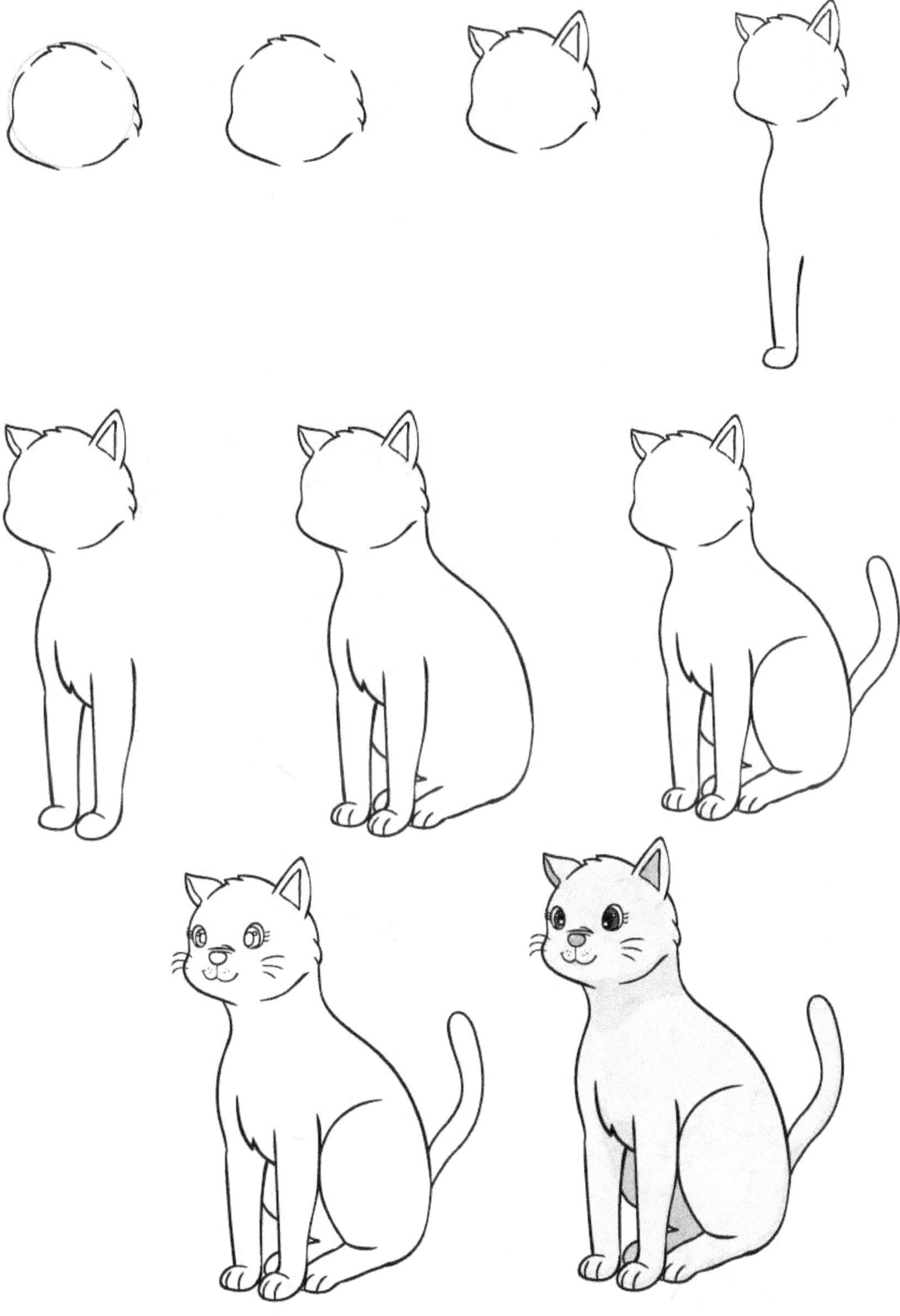

TREE

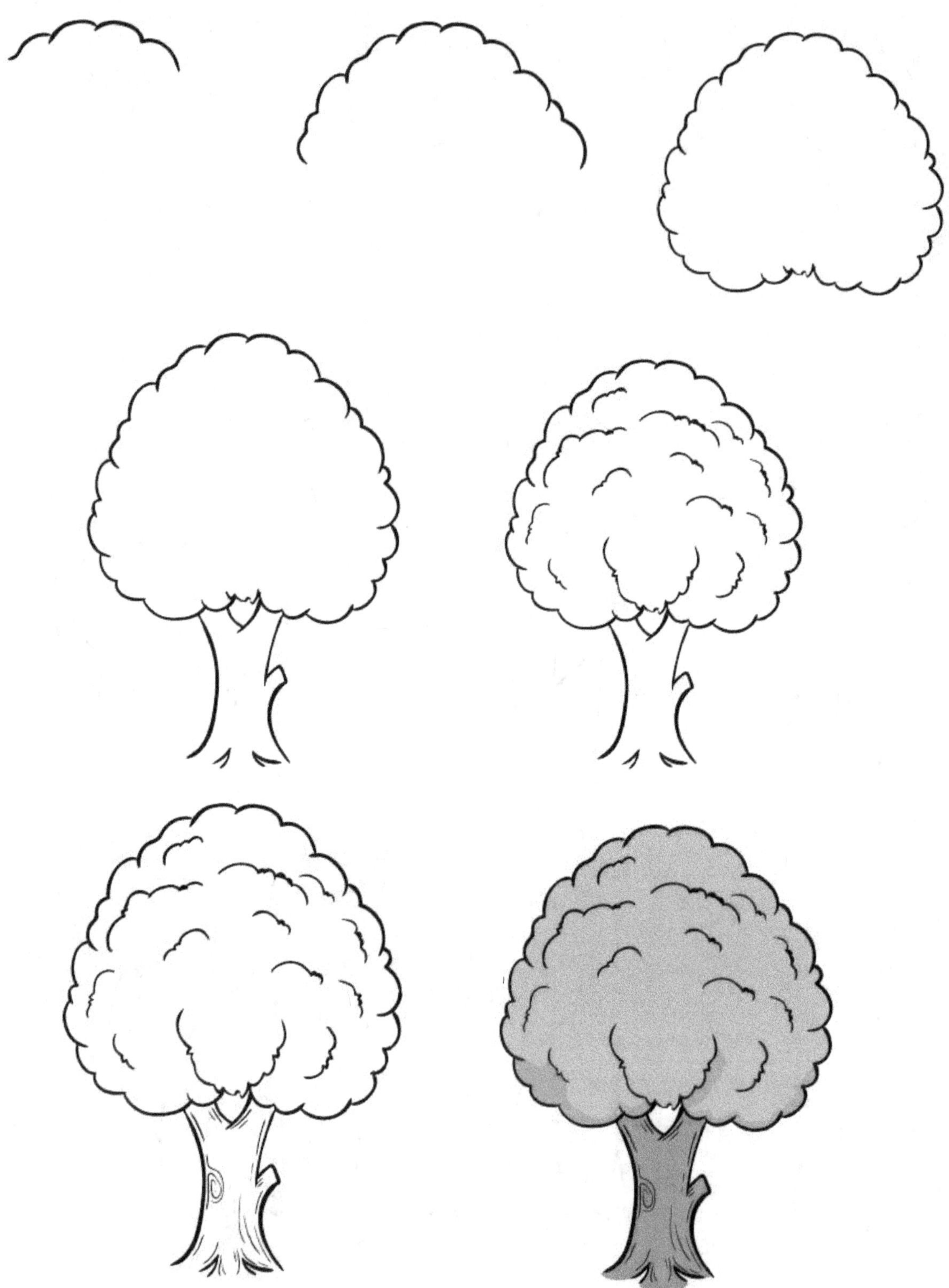

HEART

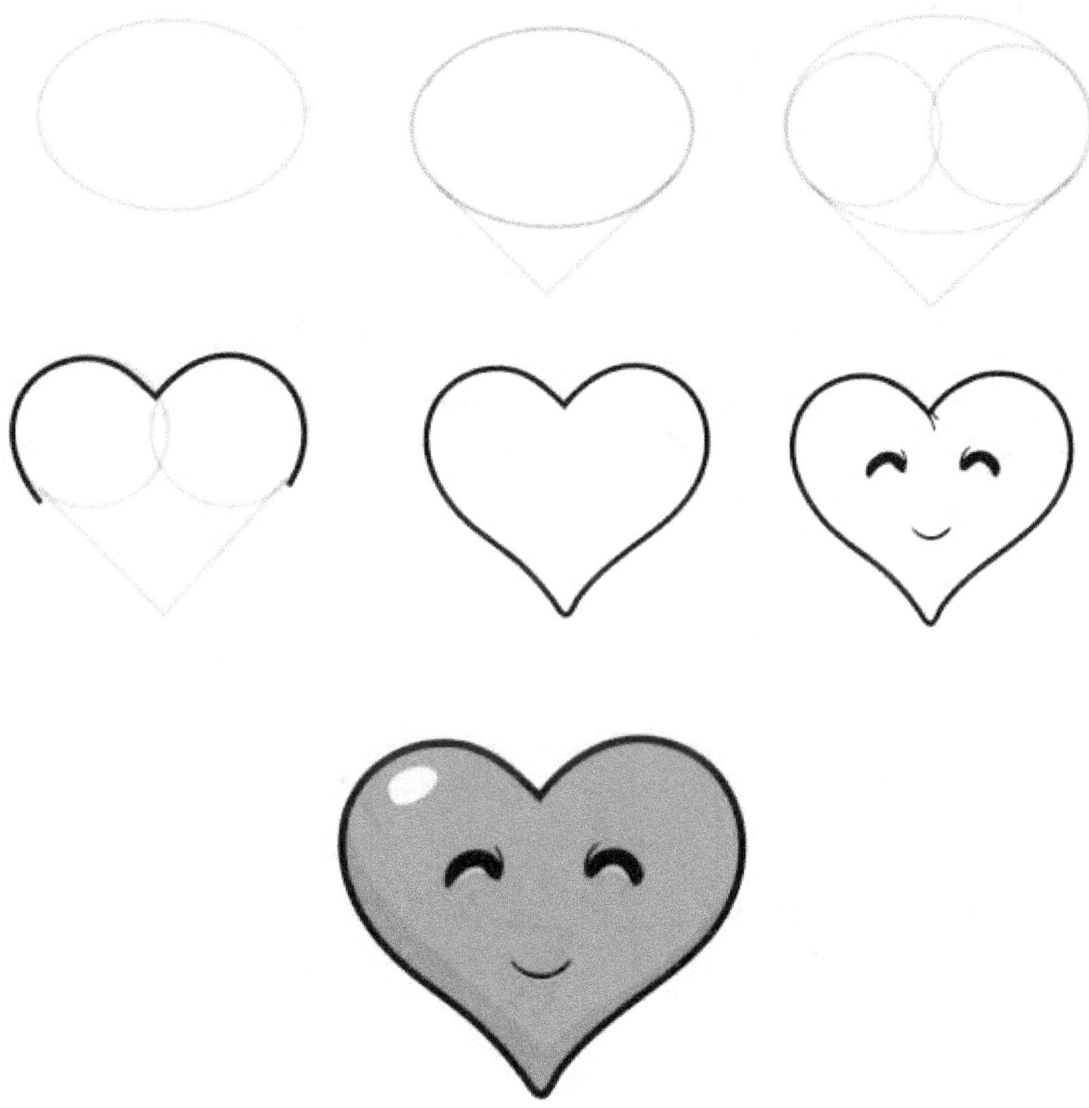

STAR

BABY CHIK

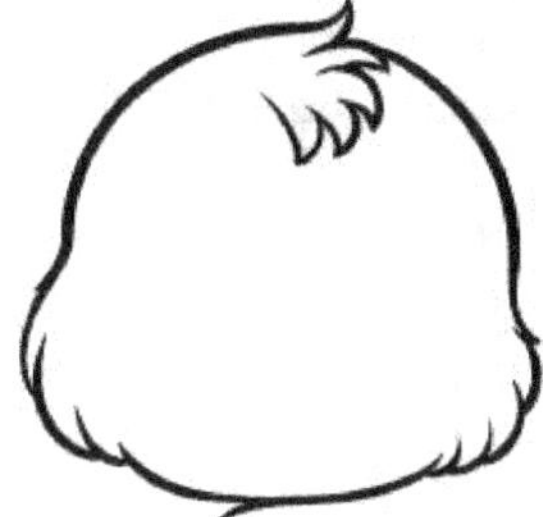 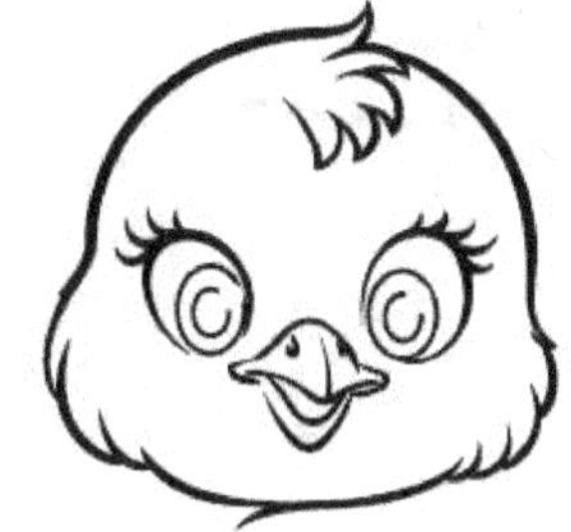

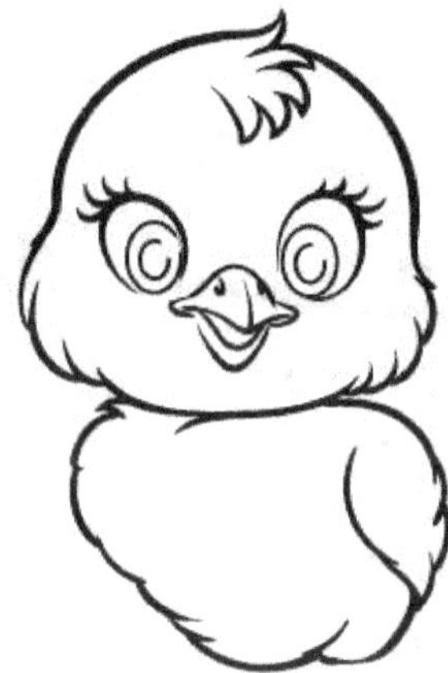 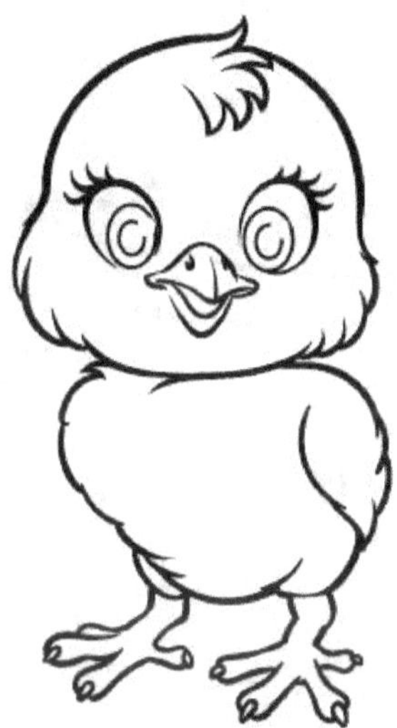

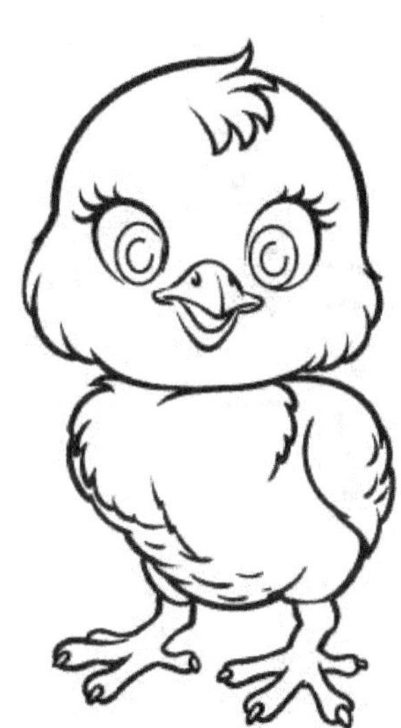 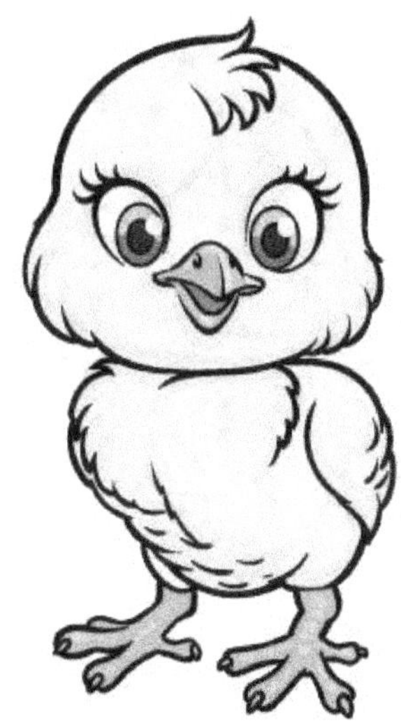

PUSHEEN

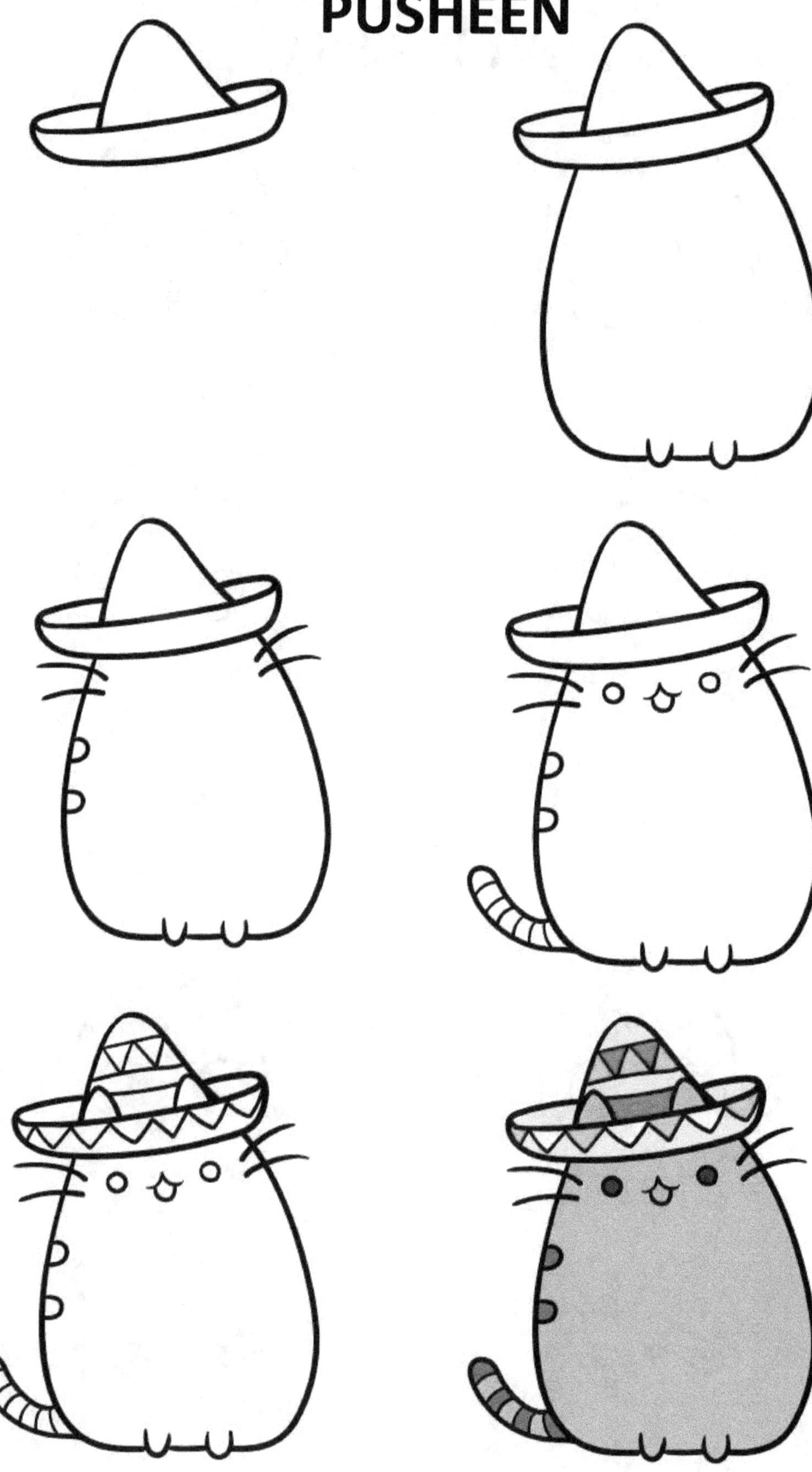